The Jamestown S'Klallam Story

The Jamestown
S'Klallam Story:

Rebuilding a Northwest Coast
Indian Tribe

Joseph H. Stauss

Jamestown S'Klallam Tribe

Cover photo: The Prince of Wales and his family digging clams near Port Townsend. From left to right: Wife of the Prince of Wales, Queen Victoria; wife of Chief Chetzemoka (the Duke of York); David Prince; and the Prince of Wales. (Photograph courtesy of the Bert Kellogg Collection of the North Olympic Library System)

Original Print Version, 2002
Substantive Editing: Stephen Hopkins, Arizona Editors
Copy editing and book packaging: Melanie Mallon, Mallon Publishing Services
Design & Production: Randy Schultz, DesignPro Graphics

Second Edition, 2019: Jamestown S'Klallam Tribe
Copy Revisions and Layout: Betty Oppenheimer, Communications Specialist
Clerical Assistance: Anika Kessler, Administrative Assistant
Editing: Leanne Jenkins, Planning Director

Illustrations: Dale Faulstich (except where noted)

Published by
Jamestown S'Klallam Tribe
1033 Old Blyn Highway
Sequim, WA 98382

1 2 3 4 5 6 7 8 9 10—03 02 01 00
First printing, December 2002
ISBN 0-9723753-0-9
Library of Congress Control Number: 2002116241

Second printing, 2019
ISBN: 0-9794510-3-4

This book is dedicated to Kenneth A. Thayer, my uncle, who was the only father I ever knew. He instilled in me the traditional S'Klallam values of hard work, self-control, and generosity. While some of the other important S'Klallam values may have escaped my grasp, it was not for lack of his being a role model as a good man and a real man.

This revision of The Jamestown S'Klallam Story *was created to make the title available electronically and make reprints available after the first printing sold out. It remains a snapshot of the Tribe and its accomplishments through 2001.*

Contents

The Jamestown S'Klallam Tribal Crest

Gregory David Prince conceived the official crest of the Jamestown S'Klallam Tribe. Gregory is an enrolled Tribal citizen and direct descendant of the original inhabitants of the Northwest coastal region.

The crest is composed of two symbols that have endured with time as totems of the S'Klallam people. The two figures have been melded together:

The Eagle is free; he is strong; he is powerful; he is silent; he is one with the Earth. For the Jamestown people, he is the enduring vision of the past and the future.

The Salmon is life; he is continuance; he is perpetual adaptation; he is the pulse of the Earth. For the Jamestown people, he is a physical link to their heritage.

If the Eagle and the Salmon disappear, the world will be a sadder place. A void will be opened that can never be filled.

The S'Klallam are a strong people; they are a proud people; they are time eternal; they live and grow as one with the land. At times unseen, but always present, their place is home to the Eagle and Salmon. Since time began, the S'Klallam people have been here, and when they are gone, they will still be here in Spirit.

The strength of the Eagle has held the S'Klallam together as a people; the Salmon is the catalyst that brought them closer together, a way for the people to maintain a continuance, a hold on their identity, a gathering sign, cause for celebration, a means of survival, a physical link to their heritage. The S'Klallam hope for our World that the Eagle and Salmon survive—let them be strong, let them relish their place. Let the Spirit scheme endure.

—**Jamestown S'Klallam Tribe**

Preface
to the Second Edition

The initial printing in 2002 of 2,000 copies of The Jamestown
S'Klallam Story sold out within about 5 years, and the book has been
requested ever since at our galleries and other sales outlets.
Fifteen years after the original publication of this book, we embarked
on a revision of the original manuscript, to prepare it for reissuing
in print and digital format. It was not our intention to substantively
change Joseph Stauss' work, which stands as a testament to the Tribe's
accomplishments as of 2001.
This revision includes corrections to certain typographic conventions,
minor errors and updating the files to 2019 print-on-demand and
e-publishing standards.

Preface

This book tells the remarkable story of a small Tribe on the Olympic Peninsula who, through maintenance of traditional character, values, and dedication to their land, have rebuilt their community. It is a story of the sustained visionary leadership of a Tribal Chairman and key community leaders who, in the face of federal, state, and local forces of change, have asserted inherent Tribal sovereignty to become an economic, political, and unique social group with influence that is reminiscent of the pre-contact powers of their ancestors.

As late as the early 1900s, most federal bureaucrats, anthropologists, and popular writers were prophesying that the Indian was one of a vanishing breed. Ironically, the 2000 census identified more than 2.4 million American Indian and Alaskan Natives.[1] This is close to the low-end estimates of pre-contact North American population (2 to 5 million).[2] American Indian languages, cultures, governments, and peoples have survived, endured, and rebuilt their unique societies across America. This book tells one of the hundreds of success stories. The Jamestown S'Klallam Tribe has been restored in dramatic fashion in just a quarter century.

Why This Book?

The need for bringing the unique Jamestown S'Klallam history together in a single volume was first voiced to me by the chairman of the Tribe, the honorable W. Ron Allen. Chairman Allen has been continually frustrated by being unable to respond to requests from non-Indians for written information about the Tribe. He and I talked about a book that would be readable for the public, perhaps with some background in Indian affairs. We discussed the need for contemporary histories of Indian Tribes.

Given my S'Klallam heritage, I was particularly motivated to make this contribution for the Jamestown S'Klallam Tribe's community members. Though I am not an enrolled citizen of the Tribe, my great-grandmother, Mary Campbell Kimball, and her two sisters each received a small check in the 1920s as part of a federal settlement between the government and recognized members of the S'Klallam. I received complete cooperation and access to Tribal materials as well as significant guidance from Tribal citizens while working for half a year at the Tribal headquarters on this book. However, the judgments on materials included in the text and the analysis of historical and contemporary events are completely mine. Neither Chairman Allen nor any other citizen of the Tribe influenced the tone, conclusions, interpretation, or other major aspects of the book. It was produced as an independent work. Any and all factual mistakes and errors of omission or misinterpretation are my own.

The Jamestown S'Klallam story must be told in two separate but, at the same time, closely linked parts. A current story of the Tribe cannot be told without drawing connections between contemporary and traditional ways of life. When looking at the Tribe's current strengths, including environmental management and restoration, governance and leadership in the state and nation, economic development, and sustaining family and community, I found that these contemporary strengths were firmly rooted in traditional ways. Though information and insights into the traditional S'Klallam way of life were only available for certain time periods and for specific subjects, these were sufficient to understand the Tribe's current success. Similarly, current S'Klallam practices gave me insights into the significance of traditional beliefs, stories, and practices. Thus, the Jamestown story, of both traditional and contemporary ways of life, came together somewhat organically through the process of my research.

> What is clear from even the European histories of the Norse and of Columbus is that the Americas were never truly "discovered" by Europeans, and most certainly not by Columbus. Indigenous people have been here from the beginnings of human history.

While some Tribes have maintained a rich and comprehensive oral tradition, the Jamestown S'Klallam are struggling today to recapture their ceremonies and relearn their language. Not everything, however, has been lost. There are significant materials left to build upon, and many are brought together in this volume. More important, as this book demonstrates, Jamestown S'Klallam people clearly exhibit important traditional values and beliefs that sustain them and maintain their status as a unique people. Indeed, they are committed to both the maintenance of older practices as well as the creation of new traditions.

Native Origins

The popular myth that Columbus discovered America is alive and well today and has received continued attention, particularly since the 1992 celebration that for many Americans represented five hundred years of progress toward increased civilization. Even the begrudging nod given to pre-Columbian discoveries has not diminished reverent Columbus Day parades nor the use of well-established signs and symbols of discovery and conquest. However, even European history acknowledges that before Columbus came to North America, the Norse visited it repeatedly. Their explorations between about A.D. 800 and 1000 propelled them across the North Atlantic from Scandinavian territories. The most famous of an array of Norse adventurers seeking their fortunes in Iceland, Greenland, and northeastern North America were Erik the Red and his son, Leif Erikson. The exact dates of their Newfoundland landing and occupation are disputable, probably between A.D. 997 and 1003, but the archaeological evidence of their presence is not. The only question is how much farther south and west Norse explorations extended.

> For a history of the Norse voyagers ,see editors William W. Fitzhugh and Elisabeth I. Ward's Vikings: The North Atlantic Saga (Washington, D. C.: Smithsonian Institution Press, 2000), particularly pages 11–25.

What is clear from even the European histories of the Norse and of Columbus is that the Americas were never truly "discovered" by Europeans, and most certainly not by Columbus. Indigenous people have been here from the beginnings of human history. However, if you open up any basic history or anthropology textbook, you will read about how and when Indians migrated across Beringia, the ice bridge that supposedly connected North America with Asia before sinking into the sea and conveniently submerging any real proof of its existence. For example, the 1,690-page, widely adopted fifth edition of America: A Narrative History begins with "The first Americans were Asians. Nearly twenty thousand years ago, nomadic peoples from Siberia began crossing the Bering Strait."[3] This migration theory has come under increasing fire, especially from scholars in American Indian Studies, and it is clear that if, indeed, a migration or migrations helped people the Americas in early times, the process was far more complex than the easy answer provided by an ice bridge.

Unfortunately, we often forget that a theory is nothing more than an educated guess about how things happened. Even though it is a widely accepted scientific paradigm, the theory that all indigenous people in North and South America came only from Asia across an ice bridge has never been proven.

> Vine Deloria, Jr., a leading American Indian scholar, has systematically challenged the Bering Strait theory on many fronts; see Red Earth White Lies (Golden, Colo.: Fulcrum Publishing, 1997).

Unfortunately, the native inhabitants of the Western Hemisphere were, from first contact, depicted as savages and pagans and were therefore considered ripe for conquest. North America, in particular, was seen as a wilderness populated by vicious wolves and cannibalistic Indians.

The right of discovery was justified by Roman Catholic monarchs because the nomadic "savages" they found were not Christians. In addition, these peoples went mostly or sometimes even fully naked and supposedly did not cultivate the land. Their biggest sin, of course, was not speaking, acting, or dressing like Spanish, French, or British people. The European thirst for gold, slaves, and land, combined with the presence of such a relatively small population of supposedly savage and godless natives, guaranteed genocide for the indigenous peoples of the Americas. The only real fight was among European powers over who would eventually keep the land.

When European and American scientists began to pay some attention to oral history, the method employed to give validity to stories was to correlate multiple sources and compare oral stories to archaeological findings. Thus, controversies like "when did native people cross the land bridge" emerged. This issue goes beyond the question of whether the land bridge was the only migration path. This argument ignores oral stories that place native origins solely within the Americas—stories that completely reject any migration theory. The real issue is why (and to whom) these questions are important at all. At the heart of this issue is the fact that a late migration from Asia justified conquest and genocide of indigenous peoples by European Americans.

See Robert F. Berkhofer, Jr.'s The White Man's Indian: Images of the American Indian from Columbus to the Present (New York: Random House, 1978) for a detailed exploration of European American views of American Indians throughout history.

Each indigenous group does indeed have its own origin story, and a few do include talk of a migration, though not from Siberia. There is as much politics afoot here as there is science or religion. It has always been a great political and legal advantage to believe a history that relegates indigenous peoples to the category of recent newcomers to the Americas. Coupled with the idea that besides being new to the area, natives were few in number and lacked the sophisticated technologies to put the land to proper use (that is, to clear the land and plant gardens) was enough rationale to provide fuel for philosophies of manifest destiny and westward expansion. Genocide, federal assimilation policies, prejudice, discrimination, and diseases nearly took care of what was perceived as the "Indian problem," but all of these efforts eventually failed.

Sources and Approach

Ordinarily, the historian would begin the Jamestown S'Klallam story with tales of Spanish, English, and American explorations and completely ignore S'Klallam history prior to contact. The anthropologist might include some "prehistory" or pre-contact stories, and thus be regarded as an ethnohistorian in today's scientific jargon. However, these social scientists' interests would end long before we reached the mid-twentieth century.

This volume is a history written from the American Indian Studies interdisciplinary approach, which combines all relevant social-science perspectives with those of the people who live the stories being told. In addition, it is a contemporary story. There are very few contemporary (meaning twentieth-century onward) histories available about American Indian nations, Tribes, bands, or urban groups. This volume helps fill this void in the literature. The benefits for the reader of this book include a concise picture of the Jamestown S'Klallam Tribe today coupled with important economic, social, cultural, family, and linguistic information from the past.

The sources of data I rely on include interviews and oral histories of the Jamestown people, observations of explorers, reports of Indian agents and missionaries, journals of settlers, editorials in local newspapers, and anthropological and other social science observations or research studies. What exists of the Jamestown S'Klallam Tribe's history has never been collected into a single volume but lies scattered among the Tribal, federal, and state governmental records, newspaper articles, and memories of Jamestown citizens. Sometimes observations contradict each other. When that happens, I rely first on Tribal oral information, then on other sources.

The term "traditional" is greatly misused and widely misunderstood in the literature about American Indians. When you see "traditional" used with Indians, you need to know to what time period the author is referring. Often, what people consider traditional is what they have seen in the movies, usually the Plains Indian warrior of the 1860s to 1880s. I use the term "traditional" in this volume to indicate cultural lifeways that have endured through time and that continue to sustain the uniqueness of the Jamestown community. It is also important to remember that traditions change over time. All traditions change by adapting to forces both within and without. For example, although song and dance have always been a part of Jamestown S'Klallam Tribal existence, some songs and dances have been lost, some have endured but changed, and some new ones have been created, which shall in the future be passed down as traditional.

Names

There are many different names used to identify today's descendants of peoples who lived here before Europeans arrived— "Native Americans," "American Indians," "aboriginal Americans," and so forth. Each of these peoples, of course, had their own name in their own language. There were more than 350 language families and 2,200 dialects in North America alone. Today, many names associated with Tribes, bands, or Indian groups reflect geographical locations (such as Spokane), English translations of languages that were not understood but were sounded out (such as Skokomish), and names that have some historical significance, such as a person who was important to the community, as with the Jamestown S'Klallam, who named their community after a village leader, Lord Jim Balch. "American Indian," "Native American," "aborigine," "native," and "Indian" are all used interchangeably in this volume. Whenever possible, group, Tribal, or band-specific names are used.

The pronunciation of "S'Klallam" involves phonetic syllables that are not found in the English language. It was difficult to transcribe into English, so early Europeans used several different versions: "S'Klallam," "Clallam," "Ns'Klallam," and "Klallam." When the three bands of this Tribe became federally recognized, "S'Klallam" was recorded in the federal register; however, "Clallam" and "Klallam" were the spellings most popular for years. Recently, however, the Jamestown Tribe has adopted the historical spelling "S'Klallam," as found in the original treaties. But confusion still exists. The county that now includes much of traditional S'Klallam territory is named "Clallam," and a variety of spellings show up throughout the scientific literature as well as in the popular media. I use "S'Klallam" consistently in this book but have not changed the spelling used by those I excerpt or quote.

Anthropological Sources and Their Limitations

Several early writers have made important contributions to the fragmented S'Klallam literature. Erna Gunther, an anthropologist, did fieldwork in the 1920s with S'Klallam informants. William W. Elmendorf, also an anthropologist, worked in the 1940s with Twana informants, but his major informant was as well connected (externally and socially) and knowledgeable about the S'Klallam as about the Twana. Myron Eells, a missionary who was stationed on the Skokomish Reservation between 1874 and 1907, was a prolific writer who also worked extensively among the S'Klallam.

George Gibbs was an important historical figure who assisted Governor Isaac Ingalls Stevens in treaty negotiations with the S'Klallam and other Tribes in the Northwest.

William W. Elmendorf 's <u>Twana Narratives: Native Historical Accounts of a Coast Salish Culture</u> (Seattle: University of Washington Press, 1993) is a volume that provides significant S'Klallam-specific stories, even though the author's focus is on the Skokomish Twana. The Jamestown-specific source for these important materials was Frank James Allen (born 1865) who had a Dungeness S'Klallam mother, was fluent in the S'Klallam language, and kept close and extended contacts with the S'Klallam side of his family.

Erna Gunther collected what she considered her best material from informants at Jamestown, Washington Harbor, and Esquimalt over the winter of 1924 and 1925. Her main contact was Robert Collier from Jamestown, though two other important Jamestown informants were John Cook (for hunting and fishing information) and Mary Wood (for information on food preparation and women's work). Gunther was a trained anthropologist who was interested in everything from language to religious life.[4]

Anthropology, of course, has a well-deserved reputation for using informants to collect information and not including them in the research process or fully acknowledging their significant contributions. This one-sided relationship certainly may have influenced the questions asked as well as the quality and quantity of information collected and its interpretation by these early scholars. For example, Gunther's works are full of value judgments exhibited by her use of words like "primitive," "war," "soul," "less-developed culture," and so on. Yet, her observations of fish traps, houses, food gathering, and myriad other ways of life are detailed and accurate when compared to oral tradition and other written materials.

Similarly, although Myron Eells, the Congregational Church pastor for over three decades at Skokomish, may have had a hard time writing about his observations of native religions, he was a keen observer and prolific writer of all other aspects of Indian life.[5] His sketches were done with attention to detail, and a significant share of his work was directly related to the S'Klallam during the 1874–1907 period. Eells noted in all his works the rapid change brought on by increasing white contact, and it was a theme for his writing on material culture. Anthropologist William W. Elmendorf added greatly to collected information on the S'Klallam during his visits in the 1940s. His main informant, Frank James Allen, spoke both Twana and S'Klallam. Allen's mother was a Dungeness S'Klallam, and he was the direct recipient of stories involving traditional S'Klallam. His stories are rich in detail and provide unique insight into pre-contact life, particularly for the Dungeness S'Klallam. Allen maintained and continued deep S'Klallam contacts and was initiated into S'Klallam secret society. Elmendorf 's collection of Allen's stories enable the reader to "hear" the oral tradition of the Dungeness S'Klallam and not just see the words of missionaries,Indian agents, and anthropologists.

Gunther, Eells, and Elmendorf (less so ethnologist George Gibbs) must be relied upon for descriptions of early S'Klallam life, although more contemporary work by scholar Barbara Lane has provided enriched detail and insight into traditional S'Klallam ways. Jamestown Elders have limited knowledge of traditional ways of life. Indeed, Gunther's judgment in the mid- 1920s was that the knowledge of what she called "the old life" was very limited. We do not know, of course, whether Gunther spoke to the right people or if they were open and completely truthful with her. What these three authors reported from different observations and informants in different time periods is more similar in agreement on important ways than it is different or contradictory. When you add to this the rich tapestry of material from the Nootka and other north, south, and central Coast Salish Tribes, confidence in what we know increases substantially. However, unique and important Tribal or village differences certainly have been lost.

For contemporary work on early S'Klallam work, see Barbara Lane and Wayne Suttles's chapter in editor Wayne Suttles's <u>Handbook of North American Indians: Northwest Coast,</u> volume 7 (Washington, D.C.: Smithsonian Institution Press, 1990), "Southern Coast Salish," on pages 485–502.

Missionaries and early non-native explorers usually lumped Puget Sound and Coast Salish Indians together, disregarding individual differences. We should not ignore these important published and unpublished works, though, because they provide us with a detailed picture of early contact life for aboriginal peoples throughout the region. We simply must stay on the lookout for biases of viewpoint, misassumptions, and incomplete information. We must also be aware of the often subtle and sometimes dramatic differences among villages and Tribes. I distinguish between Coast Salish, Pacific Northwest, Puget Sound, and Jamestown S'Klallam sources. When I describe some aspect of daily life, such as food gathering or housing, I can rely with some confidence on a multitude of sources that provide similar pictures. However, after the introductory chapter, I have written this volume using S'Klallam- and Jamestown S'Klallam–specific information.

Making a judgment about what Tribes shared, such as common fishing methods, and what they did not, such as origin stories or language, is one of the greatest challenges for all writers interested in the Pacific Northwest. The environment that the Tribes of the Pacific Northwest lived in dictated some important ways of life, such as canoes as an important mode of transportation, but did not diminish the individuality of each village, band, or group. The single most important thing the knowledgeable reader can learn about Indians is how widely they vary in language, culture, housing, eating habits, kinship patterns, political organization, reservation size, and population size (to name but a few important differences). There is not, nor has there ever been, a homogenous and static aboriginal population.

Any contemporary history has the built-in limitation of working with a dynamic, rapidly changing environment and of choosing among events or stories that may not seem as important in future years. All historical documents are built of snapshots against a constantly moving background. An author can only hope that what he or she has chosen to bring to focus tells the story as others may have known it.

> All historical documents are built of snapshots against a constantly moving background.

Acknowledgements

Many people deserve special thanks for assisting me in this project. First and foremost is Chairman W. Ron Allen, without whose support this book would never have become a reality. Elaine Grinnell, Jamestown S'Klallam Elder and storyteller, graciously allowed some of her oral stories to be put in print in this book. Much is lost when stories are printed on a flat page. These stories come alive and are so much richer when Elaine tells them.

She carries more than fifty stories in her memory and has all her life been an inspiration and role model for youth and the community.

All the very special people I worked with at Jamestown need to be thanked for their welcoming ways and unselfish sharing, but none more strongly than Kathy Duncan. Kathy took both Lynn, my wife, and me under her wing and guided us daily throughout our six-month stay with the Tribe. Linda Cawyer, editor of the Tribal newsletter, provided me with invaluable guidance throughout the project. My colleagues in the Saturday storytelling class also deserve special thanks for including me. I learned so much from their stories:

Liz Mueller, Margaret Adams, Kathy Duncan, and, especially, our teacher, Elaine Grinnell.

Dale Faulstich, who is an outstanding artist, has provided original illustrations. His work is a major addition to this book. Dale is the owner of Creative Art Enterprises in Sequim, Washington.

I could never have gotten the manuscript ready without the extraordinary editorial talents of Stephen Hopkins of Arizona Editors in Tucson, Arizona. In the final stages of publishing, Melanie Mallon took on the coordination and orchestration of all aspects of making this book a reality. Her many talents and devotion to perfection are evident throughout the book.

I also thank the University of Arizona for institutional support, including a sabbatical leave over winter semester 1999 to enable me the opportunity to work at Jamestown.

A special thank you to my wife, lifelong partner, and friend, Lynn, who was with me throughout the creation of the book.

Introduction:

An Overview of the Pacific Northwest Coast Ways of Life

The story of today's Jamestown S'Klallam Tribe begins long before their formal recognition by the federal government in 1981, and prior to the treaty of Point-No-Point signed by some S'Klallam in 1855, and even before the voyage of Captain George Vancouver into Puget Sound in 1792. Today's descendants trace their lineage to the S'Klallam, who have peopled the shores of the Olympic Peninsula, along the Strait of Juan de Fuca into Puget Sound, since the beginning of time.

S'Klallam people have been living forever in winter and summer communities along or near the shores of what today is called the Strait of Juan de Fuca and Hood Canal. They traded, intermarried, potlatched, and warred with other communities throughout what we now know as the Pacific Northwest, including southern British Columbia and

> S'Klallam words are unique in dialect and are represented in type by a combination of letters and symbols. Dr. Timothy Montler has put together an informative website of Klallam (S'Klallam) linguistics at http://www.klallam.montler.net. The S'Klallam words in this book are the benefit of his excellent work with Elwha Tribe in Port Angeles, Washington.

some of the San Juan Islands. This introduction will explore the region as a whole, including the environment and ways of life of all the native people in it, setting the stage for the detailed exploration of the contemporary and traditional S'Klallam in the chapters that follow.

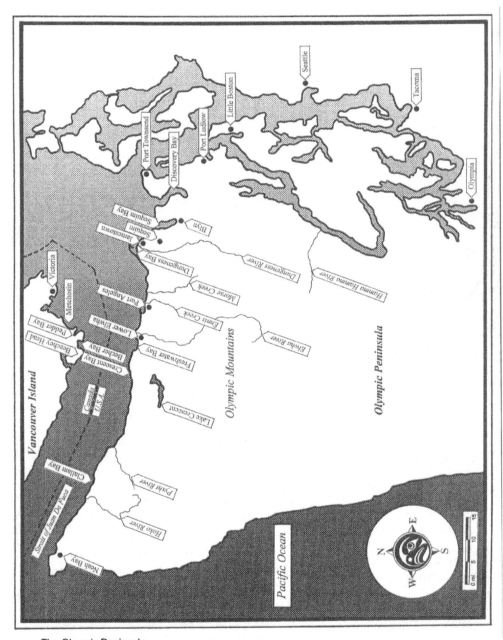

The Olympic Peninsula
map created by Dale Faulstich

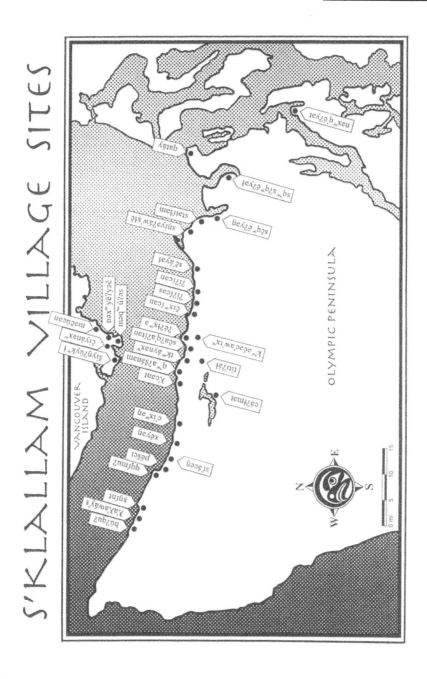

Historical village sites (map created by Dale Faulstich)
Village site names courtesy of Lower Elwha Klallam Tribe, from their 1999
Elwha Klallam calendar

Hoko	húʔuʔ
Sekiu	ƛ̓aƛawáy's
Clallam Bay	x̣ŋínt
Pillar Point	qqímuʔ
Pysht	péšct
Butler's Cove	st'ə́ceŋ
Jim Creek	xéyəŋ
Deep Creek	c'ixʷən
Agate Beach	ƛ'cəŋ
Crescent Bay	q'ʷaʔšə́nəm
Freshwater Bay	tkʷáynəxʷ
Freshwater Bay Beach, between Freshwater Bay and Elwha River	sčaʔq'a'ʔítən
Elwha River	ʔéʔɬx̣ʷə
Lake Crescent	cə́ʔɬmət
Confluence of Indian Creek and Elwha River	titiʔə́ɬ
Near one-way bridge	kʷəčəc'aw'txʷ
Port Angeles	čixʷícən
Ennis Creek	ʔiʔícəs
Beach near Morse Creek	ʔiʔícən
Green Point	sčáyəɬ
Dungeness	sŋiyəʔáw'x̣ɬč
Jamestown	stətíɬəm
Sequim	sčqʷéʔyəŋ
Port Discovery	sq'ʷaʔqʷéʔyəɬ
Port Townsend	qatáy
Little Boston/Port Gamble	nexʷq'éʔyət
Beechey Head	šiyŋʔúykʷɬ
Beecher Bay	čiyánəxʷ
Smyth Point	meq'ʷúʔəs
Pedder Bay	nəxʷyéʔəč
Metchosin	məčúcən

Potlatch

A unique traditional aspect of Pacific Northwest Coast societies was the division of groups into high class, commoners, and slaves. This ceremonial complex was most directly related to the maintenance of high status, community sharing, and strengthening of group identity. The potlatch, a ceremony of feasting and giving, held by those of high status,was so integral to the S'Klallam throughout history that their language contains words specific to the ceremony, such as the following examples:

To give a potlatch Invite to a potlatch ʔaʔátxʷ   Invite to a potlatch sʔeʔtxʷ

Although many aspects of the potlatch have changed over time, it remains today a social and ceremonial occasion, with food for everyone, gift giving, recognition, singing, and dancing.

Anthropologist Erna Gunther lists thirteen original S'Klallam winter villages and makes comparisons to ten villages identified by the early work of ethnologist George Gibbs, M.D., and twelve by anthropologist Edward S. Curtis. Research by a group interested in the language of the Lower Elwha Tribe resulted in identifying thirty-one community or village sites. Some of the differences in the lists can be explained by a largely anthropological-created distinction between winter, or "permanent," villages and summer, or "temporary," fishing sites or stations.

In sharp contrast to these arbitrary categories, we know that S'Klallam people lived at the mouth of virtually every good fishing stream and gathered on all the best beaches throughout their homeland. What did it matter if the shelter erected was not permanent? It could and would be rebuilt at the next visit.

When S'Klallam stayed seasonally at fishing sites, they certainly considered them, regardless of the type of roof over their heads, permanent and crucial to sustaining their way of life. Both winter and summer communities, or villages, were equally important and integral to S'Klallam life.

Some winter and summer places were used more than others and some changed over time, especially after European immigrants later took over some of the better fishing spots.

Elders from the Elwha Klallam have identified thirty-three community sites, including five in British Columbia. I would argue that even this expanded list may not be complete, because it does not identify sites farther down Hood Canal. More than one source in the literature cites seasonal fishing with the Twana at the Hamma Hamma River, just like the seasonal sharing of the mouth of the Hoko River with the Makah, which is equally well documented. As scholar Barbara Lane makes clear, the northern boundary of S'Klallam homeland is disputed because both the Makah and the S'Klallam had villages and fished at the Hoko River and beyond.

The S'Klallam's western boundary was the ridges of the Olympic

Mountains at the headwaters of major rivers and streams. They crossed over on a regular basis to trade. There is ample evidence of significant hunting; gathering of cedar bark, grass for baskets, and plants for medicine; and fishing for lake trout.[1]

The number and origin of S'Klallam communities on Vancouver Island is not without controversy, either. Gunther claims Beecher Bay was settled by S'Klallam who moved over from Port Angeles around 1850. She disputes artist and observer Paul Kane's reference to "Clal-lums" living at Esquimalt. Her insistence that S'Klallam were largely visitors and interlopers on Vancouver Island or were there because they married into British Columbia native groups is likely based on her informant's lack of knowledge about the communities in British Columbia.[2]

Regardless, prior to 1850, S'Klallam villages and fishing sites could be found either alone or shared on Vancouver Island as well as on the San Juan Islands.

The climate, forests, marine life, as well as the many diverse linguistic groups that interacted between the water's edge and the well-defined mountain ranges, produce what anthropologists have come to call a "culture area." Some of the things that set Northwest Coast peoples apart from other indigenous groups across America include the following:

- the existence of more than forty different languages from a dozen different language families
- a reliance on fishing and shellfish
- highly developed woodworking
- a social organization based on birth, wealth, potlatching, and marriage alliances
- an individual's ability to attract guardian spirits

Scholars often cut the Pacific Northwest Coast into smaller subareas, such as the Central Coast Salish and the Southern Coast Salish. The S'Klallam homeland is in the central area, while the Twana and numerous other distinct native groups occupy the Southern Coast Salish territory.[3] Of course, none of these individual groups thought of themselves in these arbitrary categories and European terms. European American scientists created these classifications to isolate and study what they believed were vanishing cultures.

Precontact Pacific Northwest oral history was a unique combination of personal and inherited knowledge. Community leaders and others of high status, such as shamans, inherited songs, dances, crests, and other rights, which would be displayed and shared at appropriate times. Commoners also acquired spirit guardians or helpers, songs, dances, and related rights they could share, but never with the same degree of prestige or potential power. Slaves, of course, had no spirit helpers. The bulk of this knowledge and history was not sacred, but rather was centered in interaction with places like bays, inlets, sandspits, mountains, or with animals. They were stories of everyday occurrences and were shared with everyone, especially one's family and community. People, animals, and places were all alive and possessed energy and life forces.[4]

A community leader's stories relied on precise, complex language, and criers or oracles (to use English terms) were keepers of those special chronicles. All knowledge was personal and only shared at a potlatch feast or other appropriate time or place. Sacred knowledge, in addition to being personal, was kept private unless great need demanded it be shared. Those individuals who gained a reputation as shamans or medicine men would use both their personal and private knowledge to cure others or, sometimes, for personal gain.

Anthropologists and other social scientists have rarely been able to agree on how far to stretch similarities among Tribes, or even villages that were home to more than one linguistic group. However, the unique environment of the Pacific Northwest, or even that of a smaller area like the Puget Sound, dictated that villagers, regardless of their origins, language differences, unique history, and spirituality, would interact, exchange, intermarry, and share some important ways of life. Where a Tribe like the Jamestown S'Klallam has the challenge of rebuilding and recreating much of their language and culture, reliance on knowledge still alive and well with close neighbors is given serious attention. Classical anthropological literature has roughly bonded the Nitinaht, Makah, Quileute, Central Coast Salish, Chemakum, and Southern Coast Salish with evidence from smaller social networks.[5]

Salish

The term "Salish" refers to language groups, and in this cultural area five were spoken: Squamish, Halkomelem, Nootka (or Nitinaht), Northern Straits, and Clallam. There are more than twenty branches of the Salish language family, and it is spoken as far east as Montana. The Clallam is more distinct than any of the other straits-Salish-speaking groups. Halkomelem-Salish speakers included distinctions among island, downriver, and upriver villagers at forty-six different sites, mostly along the Frazer River in present-day Canada.

The Central Coast Salish area includes traditional S'Klallam territory, with villages along the Strait of Juan de Fuca, into Puget Sound, and on the southern tip of Vancouver Island. Other Tribes occupying this cultural area in the early nineteenth century included the Squamish across the Strait of Georgia on Howe Sound and the Nooksak, or Nootkans, mostly south of the present-day U. S.–Canada border. Northern Straits groups largely occupied the San Juan Islands and the southern tip of Vancouver Island.[6]

In the Central Coast Salish geographical area, loosely bounded by both distinguishable cultural areas and social networks, kinship was largely bilateral, especially in the Puget Sound. The close neighbors of the S'Klallam, the Twana, were an exception with a more patrilineal pattern.[7] These kinship practices were important because of the commonly recognized distinctions between those with noble ancestors or those tied to immortals and those with common or slave ancestors. Genetic lineage determined whether you inherited rights to practice certain customs or pass on names, songs, or, quite important, resource areas such as good fishing places.

The Natural Environment

The creator blessed the Pacific Northwest Coast with an abundance of food and ways to live. In addition, many stories that were handed down from parents and grandparents chronicled the strength of body, spirit, and character of the S'Klallam, or "the strong people," as they called themselves and as they would come to be known by all others. S'Klallam stories tell of people and ravens or crows who became the rocks that now mark entrances to important places like Clallam Bay; of wars and agreements made with the winds to guarantee the cold north wind would never blow longer than a week or that the warm south wind would always come to mitigate the north wind; of what Slap'u may do to children if they don't mind, and where you can find Slap'u today; of how lightning came to be; and especially, how S'Klallam individuals received their guardian spirits, who brought them the power to make thunder or the power to be a great hunter or gambler. You can always find more than one version of each story, and sometimes what you learn, or think you hear this time, is different than what you might have understood the last time you heard the story.

There are many S'Klallam stories involving thunder. Most involve raiding enemies for retribution or for slaves. Men or women who had thunder as their guardian spirit were respected and feared by both their own people and others:

> The S'Klallam are alive and well today and still living in their traditional territory.

thunderstorm
ʔaʔcákʷɬ

thunderbolt, lightening
ʔaʔcáxʷɬ

rain
sɬə́məxʷ

snake
sxʷáxʷc'

> Whenever the Thunderbird moved his wings, it thundered. This bird had a belt made of a snake and when this snake stuck out its tongue there was lightning. When the thunder shook hard, the snake fell into the water. Then it crawled up a tree and burned the tree. This power could also make it rain.
> One time the Klallam had some enemies pursuing them and a man called on the thunder. It rained so hard that the enemies turned over their canoes and got under them. The Klallam then attacked and killed them.[8]

This story combines key elements of S'Klallam culture: the importance of using special powers from guardian spirits to defeat enemies and the critical need to understand and use the most powerful tools of the Pacific Northwest environment— thunder, lightning, and rain. If you have never experienced a stormy night on the Pacific Northwest Coast, then you may not be able to fully appreciate this story. The magnificent Pacific Northwest brings together people and animals in an awesome and unique environment. The oral history of the S'Klallam before written stories were penned by non-S'Klallam explorers, traders, timber men, missionaries, and Indian agents is lost or clouded by more than 150 years of intense contact. What we do know is that the S'Klallam are alive and well today and still living in their traditional territory. Each time they fought their enemies (who traditionally came from the north, across the strait) or adapted to and adopted from non-native invaders, they rebuilt their communities and re-established themselves as the "strong people" of the Olympic Peninsula.

Multiple Peoples in a Unique Environment

The S'Klallam who faced the Strait of Juan de Fuca were, of course, not the only people in the Pacific Northwest. Their immediate neighbors were the Chemakum, with whom they shared territory around present-day Port Townsend and Port Hadlock on the Quimper Peninsula. They eventually absorbed the Chemakum and moved onto their territory, making it their own. To the northwest, they camped across the bank of the Hoko River along with the Makah, who lived out their lives as great whalers in contest with the pounding surf of the Pacific Ocean.

Books abound that detail the Pacific Northwest environment and precontact societies. See in particular editor Alvin M.Josephy, Jr.'s America in 1492: The World of the Indian Peoples Before the Arrival of Columbus (New York: Alfred A. Knopf, 1992), especially Richard D. Daugherty's "People of the Salmon," 50–83. See also Philip Drucker's Cultures of the North Pacific Coast (New York: Harper & Roe Publishers, 1964) and editor Wayne Suttles's Handbook of North American Indians: Northwest Coast, volume 7, especially the chapter by Wayne Suttles and Barbara Lane, "Southern Coast Salish," on pages 485–502.

To the southeast, the S'Klallam fished the Hamma Hamma River with the Twana, who lived around the many saltwater inlets along Hood Canal. As a whole, these territories supported large populations, each with its own language and social and ceremonial lifeways.

Large bodies of water, including rivers, and mountains are the predominant geographical and environmental features of the Pacific Northwest, especially of the traditional home of the S'Klallam on the Olympic Peninsula. High mountains and dense forests crowd people along narrow shorelines and form rivers, bays, and landmarks that provide shelter from strong winter winds and rains. What we call watersheds today produced extraordinary opportunities to feed, shelter,

The Many Uses of the Western Red Cedar

The western red cedar tree and its bark provided and still do provide
• transportation
• clothing
• boxes for food storage
• housing planks and posts
• cradles for both newborns and those who have passed away
• everyday and ceremonial clothing
• mats
• canoe bailers
• rope
• baskets
• medicine for a host of ailments, from sore lungs and boils to tuberculosis (cured with boiled cedar limbs)
• cleansing of young children when they are being taught proper ways and adults when preparing for ceremonies

All of the references in the resource box on page 28 speak to the importance of western red cedar, but see also Erna Gunther's Ethnobotany of Western Washington, revised edition (Seattle: University of Washington Press, 1973), 19–21. One of the most exquisite books on this subject is Hilary Stewart's Cedar: Tree of Life to the Northwest Coast Indians (Seattle: University of Washington Press, 1984)—see especially part I.

western red cedar
x̣páy'

edible camas
qʷɫúʔiʔ

blackberry
sq'ʷiyánəxʷ

red huckleberry
píxʷ

and clothe communities. This was no paradise with overly abundant food available year-round, but over thousands of years, the natives of the Pacific Northwest learned and practiced all of the complex ways to harvest and preserve the seasonal salmon, halibut, great gray whale, seals, herring, lingcod, and so much more.

Many trees, especially conifers, provide the essentials for everyday life for Pacific Northwest Indians. The most useful, the western red cedar, grew in a region that stretched from southern Alaska through British Columbia, Washington, Oregon, and into northern California. The cedar met many of the basic living needs for the Tlingit, Tsimshian, Haida, Bella Coola, Kwakiutl, Nootka, Makah, Quileute, and S'Klallam.[9] In addition to the western red cedar, other trees that were particularly useful and an important part of the environment included the western hemlock, Douglas fir, Oregon oak, and Sitka spruce.

Pine forest, oak woodland, and small prairies overlapped throughout the Puget Sound and along the shores of the Strait of Juan de Fuca. Hudson Bay Company journals, as well as those of other explorers, noted native burning practices at the beginning of each autumn. Such seasonal burning cycles guaranteed better growth for species like camas, blackberries, bunchgrass, salmonberry, and huckleberry. This widely practiced environmental management technique also attracted deer and elk down out of the mountains and onto the prairies.[10]

Throughout this multi-Tribal area, highly skilled craftspeople employed sophisticated technologies to produce everything from small bentwood boxes to majestic canoes hewed from a single log, many over sixty feet long and standing over seven feet at the bow. Indeed, the northern Tribes of the Pacific Northwest created the most highly prized canoes on the continent.

In villages or communities, the head of a village or group of villages resided in a longhouse made of red cedar timbers and planks. As late as 1840, there was a Haida headman's home in the area that stood with eloquently carved fifty-foot-high house-front poles. The typical longhouse measured fifty-four by fifty-five feet and many of the larger homes held a terraced inner pit with a large fire pit as the focal point of activity.[11] One Nootkans chief 's house was said to be one hundred fifty feet long and fourteen feet high.[12]

The Political Environment

Throughout the Pacific Northwest, indigenous peoples governed themselves in autonomous communities by recognizing people of high rank, commoners, and slaves. The "real men," or "good people"— those whom others looked up to—possessed a number of prerogatives, from calling potlatches, which displayed their wealth, to passing on important songs to their sons or brothers. There were differences across this diverse geographic area in the ways that privileges would be passed on by descent to sons, brothers, or even, in some cases, daughters, but the basic political and social system is well known.[13] Family groups formed food-gathering and extended kin–based social villages or communities and, particularly in winter homes, through ceremonies recognized one or more male leaders based on birth, wealth, personality, and acquired spirit powers. Other men might become recognized leaders when they acquired wealth and potlatched; however, inherited wealth and spirit helpers certainly provided some with a decided advantage.

person of high class
si?ám'

slave
sk'ʷə́y(ə)c

High status was directly related to reaching out to a broader network of communities, not just one's own village. If high rank was not inherited, it could, sometimes, be achieved by exhibiting proper training through your character. You must be known by other villagers, and you must visit, arrange marriage alliances wisely, host potlatches and feasts, and be generous, especially with those in need.

ambitious
sxʷəy'ʷi?

Villagers in the Pacific Northwest have used various words to describe the good man, or real man, of a household, local group, or village.[14] There was a clear hierarchy. "Worthy people," "upper-class," "elite leaders," "descendants of noble ancestors," the "wealthiest heads of households," and "headmen" are all terms found in the literature. "Chief " is an introduced term that was later adopted and used by Indians as well as non-Indians. The term "noble," of course, reminds us of European aristocracy. The similarities with European class differences are not very revealing, though. Commoners, or lower class or "worthless people," were in the middle and could contrast themselves with slaves, who were generally captured in raids

generous
nəxʷ?í?kʷən

or purchased. The slave's fate was also genetically determined, until European American contact changed things by eventually outlawing slave holding. Intermarriage among classes was unthinkable.[15]

If you were to distinguish yourself from a commoner and aspire to higher status, you had to have the correct training by your family to instill good behavior. Others must think of you as a hard worker, serious or ambitious, able to exhibit self-control, modesty, courtesy, and generosity. You would hold an even temper, particularly in your regard to others, and you would carry yourself with pride and dignity. Although these ideal values might vary across Northwest culture groups, the basic ways to distinguish oneself largely fell into such categories. Besides lectures, various outdoor bathing and bodily cleansing methods, fasts, and vision quests to acquire spirit helpers helped educate children about their family and community responsibilities.16 All of these factors came together in the major functions expected of a person of high status.

A real man, or good man, was expected to settle disputes between parties and, in some cases, benefit from the transaction or payment. He was expected to act properly and be a role model. Supporters always thought of his advice as sound when it was revealed to others. Although no leader had absolute authority to bind villagers to decisions, rights inherited at birth, along with songs, crests, names, ceremonial clothing, rights to fishing stations, and acquired spirit powers, combined with his orator skills, the character instilled in him by his family, and the knowledge passed down to him made him a worthy person or headman in others' eyes.

Community Leaders

This community leader, or real man, however, was not what European explorers or, later, territorial governors wanted or expected from a leader. What Governor Stevens wanted in 1855 was a S'Klallam chief who could sign away millions of acres of land to clear the clouded title of the Northwest for settlement. That kind of leader never existed in the Northwest and had to be created by non-natives. The Hudson Bay Company enjoyed great success in the Northwest long before Americans had any influence by naming, paying, or otherwise supporting and dealing only with those individuals they made chiefs. This practice of creating chiefs, sub-chiefs, and Tribes from many villages was a fundamental principle used in treaty making by the U.S. government in the Pacific Northwest.[17]

What European officials never understood was a fundamental difference between natives and non-natives in the Pacific Northwest. Non-natives exerted power over groups. Individual power, not group (village) power, prevailed with natives. Every individual might possess great supernatural power, and it was always best to assume this to be true and treat others accordingly.

If you were wronged, you could, under the right circumstances, retaliate. How individual power was acquired and then acted upon according to rules defined each person's life. There might be only one headman, or leader, in a small community, but usually there were several, and in larger villages, there were many real men with unique knowledge, skills, and ambitions who were seen by others as upper class, or worthy people. The class structure has been described as looking like a pear.

Fundamental elements of leadership, especially proper character and values, have always been an important part of Northwest indigenous life. While community leaders could not, nor would expect to ever, control others in the way European Americans expected chiefs to do, the community leader and upper class both enjoyed tremendous privileges. Multiple wives, more slaves and house servants, the best location in the longhouse (which was toward the rear of the building), the authority and resources to commission works of art (like crests, paintings, and house posts), and the most ornate and special clothing were only a few of the more obvious advantages. Leaders shouldered equally heavy responsibilities. These responsibilities sometimes varied by village, but a range of examples is illustrative. A community leader would be expected to host a potlatch for varying occasions, such as a death or the onset of a daughter's puberty.

When a new leader's house was constructed, a potlatch house event was held. Community leaders could determine who fished, decide when they hunted, set limits on animals taken, or order that a trespasser be killed.[18] Marriage into the family of a community leader increased the prestige of your family. Later, for example, when a trade took place, you were entitled to the better end of the bargain.[19]

Community leaders were first and foremost leaders of extended families or households when others recognized them as such. This recognition was quite important. A leader or headman with inherited rights and responsibilities ensured that commoners and especially people from other villages recognized his position by proclaiming this authority through feast and potlatch.

Community leaders knew the rules and values involved in important ceremonial occasions: honoring others, giving thanks, showing respect, and using proper etiquette. When a close reader looks across the Pacific Northwest literature and links it specifically with cultural and social groups in the Puget Sound, a clear pattern of these three classes of people emerges.

1. Upper class and community leaders with inherited rights maintained or acquired wealth and assured their reputation through feasts and potlatches and distinguished themselves from commoners with correct training and admirable character.

2. Commoners who shared the same values and character

traits, but who neither inherited significant rights nor acquired wealth, could take leadership roles in the family group or village and could enhance their prestige through marriage or alliance. Although inheritance provided a distinct advantage, correct behavior and character acquired through proper training could signify a shift in status.

3. Slaves, who had no inherited history, no method to acquire wealth, and no ability to marry out of their class made up the bottom of the social structure.

This traditional pattern largely broke down with European contact, but the basic values held by both leaders and commoners can still be found in some contemporary Tribal people. In today's Salish or S'Klallam community, a real man or woman will maintain his or her reputation by being an active member of the community, showing up at community events, and showing respect through gift giving, modest behavior, and sharing time or unique knowledge, for example. The traditional S'Klallam character and behavior is still the expected model: hard workers who are serious about what they do and who have self-control, modesty, courtesy, and generosity, especially with those in need. They reach out to others with dignity and pride.

> A person was not expected to be successful in life without the assistance of a guardian spirit or helper. These helpers were sometimes inherited but they were more often acquired through a vision.

The Spiritual Environment

Early spiritual beliefs in the central, southern, and Nootkans cultural and social areas in the Pacific Northwest were characterized later by European observers as a world of monsters that demanded the intervention of a "transformer," or "changer." The transformer gave founding persons of a village special knowledge and skills to ensure success. They sometimes were said to have dropped from the sky knowing how to fish, hunt, or gather the correct foods with proper respect. Regardless of how the world came to be, all people interacted with the environment to ensure their spiritual fulfillment. All places and all humans were alive with energy; without knowledge of and respect for these forces, a person could never hope to live a good life.

A person was not expected to be successful in life without the assistance of a guardian spirit or helper. These helpers were sometimes inherited but they were more often acquired through a vision. As early as eight or nine years of age, a boy or girl could be sent away to bathe, fast, and purge until visited by a spirit (usually in animal form) or a human who showed him- or herself as an animal.

The spirit might also come as the sun, a tree, or some other distinctive part of the natural environment. The recipient would lose consciousness or go into a trance, where they would receive special

spiritual power
ɫqʼíyən

transformer, or changer
x̣áʔyəs

power song
syéwən

knowledge and skills and a song to evoke these gifts. A person could have several visions to gain additional helpers.

Upon returning home, the vision was not discussed, and decades might pass before the helper was needed and brought forward, usually in early winter with the onset of an illness. A winter dance would then be organized and the vision revealed through song and sometimes with dance. At each occasion thereafter, the song would be sung at other spirit dances.

The guardian spirit or helper guided the S'Klallam and other Northwest villagers through dreams, and, when evoked through song, could help one be a better fisherman, hunter, gambler, warrior, singer, dancer, and, perhaps most important, could ensure the acquisition of wealth so one could potlatch.

The helper who could assist a S'Klallam to find a wounded deer that had escaped his snare or make him a better competitor in the bone game was indeed a worthwhile guardian. Community leaders particularly needed this kind of helper, and their sons had a right to inherit this powerful spirit.

Slahal, the Bone Game

Gambling and games have been an integral part of native culture and ceremony forever. Games taught children important skills, while gambling provided individuals with both recreation and a substantive means of acquiring wealth. The bone game, or slahal, was and still is immensely popular throughout the Northwest and beyond.

Bones with specific markings are hidden, and a guesser from the opposing team points to where he or she thinks the correct bone is hidden. Helpers beat sticks, sing, and shout insults at the opposing team. Large sums of money, canoes, houses, and wives were traditionally won and lost in these exciting, intriguing, and life-changing social events.

Shamans received more powerful guardian spirits than ordinary people, but because of this, they could be considered both a healer and someone very dangerous. They had the power to cure, harm, or kill, and could themselves be the targets of other shamans. Shamans might receive their power from a two-headed serpentlike or alligatorlike being (in the case of the Twana) or from a giant elklike creature (for the Lushootseed). These unusually powerful helpers gave the shaman the special knowledge and skills to diagnose illness, especially when an ordinary person was visited by his or her guardian spirit as well. A well-known and respected shaman was first and foremost a healer. He or she could look into people to diagnose their ills. A shaman could use hands or mouth to extract foreign objects from the body, predict the future from observing water in a basket or basin, find a lost person or important object, see the health of a relative who lived somewhere else, or see an enemy preparing to attack. The shaman also could control or influence others through spells, verbal recitation of formulas, or the use of secret names.

The basic belief that an ordinary person had several parts, and that one part could leave the body and cause the person to become ill, greatly enhanced the use and reputation of shamans, who might be called upon to make the patient whole again.

European observers labeled these parts variously as "life," "person," "mind," or "shadow" and for the Twana, "life soul" and "heart soul." A dangerous being or ghost was most often identified as the source of an illness.[20]

The winter spirit dance was each individual's opportunity to announce and reaffirm his or her guardian helper gifts. In combination with a potlatch or feast, it was also the opportunity to acclaim and renew leadership rights and impress other villagers with the power of a specific group. Men or women dancers wore either red or black on the body, special clothing, and headgear. They followed timeless practices of distinctive music and dance style.

What Americans were much later to call "spirit dancing" in the Coast Salish region was deeply and devastatingly influenced by the beliefs and practices of European immigrants. Indian agents, missionaries, and settlers were all convinced that native spiritual beliefs were inferior to their own and, in most cases, evil and barbarous practices that had to be completely eradicated in order to civilize the Indian peoples. After contact, when native spiritual practices were recorded by European Americans, this basic assumption influenced their observations and descriptions.

Though biased, these descriptions are still valuable for their record of important ceremonies that later were either completely abolished or mostly forgotten. After 1900 the "invitation" to a winter dance is characterized by each individual being "grabbed," laid down, blindfolded, put in a separate enclosure, and attended by others throughout the ceremony. No food and only a little water is given for four days while the person is kept lying down, wrapped in blankets, and only carried out by attendants in the morning and evening. A song is received in a dream, and on the fourth morning, the individual sings his or her song after a meal of dried salmon. After bathing in new specially made clothing, he or she performs and is attended in seclusion for the rest of the winter dances.[21]

Before the reemergence of spirit dancing after the 1950s, descriptions for several native peoples were tied to a wolf ceremony. This ceremony could last up to ten days for the Nootkans and was often sponsored by a community leader to initiate a son or close relative. Individuals impersonating wolves captured and isolated the initiate. There was a recapture by others followed by dances taught to the new initiate. During the ceremony, dogs were eaten raw and dancers danced with skewers through their flesh. Masks, theatrical illusions, and comic entertainment were important ingredients of the occasion. The Makah practiced the wolf ceremony and whale ceremony, and the Quileute held wolf and fisherman ceremonies. Two other important winter ceremonies included for the cleansing of a disgrace, for a girl's puberty (under certain circumstances), and for naming. The secret society ceremony was an initiation of individuals, largely to maintain inherited status. The ceremony involved seizing, killing, then bringing back to life prospective members.[22]

The Pacific Northwest After Contact

Spirit dances, secret society initiations, shamanism, and potlatching were severely restricted and driven underground by Indian agents, missionaries, and others in the late 1800s and did not reemerge in a public way until the 1980s. Once it came back, spirit dancing was clearly seen as an integral public and community part of the individual's guardian-spirit power and was seen as a way to re-create traditional Indian spiritual ways of life.

These traditional ways of governance, recognizing individual status, and exercising spiritual beliefs were largely unchanged from precontact through the mid-1800s. Rapid changes occurred only after large numbers of settlers found their way to the Pacific Northwest. At first, early explorations had very little impact on the indigenous population. When compared to other indigenous groups, the native peoples in the Pacific Northwest were afforded the luxury of being geographically isolated, which made exploration and settlement more difficult.

Spanish sailors sailing from the Pacific to the Atlantic Ocean in 1774–1775 failed to identify the Strait of Juan de Fuca. As far back as 1592, Juan de Fuca, for whom the Strait was named, may never have seen this unique and spectacular area. Juan Perez, nearly two centuries later, in 1774, recorded the first European sighting of the Olympic Mountains and named them El Cerro de la Santa Rosalia. The first landing on the Northwest coast was officially recorded when five crewmen from the Sonora, commanded by Bruno de Hegeta, were killed in Quinault territory on July 14, 1775. That is when the real struggle began among outsiders to determine who would control these waterways. One of the strongest allies of the invaders was disease. The greatest killer was smallpox, and it swept through the Pacific Northwest, decimating villages in the late 1700s. Given the highly integrated and complex social, political, cultural, and spiritual societies, large-scale death (particularly of the young) severely fractured the old ways of life. The oral tradition, the very glue that held everything together, was torn asunder.

Spanish, Russian, English, French, and finally American explorers all came to the Pacific Northwest with various motives of acquiring new territory, finding shortcuts to economic wealth, and identifying potential religious converts. They came with a mandate from their religious and political leaders to claim and name the land. Early Spanish conquest in the Americas is illustrative of a persistent theme: Indians

Anglo
xʷəníəm

American
pástən

Canadian
tɬn'aʔəč

were not Christians nor were they civilized. New immigrants brought with them, and further perpetuated, the image of indigenous peoples as barbaric, savage, slovenly, naked, and cannibalistic. But most of all, the native peoples' supposed pagan beliefs branded them as uncivilized and barbaric. In European eyes, the only hope for the Indian was Christianity. Here too was the beginning of the practice, alive and well today, of identifying ways of life from one Tribe and generalizing those same beliefs or practices to all Indians.

The S'Klallam and other villagers had names for all the places that these newcomers claimed . . . then renamed. Though later adventurers in turn replaced many of the subsequent Spanish names of the region, some remain. The Strait of Juan de Fuca was "named" in 1786. John Meares, a British captain, named Mount Olympus in 1788. The Quimper Peninsula, in traditional S'Klallam territory, still bears the name of the Spanish sailor who sailed into the strait in 1790. But by far the most well-known European explorer was British sea captain George Vancouver, whose crews mapped a good portion of the Puget Sound in April and May 1792. Undoubtedly, S'Klallam people had already heard about the large ships that had been seen around the sound as early as 1790. Natives of the Pacific Northwest were already using some European trade goods when Vancouver arrived.[23]

For a recent pictorial review of early contact, see William H. T. Goetzmann and Glyndwr Williams's The Atlas of North American Exploration (Norman: University of Oklahoma Press, 1992). Edmond S. Meany's Vancouver's Discovery of Puget Sound (Portland: Beresfords & Mort, 1949) contains extensive footnotes, particularly about the people for whom Vancouver named geographic features.

It was Lieutenant Peter Puget and Master Joseph Whidbey, though, who comprehensively surveyed most of the canal to present-day Olympia. Thus, their names appear prominently. Mount Baker was named for a member of Vancouver's crew, and Rainier after a rear admiral in the Royal Navy. Vancouver named the whole mountain range the Olympics. About half a century later, American claims to the area were greatly enhanced by a U.S. expedition commanded by Charles Wilkes. Wilkes anchored at Port Discovery, in the heart of S'Klallam country, in May 1838. He also stayed at Port Townsend and further explored Hood Canal. All of these early sojourns into S'Klallam territory met a highly sophisticated, fierce, and well-respected people. The many S'Klallam villages were peopled with highly skilled fishermen, canoeists, hunters, traders, and potlatchers.

British and American claims to the Pacific Northwest are best illustrated by the spring 1792 meeting between American captain Robert Gray, in command of the Columbia, and Vancouver. Ironically, after their brief meeting, Gray sailed south and into the mouth of the river that would later be named the Columbia. He was after

furs not empire. Even with exploration and detailed mapping in the
Puget Sound area by Vancouver, the United States pushed through
its claims and forced Britain in 1846 to accept the 49th parallel as the
U.S. northern boundary. America had no serious claim to any part of
the Northwest until the 1818 Louisiana Purchase. Even then this vast
territory was in reality a joint-use area with Great Britain. Before the
Louisiana Purchase, Meriwether Lewis and William Clark mapped the
region in 1803 to 1804, and John Jacob Astor set up the Pacific Fur
Company at the mouth of the river in 1811 to 1812.

Two presidents, Tyler and Polk, pushed the American expansionist
doctrine with the help of John O'Sullivan's introduction of the
infamous phrase "manifest destiny": "Away, away with all those cobweb
tissues of rights of discovery, exploration, settlement, contiguity, etc.
. . . The American claim is by the right of our manifest destiny to
overspread and to possess the whole of the continent which providence
has given us."[24] Polk's campaign for president rested solidly on the
annexation of both Texas and Oregon. Polk used the "54-40 or fight!"
slogan to assert U.S. claims as far north as the southern boundary of
Russian Alaska, but, not wanting a war with Britain, he and Congress
settled for the 49th parallel as a diplomatic compromise.[25]

When the Hudson Bay Company built Fort Vancouver on the
Columbia River in 1824, it set the tone for the future of development
north of the river as well as for relationships with Indians. American
settlers began to arrive, in small numbers, first at the Columbia River,
then northward from 1834. By 1840 there were
six Hudson Bay Company trading centers in
presentday Washington. There was a marked
increase of intervillage economic and social
interaction because of the trade lines created
and maintained by the Hudson Bay Company.
As early as the late 1830s, the fur trade was
in severe decline and agriculture on the rise.
The fur trade, along with supplying fish and
other trade goods, fit well with the way of life for Pacific Northwest
natives. Native economy thrived around trade and resources acquired
in exchange for services like transporting foreigners by canoe, and
providing fish, shellfish, and land animal products. Slave raiding,
acquiring and potlatching resources, maintaining prestige, gift exchange,
cross-Tribal marriages, and a host of other important cultural and
economic ways of life changed suddenly and dramatically with colonial
rule. When agriculture and, later, industrialization took prominence,
Indian people were significantly marginalized in the economics of the
area.

The famous Oregon Trail dumped more than nine hundred
immigrants into the Willamette Valley in 1843, and another twelve
hundred followed the next year. Oregon Territory was created in 1844.

The S'Klallam's reputation as fierce warriors, outstanding canoeists, and expert fishermen made them a formidable force to be reckoned with by friend and foe alike.

A few moved north into Puget Sound near present-day Olympia at Turnwater, or New Market as it was originally named. The original group included Michael T. Simmons and his family. Simmons was later to play a major role as an Indian agent in the Puget Sound region and with the S'Klallam. The Simmons's group farms were the first American settlements in Washington and more followed in 1846. There were 304 white people north of the Columbia River in 1849, and by 1850, there were still only 417. However, the population of the entire Oregon Territory increased from about eight thousand in 1850 to thirty thousand by 1855. Settlers claimed Port Townsend, on S'Klallam land, in 1851, and by 1853, the U.S. federal government established a U.S. customs house to inspect the timber being cut, milled, and shipped around the world. That same year, settlers moved onto Sequim Prairie, and Washington Territory was created.[26]

Between 1775, when invaders first landed in the Northwest, and 1850, when significant numbers of immigrants appeared, the S'Klallam and their native neighbors felt secure in their homelands. The S'Klallam's reputation as fierce warriors, outstanding canoeists, and expert fishermen made them a formidable force to be reckoned with by friend and foe alike. After the 1850s this all changed for the S'Klallam and other native groups. Ultimately, it was the United States that wrested the rights to their homelands from other European invaders and invested considerable efforts to take title to S'Klallam lands, assimilate and Christianize the inhabitants, force them onto small and inadequate reservations, and end their traditional ways of life. Despite a clear federal policy that Indian title to their lands be cleared prior to colonial settlement, the Oregon Donation Land Act of 1850 gave the opposite impression. To encourage settlement, Congress illegally donated 320 acres of Indian lands to men and an additional 320 acres to a wife. The message about Indian rights to the land was clear—they could be pushed aside from more desirable places and their protests ignored. It would be 120 years of genocide and forced subjugation to a foreign culture before the Jamestown S'Klallam began the process of reasserting their inherent sovereignty and rebuilding their ways of life, which had never been fully extinguished.

Homeland

Traditional Ways

The environment in which the S'Klallam people lived during the mid-1700s, before white contact, was dominated by geography, weather, and the available sea and land food resources. Fourteen hundred square miles of mountains overshadow the Olympic Peninsula. Narrow lowlands hug the shoreline and provide ideal winter and summer village sites where rivers and streams fall rapidly into the Strait of Juan de Fuca and Hood Canal. Over two hundred inches of rain fall annually on the highest peaks, but a rain shadow shelters the Dungeness River area and results in a modest fifteen to twenty inches of rainfall a year. Long after Vancouver's famous voyage into the Puget Sound in 1792, the area along the north shoreline of the Olympics, from the Hoko River to Discovery Bay, and down Hood Canal to the Hamma Hamma River, remained S'Klallam territory until increased white encroachment a century later.

Transportation

Though there were overland trails used for hunting and trade, given the challenging terrain of the Olympic Peninsula, the preferred mode of travel was by canoe. Indeed, all Indians who lived and moved near waterways built and used canoes of varying sizes and shapes. Distance was measured by how far you could travel in a canoe in one day. Of course, weather, currents, and up-river travel were challenges. The Pacific Northwest Indians, in particular those who plied the straits and ocean waters, were greatly respected for their skills in making and using canoes. The S'Klallam—who moved extensively across the strait to Vancouver Island, throughout the San Juan Islands close to the mouth

An excellent, concise source of basic information on the state of Washington is James W. Scott and Roland L. De Lorme's Historical Atlas of Washington (Norman: University of Oklahoma Press, 1988).

An excellent discussion on both geography and archaeology of the Olympic National Park, with special attention paid to the American Indians who were there before the park, can be found in Tim McNulty's Olympic National Park: A Natural History Guide (Boston: Houghton Mifflin Co., 1996).

A recent work that brings together Indian and non-Indian changes all along the Pacific Coast, specific to the ecosystem and the economy, is Robert Bunting's The Pacific Raincoast: Environment and Culture in an American Eden, 1778–1900 (Lawrence: University Press of Kansas, 1997).

big waves
čiʔqay'áq

wind
sčuŋ

swift water
x̌ʷəŋáyəqən

war canoe
ʔuʔúʷx̣s

of Hood Canal, and throughout the canal—were no exception, as evidenced by the numerous remarks in early journals and logs of explorers and settlers.

Two types of canoes were principally constructed from cedar trees to meet the different demands of open salt water and sheltered waters. The Coast Salish sheltered water type was used for hunting and fishing in bays, inlets, rivers, and the canal. The canoe of the Coast Salish had a more gently sloping bow than its northern counterpart, and a rounded bottom. The gunwales terminated in a characteristic concave flare, with the wood only one fingerwidth at the edge. The sides of the hull measured two finger-widths in thickness, with the bottom a little thicker. In contrast, the west coast style, with its highly stylized totemic figures on the bow, was used for whaling in ocean seas and for transporting up to thirty warriors. It had a flatter bottom and a more vertical stern than the sheltered water canoe.

Myron Eells, a missionary who worked extensively among the S'Klallam during the late nineteenth and early twentieth centuries, noted, as had others, that the S'Klallam were exceptional canoeists and described the small fishing canoe: "They are used for fishing, hunting ducks, traveling on rivers, and even on the Sound when it is calm, and they wish to take only a small load. I have traveled thirty miles in this kind on Hood Canal, though we preferred to keep near shore if possible. Still I have crossed the canal in one when it was quite rough, and we were in the trough of the sea, for the larger ones withstand considerable waves. In rough water however the Indians are very careful in them. They vary in length from about 12 to 30 feet, in width from 20 to 48 inches, and in depth from nine to 20 inches in the center."[1]

Eells described several types of canoes by size and shape, but there were two primary types in use: one for travel in rivers and calmer bays and areas away from heavy waves and a larger canoe, later called a Chinook canoe. The Chinook canoes had a square stern and might measure more than thirty-five feet long, six feet wide, and three feet deep. Eells noted that the S'Klallam were better navigators and used larger canoes than other Indians in the Puget Sound.

The carving of a canoe out of a cedar tree was a complex and arduous undertaking. It was a highly skilled art that was passed down to only a few people. It was not uncommon for a S'Klallam to purchase canoes, especially the larger ones. The carving process encompasses many skills. A carver must choose the right tree and show respect before cutting it down. He or she would use stone adzes to carve, then mold the canoe features with the assistance of fire to burn out the insides. Later, canoe makers used axes and carving knives, when they became available. The sides of the canoe are spread by filling the canoe with water and dropping in hot stones to heat the wood and to allow crosspieces to be tied into place with cedar ropes. The rim is finished with fir, which is harder than cedar, to stand up to the wear from paddles, and house planks are attached to the canoe to transport goods or to dance on for certain ceremonies.[2]

Fishing

It is no surprise, given the environment and their expertise in making and using canoes, that the S'Klallam have always been highly skilled fishermen. In addition to the rich oral history about fishing, there are reports and observations pertinent to fishing from nearly all early Europeans who wrote about their travels.

A description of S'Klallam-specific fishing materials, with many photos, is found in The Indians of Puget Sound: The Notebooks of Myron Eells, edited by George Pierre Castile (Seattle: University of Washington Press, 1985), 158–59. Eells was a missionary who wrote extensively about the Indians he served. While not a trained social scientist, most of his observations appear to support those of other social scientists and writers of that period and later periods.

The Jamestown people sustained their families, fellow villagers, and, often, friends by mining the seasonal resources along the Strait of Juan de Fuca and the Puget Sound. When Charles Wilkes, commander of a U.S. expedition in the early nineteenth century, passed through the S'Klallam territory, he noted that Vancouver's earlier descriptions were "exactly applicable to the present state . . . it was difficult to believe that almost half a century had elapsed since it was written." The skill of native fishermen and hunters was duly noted: "During our stay at Port Discovery, they supplied us plentifully with venison, ducks, geese, salmon, a large species of cod, flounders, herrings and crabs. They also brought shellfish, among which were the common clam (the quahog of the Eastern states), mussels, and small oysters."[3]

The S'Klallam were astute and crafty traders who knew what foreign visitors desired and who could easily produce excess food to trade or sell. Over seventy years after Wilkes lauded the bounty available to his hungry crew, a government official noted that a hallmark of S'Klallam character included progressive and adoptive methods to sustain themselves, mixed with traditional fishing and crabbing. Selling fresh or cooked fish and crab is a natural way to make a living even hundreds of years after Vancouver floated into Discovery Bay.

butter clam
sq'x̣ə́yuʔ

mussel
ƛ'aw'qəm

little neck
clam
skʷ'ʷɬáʔiʔ

red rock crab
kʷəkʷáʔiʔ

The Jamestown S'Klallam fished throughout their traditional territory in salt water and in the rivers and streams, especially those emptying into the Strait of Juan de Fuca. (See the maps of traditional and modern-day territory on pages 2 and 3) S'Klallam people both singularly and in groups fished year-round and very proficiently for this important source of food. When the S'Klallam fished in others' homelands, they sought permission from relatives. Indeed, they were known for their strategic marriages to acquire access to good places to fish, gather shellfish and plants, and hunt land animals. Strangers without family ties might be told to move along or, if there was plenty available, might be ignored. "Ownership" of these places changed over time, of course, when lack of use by an extended family or village group signaled free access to an area. Ownership was balanced by sharing and generosity. To be seen as selfish would be considered a serious social transgression.[4]

Selling fresh or cooked fish and crab is a natural way to make a living even hundreds of years after Vancouver floated into Discovery Bay.

There is no denying the special importance of the salmon to the S'Klallam and other peoples of the region. The five most widely recognized species of Pacific salmon have different names, especially by locals, but all hatch in freshwater streams and rivers, swim to the salt water to grow and develop, then return to the rivers and streams to spawn, finally dying while struggling upstream against the fierce currents trying to carry them back to the ocean. Few people who have seen the sight of hundreds of salmon struggling against the rapids to return from whence they came fail to be impressed. The salmon continue to be revered as both a majestic natural resource for all and as a spiritual connection to the S'Klallam world. Both the current and past efforts of the Jamestown people to restore and preserve the salmon are testimony to how much a part of their way of life the fish have always been.

coho salmon
q'əčqs

sockeye
salmon
scə́qiʔ

dog salmon
ƛ̓xʷáy'

humpback
salmon
hə́nən

While the Pacific Northwest salmon has always captured the contemporary imagination of commercial and sports fishermen, as well as poets and travelers, other fish like steelhead, halibut, sturgeon, lingcod, rock and flat fish, anchovies, eulachon, and herring also filled the nets and canoes of traditional S'Klallam who lived on or near the shores of the straits, rivers, and canals.

Salmon and other fish were, of course, not the only abundant food source. Fishing in the traditional sense included the gathering, digging, and preserving of all varieties of marine resources: cockles, clams, mussels, oysters, octopus, squid, crab, shrimp, sea urchins, and sea cucumbers. Jamestown fishermen knew when the salmon came and where they came to, but more important, they knew that this resource was not always available, particularly later in the nineteenth century. This is in sharp contrast to the wildly exuberant reports from early settlers and even the oral history of S'Klallam people of the abundance of salmon available. Who has not heard the story of walking across a river on the backs of migrating salmon?

Some S'Klallam, who held fishing spots on the Hoko and Dungeness Rivers, may not have moved around as much as others because they had access to so many varieties of salmon and other fish. They made short trips from Dungeness to Discovery Bay for spring salmon. Some would fish the Hood Canal for dog salmon in August. Many S'Klallam were known to have fished at both Tahuya and Union City by the mouth of the Skokomish River. S'Klallam Tribal citizens testifying in court cases also identified the Hamma Hamma River and Brinnon as places where the Twana joined the S'Klallam to fish and visit. The Twana also fished all species of salmon that were available in the Hood Canal, except sockeye. The dog salmon run was most abundant in the Skokomish River, beginning late August into September. The S'Klallam joined the Twana for this important run in August, and some came back in September or stayed through the winter. William Elmendorf, gathering information from informants in 1940, commented on S'Klallam fishing: "My data illustrate particularly clearly the intimacy between the Skokomish and the Dungeness River people. . . . Between 1800 and 1850 it is certain that the Klallam and Twana drew ever more closely together, with accompanying intermarriage, mutual participation in ceremonies, and even joint action in raiding parties.. . . According to H.A., during his childhood (1860s) 'hundreds of Klallam' were present on Hood Canal in the summer and early fall, trolling at the river mouths on the west side of the canal alongside friendly Skokomish and other Twana.

"By 1850 the Klallam were not only friendly and frequently seen neighbors and marriage relatives, but were regarded by the Twana as an exceptionally clever, talented, and vigorous people, stagers of impressive ceremonies, worthy of emulation in almost everything, and very desirable prospects for marital and other social alliances."[5]

The S'Klallam always had a reputation among other Tribes as leaders. This especially included their fishing abilities, ceremonial powers, and propensity to raid the northern Tribes that were the most feared by other Tribes in the Puget Sound. S'Klallam intermarriage with the Twana and other Tribes was fueled by their strong reputation as fishermen and warriors with whom any alliance would benefit, be it marriage or the sharing of fishing places.

> Both the current and past efforts of the Jamestown people to restore and preserve the salmon are testimony to how much a part of their way of life the fish have always been.

Fishing Methods

The S'Klallam caught fish using various methods: traps, trolling, gillnetting, spearing, raking, dip-netting, and holes dug on the beach. A different method or combined methods were used for each species during the appropriate time of the year. For example, spring salmon

5

saltwater
fish–trap
tqápən

dip net
ʔəkʼʷáy(ə)n

creek
stútaʔwiʔ

were trapped, trolled for, or gillnetted between the middle of April to July. Dog salmon followed the silver salmon run and were caught the same way. Silver salmon, in October through December, were trapped, fished for by line in the river, gillnetted outside of a spit, and speared at night. Line fishing was used for halibut, given the depth of water they stayed in. The S'Klallam traveled as far as Cape Flattery in Makah territory to fish for halibut. Lingcod could be speared if they came close to shore but otherwise were also caught on line from April through September. Smelt were caught in September by digging holes in the beach and stranding them when the tide retreated. Candlefish were raked and dip-netted from September to late October. Dog salmon were gillnetted or trapped in late July, and humpback salmon were trapped, speared, or line fished from August to the end of October. Flounder were speared from canoes in salt water from April to September, and herring were raked from the middle of February to late March. Varieties of fish, some more desirable than others, were available year-round.

Duck Hunting Methods

Eells wrote about specially designed spears made to ensure the body of the duck would not be harmed. However, he also noticed that the introduction of firearms changed this traditional way of hunting. He described the use of nets for duck hunting:"Especially in foggy weather the Indians cover their canoes with green boughs, among which they hide, and they paddle quietly among the ducks, and shoot them. [Formerly they suspended] nets for taking wild fowl that frequent these shores in great numbers. On these poles the nets were set up at night at which time the geese searched the ground for food. Fires were then built which alarmed the birds, and caused them to fly against the nets, by which they were thrown to the ground, where, before they had time to recover themselves, they were caught and killed." [7]

Eells wrote extensively about fishing and all the tools used and created by the S'Klallam and other Indians of the Pacific Northwest. He described fishing, sealing, and whaling, as well as how ducks were captured. When discussing fishing tools and techniques, Eells wrote: "A very common fish spear is made with a long, straight handle, fifteen or twenty feet long, and not far from an inch in diameter. The handle is of fir, on account of its strength, as well as being straight, and the prongs are of some hard wood, as maple, or ironwood, sometimes hardened in the fire, and lately of iron. They are used in spearing skates, crabs, flounders, salmon and the like, and for bringing up cod fish eggs, when they are in water that is not too deep. When thus fishing, one person, sitting in the stern of the canoe, will quietly paddle, while another, sitting or kneeling in the bow, uses the spear. Because of long practice, they will see a fish partly buried in the mud, where an unpracticed eye will fail to discern it, and having seen it will rarely fail to secure it." [6]

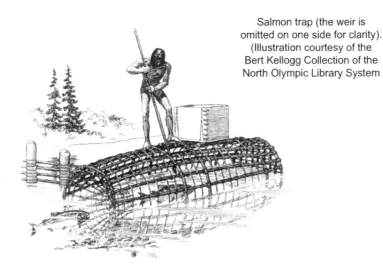

Salmon trap (the weir is
omitted on one side for clarity).
(Illustration courtesy of the
Bert Kellogg Collection of the
North Olympic Library System

For S'Klallam fishermen, a well-known technique was the weir, or fish trap, used across part or all of a river mouth. Many Tribes in the Northwest and across America used weirs. Different tree and plant materials were used for construction, depending on available resources. Erna Gunther described S'Klallam fish traps in great detail. The basic materials included young fir trees pounded into the river bottom, with the tops crossed over and tied together with cedar limbs. The trap was strengthened against the current by longer poles, braced upriver and on the sides at the riverbank. The webbing was constructed of carefully chosen small fir trees tied to the upstream side, so the current helped hold it in place. A platform is built above a trap formed by a door or window built in the center. "The fisherman sleeps on this platform with his head against the protruding posts of the trap so that he can feel the salmon beat against the upstream side of the pocket. Salmon are taken out with a gaff hook. Before the iron hook came into use they used a sack net on a pole."[8]

Of course, the construction of fish traps varied. For instance, the weir at a creek near Blyn, where Washington Harbor S'Klallam fished for dog salmon, did not have a pocket or platform, and had fewer rows of webbing and one door. S'Klallam used spears when the humpbacks ran well, which was known to be about every four years. They speared silver salmon at night with the aid of a torch for light. The S'Klallam also used a different type of fish trap for steelhead and another net for use only in rivers: "Steelhead salmon runs in December, January and February. It is not trolled for, but caught by trap. A special trap for steelheads consists of a row of vertical sticks set in the riverbed from bank to bank. The sticks protrude above the water and above the level of the platform which is erected over the trap. As the fisherman leans against the sticks he can feel the salmon striking against the trap as they

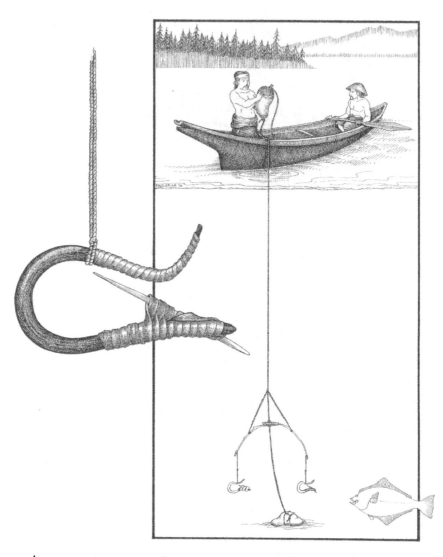

Traditional S'Klallam steam-bent halibut hook and fishing method
(Illustrations by Dale Faulstich).

Salmon traps for narrow streams (Illustration courtesy of the Bert Kellogg Collection of the North Olympic Library System

come downstream. The steelheads follow the river till it rises and then come back to the salt water. A scoop net . . . is placed on the upstream side of the trap.

"There is also a river net . . . which is used for all kinds of salmon. A basket net of nettle twine is made about six feet long, tapering, and as wide at its mouth as it is long. Fir or cedar poles about twelve or thirteen feet long are attached at opposite sides of the mouth. The mouth of the net is closed by means of drawstrings. Two fishermen take these poles and wade up the river, holding the net between them. In deep places they float on the poles."[9]

Flounder, which were eaten fresh rather than dried, were speared or caught with a nettle-twine line and two pieces of elk bone tied like a cross, with clam-meat bait. Halibut and lingcod were caught from the bank using two nettle-twine lines, with a sinker and a buoy (paunch of a seal) with devilfish bait. The steam-bent hook was created by steaming wood into a hook shape with sharpened elk bone.

The S'Klallam used a rake to catch herring. The rake was a long pole with teeth made of sharpened elk bone on a two-inch board. Nails eventually took the place of the elk bone. The rake was generally used to lift the fish into a canoe. Herring were especially available at the old wharf at Dungeness, the Washington Harbor Spit, and in a cave halfway up the south side of Sequim Bay. Herring eggs were collected by laying hemlock twigs in spawning beds, then taking them out of the water to dry.

Smelt and candlefish came in September and October and were caught by stranding them in holes dug in the beach before high tide. They sometimes splashed up on the beach on their own, or could be raked up or pulled into a basket attached to a pole by setting it in the water and walking toward the beach.

Whaling

Unlike the Makah Tribe, who are located on the west point of
the Olympic Peninsula, the S'Klallam were not primarily whalers,
though, as the following story illustrates, they did hunt them when
the opportunity arose. Even though the S'Klallam were not known
as whalers, they must have used the knowledge and equipment fairly
regularly in order to maintain them.

Whaling was both a family and a village event—watching for
whales, women paddling, men harpooning—and it was dangerous
work. A catch would be distributed among the S'Klallam, then the
extra meat would be sold to other villages and Tribes. In the course
of the following whaling story, a woman on the crew gets pulled
overboard by the harpoon line and uses the air in the bladder floats to
save herself. The whale tows two bladder floats and two canoes over a
significant distance for an entire day and night before it is beached. The
whaling story, collected by William Elmendorf, goes as follows:

A story about my mother's brother, [Captain Jack], and the whale hunters at Klallam Bay.

Now [Captain Jack]'s house is . . . on the north side of the bay,
and the house of x̣aqtə́, another relative of my mother, is on the
opposite (SE) side . . . . And they watch all the time for whale
coming, their canoes are always ready to go out after whale. And
they have men and good, stout women to help them paddle after
whales.

After a while they see a whale coming now into the bay. And x̣aqtə́
gets ready first; he goes out after that whale.

And then [Captain Jack] gets his canoe ready and goes.

And xhacatə́ gets to the whale first. He is in the bow with his
harpoon, . . . and he spears that whale first. So the whale made a
jump and dived, and a woman in x̣aqtə́'s canoe got tangled in the
line, her foot caught in the line and overboard she went, tangled
in the line. That woman was under water a long time now, and
[Captain Jack] watched where the whale went. There were two
bladder floats, . . . and he could tell by these where the whale was
going, towing those floats and that woman caught in the line.

Now the whale started to come up, the line got slack and .x̣aqt´ @'
started to pull it in, and [Captain Jack] watched for where the whale
would come up. Now that woman who had been towed overboard
had grabbed one of the bladders and held her mouth against it
and breathed through the bladder, that bladder saved her life.

And now the line was slack, the whale was coming up, and they
haul in the line, they haul that woman up into the canoe of x̣aqtə́.
She was under water a long time; it was a wonder that she could
live.

Now the whale comes up and [Captain Jack] puts his harpoon into
it. That whale jumps and starts out of the bay, with those two
canoes after him, following those bladders, with the lines tied to

the canoes. And the whale goes east down the strait now, he tows the canoes almost to Port Angeles, then he turns and comes back toward Klallam Bay. And now that whale is getting weak, they start pulling in the lines little by little, pulling up on that whale. Now the whale is weak, just swimming on the surface, not going down any more. Now they have been out following that whale one day and one night. And now he has become weak; he goes right to the shore to die. About two or three miles this side of Klallam Bay . . . he goes ashore on a sand beach. Just those two harpoons,my uncle said, killed that big whale.

The Klallam Bay people butcher that whale. They cut it up and [Captain Jack] and xaqtə́ give their own people lots of whale meat, give them the parts from the tail, and then they have lots left to sell. And people come from other places, other Klallam come and Neah Bay people come to buy whale meat from [Captain Jack] and xaqtə́. And they sell those other people the whale meat and take lots of goods for it. And at Klallam Bay they boil the fat and hang the meat up in strips to dry. [10]

All of these varied fishing techniques and unique traps had to be adapted to the type of fish, the depth of ocean or bays, and access to rivers, as well as tempered by each individual's experience and spiritual guidance. Carefully chosen fir trees were used to design gearlike buoys and steamed wood hooks. Cedar limbs, nettle twine, and hemlock twigs were used for making webbing, trays, and fishing line. Traditional S'Klallam fishermen were indeed ingenious craftspeople, which contributed to their proficiency as fishermen.[11]

S'Klallam stories have kept the fishing and crabbing tradition firmly woven into contemporary Jamestown history. Virtually any interview with a Tribal Elder or citizen reminiscing about growing up around Jamestown yields stories and memories involving fishing, such as the following excerpt from an interview with Mickie (Prince) Judson.

Gee, oh, I remember one place over here in Dungeness where there used to be so much fish that my dad would go down there in a wagon and a lot of people who didn't have cars in those days, but my dad had a wagon, and lived on the farm, we had a team of horses, and he would put hay in that . . . just put the fish in there and we would start from that end, clear down until everybody would have fish to smoke and they called that "Flumatch." 12

Current issues of the *Jamestown S'Klallam Tribe Newsletter* are full of reminiscences about fishing practices. These not only educate on traditional ways, they help identify techniques that are still useful.

At the opening of halibut season, Meredith and her grandparents, Nora and John Cook, would camp on Graveyard Spit so that her grandfather could fish for halibut. They usually stayed for two days then went back to the shore to sell fresh fish to Mr. McInnes and the other local farmers. Meredith remembers going on a fishing trip with her grandparents one summer when she was five years old. While her grandfather spent the day out on the water fishing, Meredith and her grandmother gathered wood from the beach and together they began the fire that was to cook their evening meal. Meredith's uncles set crab traps, made out of chicken wire and wood, between the McInnes farm and the Three Crabs Restaurant. Once the crabs were caught, they were put into a wood storage bin, which was sectioned off into three compartments; one section held the small crab and the other two housed the medium and large crab. This method ensured quick delivery of the correct size crab to each customer.

Meredith remembers running out to these boxes on the beach at low tide and retrieving just the right size crab for her uncles. She got quite good at making sure she did not get pinched by the live crab as she picked them up out of the bins. Some customers liked their crab cooked, so her uncles would be in the process of cooking while they sold fresh crab to the customers. Everyone at Jamestown used the salt water to cook crab . . . this was the only way to preserve the delicious natural flavor of the crab! Meredith swears by this process to this day, and wouldn't cook crab any other way![13]

The S'Klallam physical environment was a critical part of their lives, and remains so today. The ocean, currents, bays, rivers, watersheds, and species of fish and shellfish in their traditional homeland made them fishermen. The creator placed the S'Klallam there with these resources and the responsibility to protect and sustain them. In a very real sense, you cannot separate, in the past or the present, the Pacific Northwest environment from S'Klallam life.

Contemporary Ways

The Jamestown people still live amid several watersheds at the base of the mountains of the Olympic Peninsula. Seven- and eight-thousand-foot mountain peaks rapidly shed water down a vast network of rivers and streams that fan out like a web, lacing an eighty-five-mile stretch along the south shore of the Strait of Juan de Fuca. These watersheds and the ocean they feed were, until recently, bountiful food producers, ranging from elk, deer, and bear on the slopes of the mountains to salmon at the mouths of rivers and shellfish on the tidelands.

The commitment by Jamestown Tribal citizens to protect and preserve the environment today has not changed significantly from the S'Klallam people's view of responsibility since the beginning of time. The mission of this Tribe, which flows from the will of today's Jamestown citizens, is to protect, restore, and enhance the watersheds and related ecosystems within the historical territory of the Jamestown S'Klallam people. This mission can only be carried out by aggressively protecting treaty rights. This is a widely shared and well-understood responsibility of the Tribe.

The major reason for preserving and restoring the environment and securing treaty rights for today's Tribal citizens and their descendants is to allow Jamestown people to harvest fish, shellfish, and other wildlife. The S'Klallam have always maintained their livelihood from these resources, which the 1855 Point-No-Point Treaty guaranteed. Along with these rights come the responsibility to ensure the resources will continue forever.

By far, the most significant change over the past 120 years has been the negative environmental impact created by the rapid population increase in traditional S'Klallam territories. European American settlers brought with them very different ways of interacting with the environment. When the 1855 treaty was signed, neither S'Klallam nor settlers were worried about future supplies of fish or game. In everyone's view, there would always be enough fish and shellfish. Today, few people argue that there has not been a serious, and for some places and species catastrophic, degradation of the Olympic Peninsula watersheds and overall ecosystems.

Fishing Rights

All Indian Tribes who signed treaties with Governor Stevens in 1854–1855 face a continuing challenge to interpret and allocate natural resources within traditional territories. In 1999 the U.S. Supreme Court upheld the 1994 U.S. District Court's ruling that Tribes in Washington had the right to harvest clams, oysters, and other shellfish from private beaches. The terms of use include that written notice be given after surveying for an adequate population (citizens may take no more than half the population), and access to the property must be from the water. In addition, the harvests can only be made during daylight hours and only over five days each year. Current issues include shellfish allocation, interTribal allocation of the 50 percent share of fisheries mandated by the Boldt decision (see below), and the treaty right to 50 percent of the harvestable surplus of halibut, which was recently reaffirmed by the federal court.[14] However, intertribal allocations are still annually in dispute.

Other issues include hunting and Tribal rights to protect and manage habitat. A court case known as "Phase II of the Boldt Decision," which dealt with protecting fish and shellfish, was dismissed without prejudice in 1993, so future court action depends upon the

Threats, fraud, force, and the English language were just some of the barriers to negotiating a fair treaty. The playing field was never level.

continued success of cooperative management of the environment. Several other court cases are pending that focus on boundary disputes between Tribes, equitable adjustments of annual catches, prior interceptions by Alaskan fisheries, and registration and taxation of Tribal boats.

The Boldt Decision

After the War of 1812 and the departure of the British, Indians could no longer negotiate treaties from a strong position. The Americans had no further need of Indian fighting forces, and Indian policy shifted to removal of Indians to enhance westward migration. Threats, fraud, force, and the English language were just some of the barriers to negotiating a fair treaty. The playing field was never level. However, one of the rules of law that evolved, called "canons of constitution," was that each part of a treaty must be read today as the Indians would have understood it when they made the agreement. This rule of law laid the framework for one of the most hotly debated court decisions in modern times, *United States v. Washington*, commonly referred to as the Boldt decision.

> For a succinct legal description of the Boldt decision, see David H. Getches, Charles F. Wilkinson, and Robert A. Williams, Jr.'s <u>Cases and Materials on Federal Indian Law</u>, 3rd edition (St. Paul: West Publishing, 1993), 158–62. A more general discussion is in Robert E. Ficken and Charles P. Le Warne's <u>Washington: A Centennial History</u> (Seattle: University of Washington Press, 1988), 174–77. There are a large number of other sources on the Boldt decision, but a current and particularly insightful source is Alexandria Harmon's <u>Indians in the Making: Ethnic Relations and Indian Identities around Puget Sound</u> (Berkeley: University of California Press, 1998), especially pages 218–44.

in office
čačtəʔ

all
ʔuʔ x̣ənʔə

part of it
sqʷúʔs

half
ʔəɬčəx̣

It is not often that court decisions become known by the name of the judge who issued them. At the time of the case in 1974, George Boldt had already amassed twenty years of experience on the federal bench and was a senior district judge for the western district of Washington, presiding in Tacoma. His name became a household word when he held that treaty fishermen would have the right to take up to 50 percent of the harvestable number of fish, using traditional methods and at their usual and accustomed fishing stations. When the non-native people of Washington heard that the Indians were guaranteed half of the salmon catch, over 120 years of racial tension, Indian stereotypes, and depletions of a scarce resource overflowed an already simmering pot.

The state of Washington had banned commercial net fishing in 1907. Throughout the 1940s, many Tribes, such as the Makah and Yakima, challenged this and other state fishing laws. In 1954, the "fishing wars" began when two Puyallup Indians, Bob Satiacum and James Young, were arrested for fishing with nets and hooks, which the state said were illegal. The fish-in was a nonviolent protest mirrored after the sit-ins held by African Americans in the South.

More than twenty years before the Boldt decision, fish-ins had received considerable publicity (particularly when attended by noted celebrities like Marlon Brando and Dick Gregory) and had created some deep divisions in the region that the Boldt decision brought to the foreground. Twenty years of fish-ins and other demonstrations and counterdemonstrations finally forced the federal government to intervene on the Indians' behalf.

Governor Stevens's nineteenth-century treaties had used nearly identical language concerning the Tribes. He knew they relied on fishing for a living. Stevens had also included language that white immigrants should be allowed to fish. Although those Indians at treaty camps may have understood that the whites would also be fishing, they certainly had no understanding that their own fishing would be interfered with or completely taken over by the newcomers.

Chinook jargon and English were the primary languages used to explain the treaties, and these had to be interpreted into a wide variety of native tongues. Boldt held that Chinook jargon was totally inadequate for this kind of transaction. There were no words in the jargon at that time to explain terms like "usual," "accustomed," or "in common." When violence escalated after his decision, Boldt assumed personal responsibility to assure his decision would be enforced by creating an advisory board and empowering its chair to deal with disputes. The Boldt decision was affirmed by the 9th Circuit Court in 1975, and the U.S. Supreme Court denied an appeal in 1976.

The Washington state government has over the years consistently attempted to assert its sovereignty over Tribal sovereignty, particularly in the arena of fishing and shellfishing. The dwindling resource of the salmon has become the central battlefield. Commercial and sport fishermen lobbied the state to stop Indians from fishing in "usual and accustomed locations" with traditional traps and nets, despite their having been guaranteed these rights by treaty. The thrust of the argument has always been that Indians were taking the majority of the catch and negatively affecting the resource. The reality, of course, is that in the decades preceding the Boldt decision, Indian fishermen rarely took more than a very small portion of the catch and that the fluctuation in salmon runs was caused by many factors, including commercial fishing in international waters. State courts, as might be expected, made inconclusive and contradictory rulings for several years before the federal government began suing on behalf of the Indians.

The landmark Boldt decision to give Indians one half of the salmon catch made clear that no act of Congress or other rule of law had taken away or nullified Indian treaty rights. Indeed, Boldt's interpretation of Indian rights was that the Indians had agreed to share their resource with non-Indians, not the other way around.

There is no way to tell how many salmon once flooded the rivers and streams along the Olympic Mountain watersheds, but many stories tell of striking abundance. The pink salmon run in 1963 was more than four hundred thousand in the Dungeness.[15] However, the promise of returning salmon and their former abundance are now threatened. Using data collected by the Washington Department of Fish and Wildlife, the Jamestown S'Klallam Tribe natural resources director notes the seriousness of the situation: "Unfortunately, the Dungeness is not the abundant source of fisheries that it was in the last century with chinook and summer chum salmon now listed as threatened under the Endangered Species Act. The returning run of adult Dungeness chinook in the 19th century has been estimated as high as 26,000 fish, but less than 300 chinook now straggle back to their home watershed to spawn annually. In 1998, only 44 nests, or 'redds,' of chinook eggs were counted in the river. Other species of Dungeness salmon, including pink and wild coho, are also considered to be depressed or critically low."[16]

A seminal Supreme Court decision in 1908, *Winter v. United States*, affirmed the rights of Indian Tribes to have enough water to support their nations and communities. The combination of the Winters and Boldt decisions, along with Point-No- Point Treaty rights, laid the foundation for the S'Klallam to take a leadership role with the state, county, and international groups committed to water and salmon restoration.

Resource Protection

The S'Klallam/Klallam Tribes join state, other Tribal, and industry representatives to regulate salmon harvests each season. The Jamestown S'Klallam Tribe has a representative on the Pacific Salmon Commission, which controls salmon harvest shares, seasons, and regulations with Canada. In 1999, several salmon runs, including the Dungeness chinook and Jimmycomelately Creek summer chum, were listed as threatened under the Endangered Species Act. S'Klallam biologists collect weather, water, and related data to submit forecasts to the Pacific Fishery Management Council, which regulates such things as the type of gear used to catch fish and the area or time to harvest endangered species of salmon. Both Tribal and non-Indian fishermen have reduced their catch by 80 or 90 percent in recent years, but still there are sharp declines because of El Nino, ocean overfishing, and freshwater habitat degradation. The Tribe has tagged more than four hundred thousand young chinook salmon in a year and released them in order to locate where they are captured and how well they survive. Other scientific studies sampled juvenile salmon in every area of the Dungeness River to determine where they lived before migrating out to sea. While hatchery production was seen as an answer at one time, we now know the competition for food and cover, poor survival rates for hatchery fish, and past hit-and-miss practices by hatcheries still show that, overall, the salmon runs for critical species remain in decline

or fluctuate sporadically, making resource management
difficult.[17]

Salmon runs vary each year and are both commercially profitable
and highly popular with sports fishermen from the mouth of the
Columbia River, north to Neah Bay, around the tip into the Strait of
Juan de Fuca, and down into the Puget Sound. A *Seattle Times* article
in June 2001 attributed the prediction of a surprisingly stronger than
usual salmon season to improved ocean conditions, good river flows
for outmigrating fish over several years, and the end of El Nino.[18]
Both wind and current are critical factors for outmigration. The
nutrients juvenile salmon need are negatively affected by drier and
warmer conditions along the coast.[19] Because these fluctuations are
normal but can also mask serious changes in salmon population,
careful study and assessments must be continually undertaken.

Only a few Tribal citizens troll for salmon or pursue a limited
set-net fishery from shore at Dungeness Bay; however, the Tribe
remains committed to restoring and protecting this resource for future
generations.[20] Indeed, if you visit the Jamestown S'Klallam Tribe, you
will find highly trained, committed professionals (habitat biologists,
shellfish biologists, water resource experts, and so on) working every
day through scientific programs to restore and protect the habitat and
recover or enhance stocks of fish and shellfish.

Jamestown is not alone in this struggle to restore the salmon and
shellfish and protect the watersheds. Federal, state, and county agencies
are equally involved and committed. However, the arena of fishing,
hunting, and shared responsibility for environmental protection
continues to be one of the most hotly debated, widely misunderstood,
and litigious issues for Indian Tribes today.

Indian Tribes across America are used to being forced to go to
court to protect their rights. They have won (and sometimes lost)
landmark cases and have been involved in thousands of minor court
battles, especially over the past two hundred years.

These court battles are not surprising. It is a cliché today to talk
about lawsuit-happy Americans; environmental groups sue large
corporations or the government, reporters sue for the release of
information, and family members sue each other
over inheritances.

"If we can apply the same energy
to a team effort to protect natural
resources that we have to fighting
over them, there is hope for future
generations."

In sharp contrast to this national trend,
the Jamestown S'Klallam Tribe has taken
the leadership reins to facilitate cooperative
agreements with county, state, and regional
groups, particularly in the area of natural
resource rehabilitation and protection. Anyone
familiar with the spirit and heritage of the Jamestown S'Klallam
people would not be surprised by these actions. The S'Klallam have
always shared fishing stations and shellfish beaches, intermarried with

other Tribes to strengthen political and sustenance ties, and worked reciprocally with early white explorers and traders needing food or wanting furs.

Water Resources

There are several recent examples of the Tribe's commitment to working with all the stakeholders who share in the future of the watersheds and ecosystems within S'Klallam traditional lands. The Tribe was the coordinating body for the successful development of a water-resource-management plan in 1994, flowing from the Chelan Agreement. The historic Chelan Agreement illustrated how a locally based consensus process, committed to negotiation and not litigation, could work. A brief excerpt from the Tribal position paper supporting the Chelan Agreement will illustrate these points: "For many years, the Indian has had to endure the devastation of natural resources on which we have always depended for our sustenance, our culture . . . our very life. We have seen water, the blood of the Earth, treated as a sewer. We have seen rivers dry up, great dams constructed across salmon channels, and poison poured into creeks and streams.

"It seems impossible for there to be a water crisis in Washington State, but there is one. All living things utterly depend on water for their survival, yet clean water is already in short supply. With hundreds of thousands of new people expected to arrive in the Puget Sound region in the next few decades, and a greatly over allocated resource problem in Eastern Washington, the availability of adequate

S'Klallam natural resources professionals performing water-quality testing. (Photograph courtesy of Jamestown Tribe photo collection)

water supplies is in serious jeopardy. If our precious water resource is
to be saved, we must go to work to save it—all of us—now.

"We must get out of the courtroom and into the field. We
must stop fighting over dwindling resources, recognize that we have
common enemies and join efforts to find common solutions. The
enemies are waste and pollution. The solution is cooperative resource
management. If we can apply the same energy to a team effort to
protect natural resources that we have to fighting over them, there is
hope for future generations."[21]

This agreement, with a major goal to develop a model
comprehensive water-management plan, was reached among a broad
representation of people in key positions with Tribes; state, county,
and city governments; environmental groups; agriculture; business;
recreation; and fishing. The Dungeness-Quilcene (DQ) region in
traditional S'Klallam territory was chosen as a focus area, along with
the Methow area in eastern Washington. The Dungeness River was
nominated as a pilot project because of its historical importance to
both S'Klallam and non-S'Klallam people and the critical nature of the
problems facing it.

The average flow in the Dungeness during late summer is about
180 cubic feet per second (CFS), but 581 CFS were allocated to
various uses by the state around the turn of the century. No minimum
instream flow was ever established, and today, hundreds of miles of
ditches and laterals fan out over the Sequim- Dungeness Valley. Water
flow is only one issue, and emphasis has also been placed on restoring
the integrity of the channel structure, particularly efforts to reduce
flooding. By far, however, the key ingredient is providing enough clean
water for salmon. Salmon restoration is a driving force propelling
the Tribe toward a major leadership role with federal, state, and local
communities.

The most fundamental element in the equation affecting salmon
restoration is water resources. The Dungeness River ecosystem, which
has always been the primary resource in the Tribe's territory, contains
more than fifty-three mainstream river miles across 270 square miles
with the upper portion of the watershed on national forest and

river
stú?wi?

murky
(water)
ɬčá?mən

clean
c'á?c'u?

The Seven Pillars of Dungeness River Restoration

1. Reestablish a functional estuary and floodplain in the lower 2.7 miles through managing dikes and reducing river constrictions.
2. Reduce manmade constrictions upstream of the Corps of Engineers dike (everything above River Mile 2.7).
3. Create numerous, stable, long-term log jams.
4. Manage sediment to stabilize the channel and reduce the risk of flooding.
5. Construct and/or protect side channels.
6. Restore suitable riparian (streamside) vegetation and riparian-adjacent upland vegetation.
7. Conserve instream flows.[23]

national park land and the lower part on private lands, where more than sixteen thousand people live. The primary tributary is the Gray Wolf River. There are more than 150 miles of irrigation canals, ditches, and laterals throughout the valley floor on the Sequim prairie.[22]

Beginning in 1991, the Jamestown Tribe took a leadership role in restoring the Dungeness watershed. This began the process of reversing over 130 years of watershed degradation, mainly from clearing land, logging, farming, and building dikes to prevent flooding. Logging around Dungeness Bay began in earnest in the 1860s, and the first irrigation ditches started taking the water away from the salmon in 1896. Still, there were strong salmon runs, so in the early 1960s commercial fishing licenses were in high demand. Between 1963 and 1972, dikes were built to protect communities from flooding and the practice of clearcut logging in the watershed continued into the 1980s. When measurements of water flow were taken in 1987, the Dungeness was losing 82 percent of its flow, largely due to irrigation. Given its location on Olympic National Forest and Park lands, the upper portion of the watershed still has a good share of the natural characteristics that salmon and other fish need to thrive. Large trees still fall into the water and slow the flow or sink to the streambed to provide shelter. Trees that were not clear-cut right to the edge of the bank can still provide shade and roots to hide in, and can still drop leaves and insects into the water for food. Clean gravel, stable streambeds, side channels, and wetlands are also important, but very few of these functions are left in the lower ten miles of the Dungeness, where they are needed most by the Dungeness salmon.[24]

One vision for the future includes the hope that more than half the water in the Dungeness can be left in the river at all times. However, everyone recognizes that achieving this goal will call for even more significant sacrifices by all users.

The Jamestown S'Klallam Tribe has helped the Dungeness River Agricultural Water Users Association to acquire over a million dollars in grants since 1995, primarily to replace fish screens on irrigation ditches or to reline leaking channels. The association has negotiated reduced withdrawals during the chinook-spawning season that have reduced the burden on the river by one third in August and September. The association has won both national and state awards for its accomplishments.

Restoration factors for pinks and chinooks include work that increases stream flow (especially during spawning), stabilizes the spawning habitat, creates side channels for use during high flows, and creates good quality pools and riffles.

The focus of the DQ water resources management plan is on water quality, flood management, water quantity, and fisheries restoration.[25] The key provisions of the Dungeness portion of the plan included agreements with nine irrigation districts and other water companies to reduce their late summer consumption to no more than 50 percent of the flow, even though they could legally draw significantly more water if they wished. When the fish need the water in the river, everyone is cooperating to make sure more of it is there. One vision for the future includes the hope that more than half the water in the Dungeness can be left in the river at all times. However, everyone recognizes that achieving this goal will call for even more significant sacrifices by all users.

The results of the Tribe's leadership in resources management and protection include the following:

- development and maintenance of long-term relationships among all stakeholders across these communities
- more effective and efficient management of the Dungeness River watershed
- generation of much needed scientific knowledge

Clallam County and the Jamestown S'Klallam Tribe passed a joint resolution in 1995 to reactivate a management team for the Dungeness River.[26] The watershed council is composed of representatives from the Tribe; county, state, and federal agencies; property owners; farmers; fishers; and scientists. The purpose of the resolution was multifaceted:

- Exchange information on technical studies, issues, and projects occurring in the Dungeness Watershed.
- Pursue implementation of the Dungeness River Comprehensive Flood Control Management Plan (1989), Dungeness River Area Watershed Management Plan (1993), and the Dungeness-Quilcene Water Resources Management Plan (1994).
- Coordinate the use of staff, funding, and other resources among agencies and representatives.
- Promote public education on watershed processes and activities.

The Tribe is involved in a number of other critical environmental initiatives. For example, habitat protection efforts have increased under the auspices of the Timber, Fish, and Wildlife Multiparty Agreement. Forest initiatives, construction, and closely related activities are reviewed under this agreement if they fall within the Tribe's management area. Habitat inventories are also conducted in cooperation with the Forest Service, state agencies, and the Point-No-Point Treaty Council. Tribal citizens have consciously increased their public presentations, which promote ecosystem protection, and have joined the Washington Department of Ecology, the Clallam County Water Quality Program, and the Puget Sound Water Quality Action Team to produce and distribute educational publications. The Tribe used a state watershed partnership grant to make improvements to irrigation systems and to install new fish screens. A federal watershed restoration grant was used to replace leaking siphons on irrigation systems.

In 1992, the Tribe joined the state's Department of Fisheries and the North Olympic Salmon Coalition to try to save the Dungeness River chinook run, which had dwindled to less than three hundred adults. Some fry were pumped out of the redds (fish nests) in the river and transported to Hurd Creek Hatchery to be grown to adulthood, then released back to the river. Another joint project with the state was a memorandum of agreement, reached in 1993, to increase coho production.

One of the other primary responsibilities the Tribe has, through comanagement of fisheries with the state of Washington, is to oversee the harvest of resources. In this regard, the Tribe promulgates ordinances and regulations for the harvest of fish, shellfish, and wildlife. They regularly notify S'Klallam fishermen about season dates and restrictions, and they license fishermen and hunters. Enforcement officers are employed to police harvest rules. Another major responsibility is to regulate Tribal ceremonial and subsistence harvests. The Tribe reports on the annual harvest to fellow Tribes and the state. The Tribe also negotiates with international, federal, interTribal, and state agencies for annual harvest quotas and provisions.

One of the most important outcomes of this kind of work is increased opportunity for Tribal citizen use of the ecosystem for their livelihood. For example, today there are many more shellfish plantings on reservation tidelands, and Tribal citizens have trained themselves as

The Railroad Bridge Park

As recently as 1990, there was virtually no public access to the lower Dungeness River. The Railroad Bridge site started as an unpaved trail, was developed into a sixteen-acre park, and today is one of twenty-eight Audubon interpretative centers across the United States. The park includes a one-half-mile paved trail through meadows and forests, which leads to an historic wooden trestle bridge.

The park encompasses fourteen hundred feet of riverfront, picnic tables, interpretative signs, a covered picnic classroom shelter, and a one-hundred-seat, open-air amphitheater along the approach to the bridge. A classroom was constructed in 2000. The park offers a unique physical environment for recreation and education.

The sights, sounds, and smells when you are on the river provide a special place for a walk, a bike ride, bird watching, fishing, and learning about the peninsula's natural and human history.

Annual educational programs include the following:

- Rainshadow Spring Lecture Series
- Watershed Week for all Sequim sixth graders
- Summer River Talks for the general public
- Summer Science Day Camp for sixth- to twelfth-grade students
- a variety of classroom seasonal visits for area elementary students

By far, the largest event is the biannual Dungeness River Festival, a two-day celebration of the Dungeness River and all of its natural resources. The festival attracts large crowds to an array of activities such as storytelling, workshops, music, talks, educational exhibits, food, nature craft booths, and 10K fun run-walk.

divers to harvest geoduck clams, which live on the seafloor under forty feet or more of water. (This unique farming business is described in greater detail in chapter three.)

Highlights from the past several years of Jamestown Tribal Natural Resources Department annual reports provide a good picture of the current success and significant impact the Tribe's protection and preservation of the environment has had. Dive surveys were conducted on 710 acres of shellfish beds for future commercial geoduck harvesting. The total 1994 run of Dungeness chinook

Other Tribal Projects

- Ongoing efforts to help find a solution to the city of Sequim's sewage problem came to a successful close when the city constructed a longer outfall and reclaimed-water treatment plant. The treatment facilities will make it possible to safely harvest clams and geoducks on Travis Spit and parts of the Middle Ground. The treated water will be of a high enough quality to reuse in area creeks or for irrigation, resulting in future savings of Dungeness River water.
- Tribal natural resources staff led or participated in a number of technical studies and projects to improve the level of scientific information of natural resources.
- Monitoring of wetlands near the 7 Cedars Casino, wetlands the Tribe created as part of the environmental mitigation for construction of the casino parking lot, has continued. The Tribe's new wetland at 7 Cedars is considered a model project. A grant from the Environmental Protection Agency (EPA) is funding a map of the wetlands and habitat along Bell Creek.
- An EPA grant was funded to study what portions of the Dungeness River are used by young pink and chinook salmon at different times of the year. This will help to find the best locations for habitat restoration and salmon release.
- The Tribe is also working with the U.S. Bureau of Reclamation and the U.S. Geological Survey to study movement of gravel and sediment in the Dungeness River, which has been extremely harmful to salmon eggs.
- The Tribal Council has provided funding to take air photos of the Dungeness River for several years. The Tribe and many other agencies use these to look at changes in habitat. In addition, continuous sampling of water quality is performed throughout Sequim Bay and Dungeness Bay to ensure shellfish certification.
- A threatened closure of Dungeness Bay to shellfish harvest due to water-quality problems was the focus of extensive sampling and analysis in 1997–1998. Tidelands are mapped; shellfish and pollution data, and other Tribal habitat projects and technical information, are gathered and entered into the Tribe's computerized Geographic Information System.
- The Tribe is working with Clallam County and others to prepare a plan for the restoration of Jimmycomelately Creek at its mouth. The summer run of chum salmon in the creek is also proposed for listing under the Endangered Species Act.

S'Klallam citizens are participating in a wide variety of professional and honorary roles to bring this all about. Tribal Chairman Ron Allen, appointed Tribal commissioner to the Pacific Salmon Commission, serves as the lead Tribal representative for negotiating harvest shares between the United States and Canada. Natural resources staff represents the Tribe in negotiating fishing seasons in U.S. waters and allocating the available resources between the non-Indians and treaty Tribes, and among the treaty Tribes.

numbered less than eighty fish. Because of cooperative work between the Tribe, the Washington Department of Fish and Wildlife, and volunteer sport fishermen, approximately 1.8 million chinook fry from an experimental captive breedstock program were released into the Dungeness River in 1997. Four hundred thousand of these chinook were marked with coded wire tags to track the success of the experiment. The restoration of the lower river run of pink salmon included approximately fifty thousand eggs collected from a total return of approximately 260 lower river pinks.

Dungeness River property owners were assisted with habitat restoration projects at three locations in 1997. Logjams were engineered and installed to help stabilize the river channel and to provide cover and pools for salmon. Natural resources staff worked with a habitat work group and completed a report in 1997 titled "Recommended Restoration Projects for the Dungeness River."[27] Work continued with irrigators to protect instream flow in the Dungeness River. Eighty-nine weekly flow measurements and 119 gauge readings at irrigation ditches were collected in one summer to record progress.

Resource Education

The Tribe's efforts to protect and restore their environment and ecosystem have increased dramatically in the past quarter century. The benefits of cooperative management seem to far outweigh going to court. However, no one believes that every issue can be resolved out of court, and the Tribe remains prepared to aggressively defend its treaty rights when it is forced to do so. The Jamestown S'Klallam Tribe's commitment to maintain, restore, and educate the public about the unique ecosystems of the Olympic Peninsula is highlighted by the partnerships created to develop the Railroad Bridge Park and Dungeness River Natural History Center.

An excellent and comprehensive overview of the Dungeness River Natural History Center is contained in a self-guided brochure available on site. Further information is available on the web at www.dungenessrivercenter.org. "The Rainshadow Natural Science Foundation Annual Report" (1996) is useful as well as articles in the *Peninsula Northwest*, 30 September 1997, A3, and the *Gazette: Second Front Page*, 8 October 1997.

In 1993, the Tribe joined the Rainshadow Natural Science Foundation, which is dedicated to expanding scientific understanding about the eastern Olympic Peninsula. Rainshadow has been the caretaker of the Sequim Natural History Museum and hoped to move to a permanent home at Railroad Bridge Park.

The Jamestown S'Klallam Tribe became the government sponsor and now owns the twenty-six-acre park land, which is just beyond the western city limits of Sequim and north of Highway 101. (Access is from 5th Avenue north and Hendrickson on the east side and Carlsborg Road and Runnion Road on the west.) In 1997, the National

Audubon Society and the Olympic Peninsula Audubon Society also joined the Tribe and Rainshadow to create an interpretative, interactive Dungeness River Natural History Center at the park.

This was the first Audubon center in the state—the National Audubon Society was attracted to the site because of the Tribe's leadership and involvement.

The Railroad Bridge Park and Dungeness River Natural History Center have been an unqualified success for the Tribe and the surrounding communities. They demonstrate the Tribe's continued commitment to reach out and form partnerships with other organizations. The site and its educational activities are also a natural extension of the Tribe's commitment to maintain its leadership as a steward of the river, watershed, and peninsula.

The importance of the environment, and particularly the salmon, to the S'Klallam Tribe both traditionally and today cannot be overstated. The Jamestown S'Klallam people have inherited cultural and legal rights and responsibilities to restore, maintain, and manage all the resources of their homeland. Their record of achievement, particularly through cooperation with other Tribal and non-native neighbors, is remarkable. Despite colonial rule, the S'Klallam have been blessed by forever remaining, adapting, and prospering in their homelands.

S'Klallam
nexʷsx̣'áy'əm

salmon
sčánənəxʷ

Why the Salmon Always Return
as told to the author by Elaine Grinnell, Jamestown Elder and storyteller

A long time ago, the S'Klallam weren't getting any salmon, and, gee, the people were really hungry. People were asked to help—two were assigned to go find the salmon, wherever it was. So they went to the west. They finally found the chief of the salmon. After they gave him a lot of gifts, he said, "OK, I'll send my salmon people to you and you may eat them. But you have to make one promise and you have to be very careful about this." "Yes," they were willing to agree.

He said, "As you eat them you have to make sure that the bones are all put in one particular place and you keep them together. And when you're through eating, you must commit the bones back to the sea again and they will find their way back to me." So that's what the people did. They would receive the salmon and they would keep all the bones just the way they took them out of the fish. They would send them back. They treated the first salmon with respect, as we still do today. That way they were assured that they would bring more salmon back to the people the following year.

All the salmon came at different times. King salmon, coho salmon, sockeye salmon, and then the humpie salmon was the last one.

Way of Life

Traditional Ways

The S'Klallam way of life revolved around the everyday tasks of feeding, housing, and clothing family and extended family, as well as any others in the village who could not provide for themselves. As in all families, marriages, births, and the passing on of loved ones were important events. These events provided occasion for practices and ceremonies that greatly helped the S'Klallam deal with the realities of their lives and surroundings.

The S'Klallam way of life revolved around the everyday tasks of feeding, housing, and clothing family and extended family, as well as any others in the village who could not provide for themselves. As in all families, marriages, births, and the passing on of loved ones were important events. These events provided occasion for practices and ceremonies that greatly helped the S'Klallam deal with the realities of their lives and surroundings. The practices were often gender specific. For example, a man, particularly one of high status, endured hardships and sometimes ridicule when seeking a bride because it was often a costly undertaking for his entire extended family and village. The bride and her family were certainly the focus of marriage proposals, and women's prerogatives continued with pregnancy and child rearing. Men and women shared equally important roles when someone left this life and passed on to another place.

As discussed earlier with fishing practices, the environment and resources also necessarily dictated many practices and beliefs. For example, the cedar tree was as important a land resource to the S'Klallam economy as the salmon was a sea resource. Housing, clothing, transportation, and art all stemmed from the western red cedar and a variety of other hardwood trees and vegetation. Marion Taylor, a S'Klallam elder, wrote, "It has been said that the cedar tree served them from cradle to grave." She noted in particular baskets, cradleboards, sleeping mats, clothing, canoes, and the newborn wrapped in the shredded fibers of cedar bark.[1] Indeed, Myron Eells's descriptions of the use of cedar in daily S'Klallam life are worth careful study by anyone interested in traditional S'Klallam life.

Many of the ways the S'Klallam interacted with each other and their surroundings are still evident today. Even those practices that are no longer continued can give great insight into the formation of new traditions and even the business philosophy of the Jamestown S'Klallam Tribe.

Gender Roles

Men's and women's roles followed well-established practices: men fished and hunted for food and women gathered, dug for, prepared, and preserved food. Everyone worked together when winter or summer dwellings had to be built or rebuilt. The building of a potlatch house demanded the intense work of everyone in the village and even neighboring villagers. While men shouldered the heavier planks and logs, women and older children joined in on the construction, as well as the preparation of meals. Women made most of the clothing, although a hunter might make some of his own coverings for the mountains or rough sea. Women wove blankets and men made boxes.

Hilary Stewart's book Cedar: Tree of Life to the Northwest Coast Indians (Seattle: University of Washington Press, 1973) has the very best illustrations (done by the author) I have seen on the many native uses of cedar. Her text is precise, clear, and interesting, and I am greatly indebted to her work. Myron Eells and the Puget Sound Indians, by Robert H. Ruby and John A. Brown (Seattle: Superior Publishing Company, 1976) contains exhaustive drawings and descriptions of the many ways cedar has always been important to the S'Klallam. See also Allan Lobb's Indian Baskets of the Pacific Northwest and Alaska (Portland: Graphic Arts Center Pub., 1978).

While the general patterns of men's and women's responsibilities and rights were recorded in oral history and later in some observations, one of the earliest written records with significant detail was by the missionary Myron Eells. Eells's observations of men's and women's roles during the late 1880s are very telling: "The business of the women was to cook, get berries, roots, and sprouts, dig clams, clean the fish, dry the berries, clams and fish, make the mats, and baskets, spin yarn and make the old fashioned blankets, and clothes, and some of the ornaments. Since the introduction of white industries, they have been accustomed to do much the same work in the house as the white women. Basket making, mat making, gathering berries, and digging clams, spinning yarn and knitting socks, sewing, washing for whites, and digging potatoes for the whites as well as the general duties of housekeeping are their principal industries now. Socks, washing, berries, and potatoe [sic] digging are their principal sources of money revenue.

"The men's business was to hunt, fish, make canoes, planks, build houses, and take care of the horses. They still do these things, except making planks. They also do much work at farming. Many of them work in sawmills, and a large number are loggers, preferring this business to farming, even when they have good land, if they can only make it pay. Canoeing for whites has been quite a business with Clallams, until lately. Steamers have ploughed their waters so often and regularly, as to almost entirely destroy the business. Hop-picking in the White river, Puyallup and Duwamish river bottom has for ten or twelve years been a great business for all the Sound Indians in September, as well as for more northern Indians and those east of the Cascades and west of the Olympic mountains. They have made money very fast in the short season of the business. For the last two or three years, white pickers have begun however to crowd greatly on this source of revenue, as the times have grown harder. A dozen years ago they had almost the monopoly of the business, and those who have kept sober, attended to their business, have held their own with the whites to the present times. Many growers prefer them as they are more willing to live out doors, begin early, and complain less than most of the whites."[2]

As contact with European Americans increased, gender roles started to subtly change to more nearly match that of period whites.

Meals and Food Preparation

The S'Klallam had two meals a day, around 8 or 9 A. M. and around sunset. These consisted basically of fish or meat (fresh or dried), grease, a vegetable, and berries. Shellfish was always present and eaten raw, roasted, steamed, or in soup. Meat was dipped in oil, when available. But the collection, preparation, and storage of food were continuous and daunting tasks. Dried and stored foods were particularly essential. S'Klallam women, assisted by children and slaves, worked constantly with digging sticks to provide needed food. Available shellfish included cockles, various clams (little neck, steamer, little round, rock cockle), mussels, oysters (native or Olympia at the mouth of Hood Canal or on the beaches of Vancouver Island), and geoduck (although it was not popular because of the work involved). Butter clams were important because of their larger size and fat. Horse clams were also harvested and preserved with smoke, strung, and used in trade. Although shellfish and plant products were plentiful at different times, the work never ended. Collection was only the beginning. Then

When china shoes had to be pried off rock cliffs or seagull eggs collected from cliff-face nests at locations away from the village, women knew they had to be careful. A sudden squall could tip a canoe, or slave traders from the north, always looking for isolated prey, could be nearby.

there was transporting, preserving, and preparing ahead. Then there was transporting, preserving, and preparing ahead. When china shoes had to be pried off rock cliffs or seagull eggs collected from cliff-face nests at locations away from the village, women knew they had to be careful. A sudden squall could tip a canoe, or slave traders from the north, always looking for isolated prey, could be nearby.

Women favored ironwood for the digging stick they used. The stick needed a sharp point, gentle curve, and a good grip. Most were three to six feet long, with a curved shaft and firehardened pointed end. This tool was essential for digging butter clams, horse clams, cockles off the beach, the roots of ferns, wild carrots, wild onions, or the bulbs of camas and tiger lilies. Shellfish were harvested year round; even at night, by the light of the full moon or with a torch fired by pitch. Other essential tools included shell scoops and prying/scraping sticks or large shells. The extensive use of various shells is often overlooked in the literature. Clam, abalone, dentalium, and snail shells were used for everything from rattles, knives, spear or harpoon points to ornaments for earrings, nose rings, necklaces, bracelets, breast plates, pendants, and ceremonial clothing, such as headdresses. The S'Klallam visited the west coast of Vancouver Island for dentalium (often called Indian money throughout the west because of its high trade value).

In addition to digging for food, women and slaves collected a broad variety of berries, including the blackberry, elderberry, gummy gooseberry, huckleberry, Oregon grape, red-flowing currant,salal, salmonberry, strawberry, and thimbleberry (sprout). Spring, when both fish and berries were plentiful, was a particularly busy time. Some berries, like strawberry, currant, and Oregon grape were only eaten fresh, not dried. For berries that were eaten dried, the S'Klallam used different drying methods for different berries. For example, they heated the elderberry over rocks all night, then stored it in maplewood boxes, but they dried salmonberries in the sun and air and stored them in baskets.

For preserving butter clams and cockles, they dug a hole in the beach, filled it with larger rocks, lined it with seaweed, and then built a fire in the pit. When the fire burned down, they put the clams in the hole, covered them with mats, and let them steam in their own juice for about a half hour directly on the rocks. Afterwards, they washed the clams and poked the stomach and head onto an ironwood stick and dried them over a fire. When dry, they laid them on a plank and covered them with fern leaves. The women would walk on them to flatten them for stringing and tying into a ring of about forty clams. The rings were placed near the fire for another week before being stored in an open basket.

Men would help when large amounts were needed for storage. Spring and summer were the best times to produce large quantities for trade. Horse clams, which were larger, were processed similarly

salmon stew
sčáyəɬ

digging stick
kʷúkʷ

herring rake
ɬə́t̓əm

but were not walked on, and only fifteen would be strung together. Anthropologist Erna Gunther discussed what such clam rings were worth at the time of her research in the mid-1920s: "In the old days a string of dried horse clams sold for one small store blanket worth about $1.50. Now any kind of dried clams sells for $.50 a string. Neah Bay people used to buy dried clams when they returned from hop picking. In the hop field the Klallam used to meet the Yakima who paid as much as $3.00 for a string of dried clams."[3]

Useful Byproducts

Often cooking would produce useful byproducts for the S'Klallam as well. For example, when skate (a type of fish) were boiled, the grease was skimmed off and used on paddles or other wood implements that needed protection.

The S'Klallam dried the spring salmon on newly cut poles each season over alderwood fires. Because of their size, the salmon had to be cut into strips, while other varieties were dried open and flat using cross-sticks. The S'Klallam ate the heads fresh after boiling and roasting them over the fire. Heads kept in the house overnight or dried to eat later were thought to interfere with a fishermen's next catch, so they were never preserved. While the salmon was drying, the women would break the fibers to allow air to reach all of the meat. The bending and twisting also made it pliable so it could be folded and stored in cedar baskets that were woven so as to allow air to circulate. Halibut, lingcod, and dogfish were dried either in the sun or over the fire for varying amounts of time up to two weeks.

smoked salmon
ʔəsx̣áč

S'Klallam women boiled food in watertight baskets by dropping in red hot stones, roasted food over the fire, or steamed or baked food in a pit. Fresh fish, meat, and vegetables were baked in a pit with varying cooking times. Hot stones could cook meat in about an hour and vegetables in ten to fifteen minutes. For example, tiger lily bulbs were put in a hole in the house floor lined with cedar boughs, then hot stones were added. Scholar Barbara Lane identified regular usage of a variety of plants and berries:

cook under hot gravel
t̕ə́yəq

dig clams
q'x̣'əyu

eat fish heads
ʔəɬsqʷuʔúʔŋiʔ

- wild carrot
- tiger lily
- licorice fern
- Oregon grape
- wapato
- camas
- blackberry
- blackcaps
- elderberry
- gummy gooseberry
- huckleberry
- red-flowering currant
- salal
- salmonberry
- strawberry
- thimbleberry
- serviceberry

Common S'Klallam Meals

Informants who worked with Gunther provided extensive information on S'Klallam food preferences and which foods were always served together and which were not. These preferences seemed to evolve given seasonal availability, ease of preservation techniques, and preferences for what tasted good. Following are common meal combinations.

- baked wild clove roots with grease
- baked horsetail with dried salmon eggs
- baked salmonberry sprouts with grease
- flounder, boiled or roasted, with thimbleberry sprouts
- fresh or dried salmon with potatoes
- fresh lingcod, boiled with grease
- halibut and potatoes
- dried salmon, cold, with whale or porpoise oil (the latter is preferable because it has no taste)
- dried clams and potatoes
- dried clams with whale, bear, or duck grease (seal oil is not considered good with clams)
- camas and seal oil
- fern roots with seal or skate oil served with any kind of meat[4]

Different foods required differing methods and, much like today's gourmets, the S'Klallam highly regarded expertise. They ate the center of fern roots as a breadlike substitute. They roasted it on sticks laid out on a stone and pounded it with a stick. After scraping off the skin with a mussel shell knife, they would split open the root. Dried foods, like horse clams, butter clams, and cockles were often soaked for a few hours to days in wooden boxes or baskets before cooking or eating. They would cover camas with mats in fern or salalberry leaf-lined pits for three days and nights. They sometimes toasted dried salmon over the fire as well as mussels in the shell. They would burn the shells before turning them to the other side.

A Salish-style burden basket used by women, shown here with a tumpline that was worn across the forehead. (Illustration by Dale Faulstich)

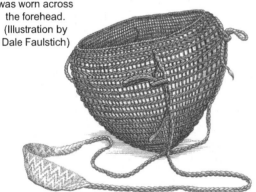

The S'Klallam used alder and maplewood to make plates and other dishes. Feast dishes were reported to be as long as twenty feet, were shaped like a trough, and were finished into a beautiful dark surface with grease. Spoons were made of madrona, or a nice horse clamshell could serve either as a spoon or grease dish. Bentwood cedar water boxes with handles served as buckets for water, which was preferred at mealtime (though a tea boiled from blackcap leaves, cranberry, blackberry, or hemlock might be served instead).

Baskets

The Northwest Coast is known worldwide for native baskets and boxes of unparalleled quality. Baskets, collected for their beauty and novelty, were of course utilitarian for Northwest Indians. They were used for collecting, gathering, cooking, and storage. A wide variety of materials were used besides cedar and cedar bark or root, including spruce root, cherry bark, tule, cattail, moss, and willow, to name but a few. Each unique Northwest Coast environment provided different materials that varied over the seasons. This contributed to the different weaving techniques used from Tribe to Tribe. Making baskets is a cultural art that was never lost and is practiced today among S'Klallam.

Hunting

The S'Klallam used various methods to harvest blacktail deer, Roosevelt elk, black bear, beaver, and cougar. Bow and arrow, pits with stakes, nets hung from poles, and driving the animal into water to make it vulnerable were most common. Besides larger animals, marmot, mink, muskrat, otter (land and river), rabbit, raccoon, wildcat, wolf, and panther were hunted.

The S'Klallam harvested an equally impressive array of birds (land and water), including eagle, grouse (many varieties), hawk, kingfisher, pheasant, quail (multiple varieties), and woodpecker. They hunted more than thirty types of water birds, especially multiple varieties of geese, brant, loons, cranes, and ducks.

Observations of duck nets thirty feet by sixty feet in the path of the ducks' usual departure lane were made between 1792 and the mid-1850s. Many animal products were used for trade, ceremony, or personal enrichment. For example, the Roosevelt elk provided bone and horn, arrow points, seal harpoons, pegs for cedar boxes, fish hooks, and tallow. Blacktail deer also provided tallow, used as a base for black charcoal on the face for a potlatch initiation into the secret society. Beaver teeth were used in a gambling game popular among women.[5]

Making baskets is a cultural art that was never lost and is practiced today among S'Klallam.

Lodging

While permanent villages made use of planks, summer dwellings might consist of rush mats over cedar poles. Most villages housed a relatively small number of families. These homes were small, but larger houses were constructed for feasts, other ceremonies, and the potlatch. Not every village had a longhouse large enough to host a big potlatch. Although the number of houses and sizes varied within each village, the basic construction and shape for traditional S'Klallam homes are well documented. Most houses were rectangular, about twelve feet high and more than thirty feet long. House posts about ten feet in length supported crossbeams and a ridgepole, all held in place by a system of notches created with adzes. Cedar planks, several inches thick, were

longhouse
čəqáw'ʷ

dancehouse
čaqáwtxʷ

ledge in
longhouse
for sitting
šxʷʔáʔmət

grooved to fit together in a joint. Gunther based her observations on descriptions from informants specific to the 1875 to 1880 period. "The potlatch house at Washington Harbor is fifty by two hundred feet in dimension, standing with the long side facing the water. It has a shed roof with the high side facing the shore. The high side of the house is twenty-five feet tall, the low side ten to twelve feet. The roof is made of planks that overlap. The house posts along both sides are about ten feet apart. To help support the roof there are three posts in the center of the house which are larger than those at the sides. These are about two and one-half feet in diameter, carefully adzed and made of cedar. On the center post is painted a large white circle symbolizing the sun which is the chief 's guardian spirit. Such a circle is painted on the front and back of the post, which stands directly opposite the two doors, one on each of the long sides of the house. The posts along the side of the house are painted with bands of red, white and black about one inch wide running around the post.

"Outside the house is a series of tall slender posts set about ten feet apart. They are six inches in diameter and painted with alternating stripes of red and white. On top of each post is a small figure of a bird with spread wings. The chief . . . who built the house, also carved these figures because the sun, his spirit, told him how to do it."[6]

Traditional S'Klallam longhouses and canoe types.
(Illustration by Dale Faulstich)

Two smoke holes in the center, under the ridgepoles, are in constant use in a house twenty-five to more than thirty feet long; these houses also have the advantage of opening other smoke holes, if needed. There are five-foot-wide benches all around the interior, with storage underneath. The walls and benches are covered with rush mats.

Over time, oval doors eventually gave way to square ones, which were originally attached to elk skin straps that acted as hinges. Early doors were often red or horizontally striped in red and white. Shed roofs gave way, later, to gable roofs. The S'Klallam adopted new practices and used new types of construction as such became available. However, the potlatch house retained, through time, its original design and function.

For all Coast Salish Indians, an important consideration for choosing a village site was if canoes could be easily beached and would be sheltered from the wind and protected from the tides. Houses were generally built in a single row with a door facing the water. Traditional S'Klallam communities separated the upper class from commoners with a line of poles that also served to hold the heads of enemies killed in battle. The slaves were housed where the enemy might attack, such as out on a spit that created a cove. The wealthy homes more likely would be stockade with cedar poles twelve to twenty feet high for protection and built deep in the back of the cove below a high bluff.

Clothing

The S'Klallam, like their neighbors throughout the region, wore little or no clothing when weather permitted. This was particularly true for the men and children. Women, after puberty, often wore cedar skirts made by folding cedar strips over a buckskin thong tied like a belt and a robe across the shoulders. These gave way to wool blankets as soon as they were available in trade. Blankets or capes were made from a variety of materials and were worn over the shoulder and pinned with wood near the chest. Skins of beaver, sea otter, and bear, or woven coverings from mountain goat, dog, or duck feathers with fireweed cotton were common.

skirt
ƛqít

rain hat
sƛəm'əxʷay'éqʷ

shawl
ƛišán

dress
ƛqít

Clothing for colder weather and specialized purposes like hunting and fighting were much more elaborate: "In colder weather both sexes wore a shirtlike garment made of down-and-nettle fabric, covered with a robe or, in wet weather, a poncho of cattail matting or woven cedar bark. Men who went hunting inland wore a hide outfit consisting of a pointed hood, shirt, leggings, mittens, and moccasins, and they used snowshoes. Warriors wore a knee-length shirt of several thicknesses of elk hide." [7] Hunters were more heavily equipped for the dense forest and mountain climate with knee-length leather aprons or buckskin shirts, which laced in the front.

Myron Eells's descriptions of clothing contained many references to the use of cedar, including hats for infants, bark dresses, and capes.

In addition, many other materials were used, such as cattail rushes for coats, mountain goat wool for coats and blankets, or robes made from rabbit or other small animals. A special breed of dogs was maintained by S'Klallam and other Northwest Pacific Indians and, when writing about blankets, Eells noted: "One was made of dog's hair, geese or duck down, and the cotton from the fireweed. These were twisted into strings and woven together. This special breed of dog was kept for its hair, but is now extinct. It was not large, but the hair was long, and the number of such dogs she owned often estimated a woman's wealth. I have never seen any of these blankets. Vancouver speaks of the dog as resembling those of Pomerania but larger. They were white.

"Another kind of blanket was imported from the Makahs who made it. It was made from the inner bark of the cedar slightly beaten, so as not to be too stiff, and woven with strings of geese down twisted. The only one I have seen was at Dungeness in 1878, and had a border of fringe of black hair. The third kind was of the wool of the mountain goat twisted into coarse strings and woven together. All of these blankets were woven on a loom."[8]

The S'Klallam reportedly did not make any of the conical rain hats so popular in the Pacific Northwest, but they did wear them. The oral record on this point probably needs some additional investigation. Given the extent of weaving and the weather, it seems unlikely that the S'Klallam did not make hats. In light of so little information on this point, it is just as easy to assume they made them as it is to assume they did not. Ceremonial and potlatch clothing, however, called for something special. Cedar bark dyed red, tied around feathers, might be used as head gear. Face masks carved from maple or cedar and whistles or rattles from cedar or cherry bark were important additions to everyday clothing.

After about age six, both men and women painted their faces daily, especially for ceremonials. Red clay over a base of deer tallow, augmented with charcoal over the cheeks, was common. This was in sharp contrast to the black face used by participants in the secret society initiations (see page 73 for more information on the S'Klallam secret society). Other parts of the body, such as the hands or forearm, might be painted for a ceremony if the person had a powerful guardian spirit. Early observers noted very little tattooing, and those who did have tattoos usually had them only on the hands and forearm. Indeed, the S'Klallam favored light skin and had words specific to shades of complexion.

Marriage
S'Klallam marriages followed the widespread practice in the Pacific Northwest of securing alliances with other Tribes, particularly by marrying into a community leader's family. Even as late as 1880, a census revealed that approximately two hundred of five hundred

marriages were outside the Tribe, largely with the Cowichan, Makah, Twana, "Victoria Indians," and the Quileute. Forty years after this census, Erna Gunther collected stories about how marrying into British Columbia Tribes was a particular honor. During this period, the out-marriage preference had shifted toward the Makah and Skokomish. Commoners who had neither the social standing nor the appropriate wealth to marry outside the Tribe would marry S'Klallam from other villages. Immediate family and other relatives carefully watched young women from puberty until they were married.

It was never acceptable to marry too close a relative, such as close cousins. When two young Jamestown people of "remote kinship" were married in the 1920s, the Prince of Wales (community leader at the time) gave a speech pointing out that the union would not have been allowed in earlier times but could be today because of the small number of S'Klallam left.

If any sort of an affair or elopement occurred, even between cousins, then the S'Klallam attitude that such an event must end in marriage overrode marital taboos. Of course, these unions would not earn the couple any respect. Even in this situation, a marriage to a slave by a higher status commoner would not be dissolved. If a family of wealth were faced with this situation, they would be obligated to give a feast with gifts to help their new in-law gain some acceptance and respect. However, people kept track of who had or was thought to have slave blood and even the children of such a union, regardless of their inherited wealth, would still be considered part of the slave class. This class system, and particularly the treatment of slaves, gradually eroded. However, even in contemporary times, family names and their associated histories and place of prominence in the S'Klallam Tribe are well known.

The traditional S'Klallam suitor with adequate family resources to seek a bride of high prestige would travel to the girl's house and sit near the door, away from the fire. Word of his coming would have already reached the village. He would be ready to be tested by the prospective family with any manner of insults for days or even a week. All of the

Marital Separations

A person with the spirit power to make a wish come true could sometimes repair separations. They would speak of every body part, in order, and wish that the person's mind would become right. If there were unsolvable problems, a wife would leave all the children with her husband and his family, though she might take a new baby with her. The bride price was expected to be returned and would be offered to the husband but was usually not accepted. Reputations were always important, as were the reasons behind a separation. If things were known to be the husband's fault, then it would be easier for the woman to remarry, but without the requirement of a large wedding feast. In the case of a wife's infidelity, the husband had the right to kill the other man without fear of revenge from that man's family. If he did not also kill his wife, to save face, he would have to leave the house until she returned to her village.[9]

Masked dancers in a wedding party. (Illustration courtesy of the
Bert Kellogg Collection of the North Olympic Library System)

girl's family would be notified so they could come and be part of the
decision to accept or reject the proposal. Of course, the groom would
not have traveled alone. His family would have loudly announced his
arrival to the entire village by singing from their canoes. If the proposal
was accepted, then the suitor's family would give blankets, shell money,
and other gifts for the girl's family.

It was the responsibility of others in the village to house, feed,
and entertain these visitors while the prospective bride's family ignored
them and concentrated on evaluating the prospective groom. If half
or more of the bride's family could not agree on the worthiness of the
groom or the appropriateness of this strategic union, then he would be
turned away. However, if the proposal was accepted, the marriage feast
began immediately. Headmen of both villages would give speeches
proclaiming that from now on these two people were married. As
times changed, a suitor might not be tested but instead the word was
put out questioning the desirability of the marriage.

The bride's father might give the groom a suit made of the finest
materials and would sing his inherited family songs. He also would pay
the groom's people for the food and for coming, including the men
who steered the canoes, since they were generally of high standing
or wealthy. The spokesperson for the headman of the bride's village
would start the wealth songs and others would join in. When the
couple left for the groom's village, her relatives would carry her to the
canoes, or the path would be covered with skins or blankets that then
became her property.

Within a year, the bride's family would be expected to travel to the
groom's village with food and gifts for a reciprocal feast. As befit their

marry
məɬíyíti

elope
ɬuʔísti

wife
sɬáániʔ

husband
swə́y'qəʔ

status, they would bring more food and gifts than the groom's people did for the wedding feast.

Leaders, since they could afford it, might have many wives, though two was the common number reported from data collected in 1880 and the 1920s. However, stories of twelve to fifty or even eighty wives circulated. Widows were expected to marry the husband's brother. If he was already married but could afford another wife, he would be expected to accept her. A male who was a good provider, someone worth keeping in the family, would be given a sister, aunt, cousin, or, particularly, a niece, if his wife passed on. The age difference between husband and wife was of little consequence as long as the girl had reached maturity.

Pregnancy and Birth

S'Klallam beliefs included keeping menstruating or pregnant women away from others, especially men and, most particularly, any man with strong spirit power. The woman would continue with her work but sleep in a corner of the house behind a screen or on a porch. She would fast the first day of her period and would not use a wood scratcher on her body or a tube for drinking. A man who accidentally came in contact with a menstruating woman had to fast, bathe, and sleep outside without blankets for a few nights.

A pregnant woman faced many things that could go wrong. For a child to be large and healthy, a woman was expected to sacrifice everything.

- Bathing each morning and evening was essential—several stories were told and retold of thin and weak children being born to S'Klallam women who did not bathe frequently enough.
- She could not eat food or drink water that was stale or a day old.
- She especially would avoid eating any meat from an animal that had suffered when killed because her child could suffer the same malady when born.
- Her husband could not hunt raccoon or wildcat for fear that the newborn would end up acting like these animals.
- She kept the child from sticking to the walls of her womb by rolling in her sleep and, to ensure the child came feet first, she always laid her blankets crosswise where she slept.

One or more midwives would attend the birth. They received a dollar each and a blanket. A shaman would only be called if there was a problem. He would call out and use his hands to swirl water and throw it toward her, but he would never rub or touch her as he might for another type of illness.

The woman would deliver in a half-squatting position over shredded cedar bark while holding onto a rope tied to the ceiling post. She would chew on leaves of the Indian plum. Quiet was expected

be pregnant
skʷ'ákʷi

give birth
néʔət

baby
ŋaʔŋáʔnə

Head Flattening

Flattening the head was very important to traditional S'Klallam social life and the cultivation of prestige. Head flattening was a common practice to enhance an individual's attractiveness. Indeed, round heads were often compared to rocks and were the brunt of jokes and insults. To assure their low status, slave children were forbidden to receive head-flattening treatment.

The process varied in several distinct ways among Pacific Northwest Tribes; the S'Klallam inserted a flat rock into a cedar-bark pad and placed it directly on the child's forehead with a second stone and pad on top of that, all tied to the cradleboard. Buckskin thongs would keep the pad from slipping down over the child's nose and mouth. The procedure took about two weeks, and experienced women would judge when the right pressure had been used for the appropriate amount of time.

so the child would not get caught in the womb. Everyone would pray while the child was being born. The father would then take the afterbirth miles from the house and bury it. The child would carry a piece of the umbilical cord in a buckskin bag around the neck or wrist until puberty. Children grew up knowing that they would be foolish as adults if they lost their bag.

Dogfish oil was put in the eyes and rubbed on the newborn's body as soon as it was bathed. Each part of the body was rubbed, even the fingers, so the child would be well proportioned, strong and not fat. Dogfish grease would also be the baby's first meal to clear the stomach. A horse clam, prepared in a special way, was the second meal. The meat was chopped very fine and made moist from the milk of another nursing woman. The mother could begin nursing in about twenty-four hours, after she had "cooked her breasts" over steam rising from hot rocks for about an hour. If her milk was not rich and plentiful, she would repeat the procedure. She would also drink water with ground mussel shells to increase her milk. The S'Klallam believed the first milk was never good and that an adult must suck it out. Clams, because of their milky consistency, were the favored meal for a nursing mother She would also eat fish and other game, but never berries or their sprouts because this was thought to cause colic in the newborn.

The S'Klallam used a temporary mat cradle before tying the child to a cedar cradleboard about two-and-a-half feet long and a foot wide. There was always a handle at the top where a hand could easily fit because the child's cradle was always being moved and laid against a tree or rock. The shape was like a dugout canoe, but the walls were only about an inch thick and very low so the child rode up high. Gunther described these cradles in great detail: "Along the sides are holes . . . for binding thongs, four on each side, while on each side of the head are two holes for the buckskin thongs which fasten the head pad. . . . Tied to the lowest cross lacing is another thong which is carried around the feet and fastens them to the lower end of the cradle."[10]

The child's neck and knees would have cedar bark rolls under them, and the feet were raised with cedar bark to help digestion. Blankets were made of doubled over, slightly shredded cedar bark with twined edges and twining at the fold. If a woman wanted to be considered a good mother, she would wash and dry the cedar padding and blankets each day. The cradle was built for the first six months, and often another was built if the mother was going to be out picking berries and digging roots. Even after a child started walking, he or she might sleep in a cradle.

Childhood

Boys and girls played together until about age twelve; however, they were expected to learn their roles, which would prepare them for adulthood. Although all children were made to rise early, before the sun, and run on the beach and swim each morning, boys were particularly encouraged in order to build strength and endurance. Boys carried packs, picked up wood, and went fishing when they were older. Girls dressed wooden dolls, made clothes and mats with small needles, and wove baskets.

Children shared games and play performances, and both kept pets. Small seals were a favorite, which they took swimming with them. Birds were not allowed inside the house, and girls could not keep a dog as a close pet. It was thought that if she grew to love a dog and slept with it, she would have pups. Wellknown stories supported this belief.

Beliefs and Practices Learned in Childhood

- Swim every morning because the water goes through your skin and makes your blood healthy.
- Do not eat anything before the family's morning meal, or you will grow up a
- glutton.
- Keep your teeth clean with the quill of a duck.
- Wash your mouth out with water before bed.
- To get white teeth, throw your baby teeth into the salt water and call out to the blackfish and sawbill duck.
- A boy who touches a doll will always be laughed at.
- The father of a boy who catches his first salmon or kills his first animal will give presents to mark the occasion

grandparent
síyə; sé?yə

**aunt or
uncle**
cáčc

woman
sɬáni(?)

Coming of Age

A S'Klallam girl could not receive a marriage proposal without a feast announcing her new social standing in the village. This ceremony would be planned and given by her mother or a close female relative, and only her female relatives and the women in the community would be invited. The girl would attend the feast in her honor after a week or two of isolation, without food, water, or a lot of sleep. Traditionally, this was to prepare her for war, if it came. Later, this occasion became more important for judging the personal characteristics and work ethic of the bride. Her behavior during isolation was very important. Too much laughing or talking would forecast bad times later in life.

Other rigors she would undergo during the seclusion included rising early to rub her eyes with dew-covered grass to ensure good eyesight in older age. After bathing in cold water, she would rub her body with cedar twigs to guarantee soft skin later in life. To keep her hair from falling out when she was older, she would not be allowed to touch her hair and would cover her braids in red paint. Her forehead would be accented by plucking out the hairline to make it look higher.

During her isolation, she would make mats and blankets to give to an aunt or grandmother as gifts for attending her. She would work without clothes on so she wouldn't perspire and leave her smell on anything. These behaviors were a direct indicator of how industrious she would be later.

The ceremony ended when women from the village were invited to come and sing their puberty songs. Each woman owned her own song or songs, and only she could start her song, but then everyone would join in. Both a drum and sticks beat on boards and planks were used for accompaniment. These songs were from the women's world. They would sing of jealous husbands and of lovers and love affairs they had when they were young. Those who came were given presents, especially calico, and on the last day, men were invited for a feast but received no presents. The young woman who had come of age would then give up the straight buckskin dress she had worn for a fringed cedar-bark skirt and, when needed, a blanket over the shoulder.

Naming

Naming ceremonies were another important practice to the S'Klallam. Names were considered family property and were given to boys and girls at a potlatch or feast. A first name, given by the time a child was walking, was of no significance. Traditionally, an inherited name was announced and assumed when a man or his family had the resources to bestow this honor. There were no set times, like puberty or marriage, but just before or after a man or woman married was a favored time to assume a new name.

Over time, changing beliefs caused the S'Klallam to give up some ceremonies. It is not just because the details were forgotten. For example, Gunther reported that, according to her informants, the Jamestown S'Klallam gave up the puberty ceremony when some girls died young and stories circulated that the ceremony was to blame.[11] There were certainly other beliefs and practices associated with a girl coming of age, but the ceremony is no longer practiced at Jamestown and would have to be revived in order to identify additional traditional ways related to that period in a girl's life.

Passing On

The S'Klallam used various methods over time to bury those who had passed on. They preferred sandspits as places for burial and laid the body on a wood platform or in a canoe supported about two or three feet off the ground. A small shed was also used at times, and the body may have been placed in a sitting position. Other observers found burials in canoes covered with planks about twelve feet in the air held by one or more tree branches or laid on the sand and covered with a shed or canoe. Burials in the woods might also be in the ground. Reportedly, bodies were never cremated.

When a person died at his or her house, the body was never taken out the front door but, rather, through a hole cut for that purpose, or in recent times, through a window. The body would be wrapped in new blankets and mats tied with cedar thongs. After mourning, older men with powerful guardian spirits would carry the body to the gravesite. They would do this alone and were given some of the deceased's possessions as payment. These possessions could be left at the grave or taken with them as they saw fit. The remainder of the dead person's belongings would be buried the day after the burial at a separate location.

The wailing ceremony was very important, and the number of days and participants varied with a deceased person's rank and prestige. A shaman, however, would be buried immediately because of his power. The wailers were women, including some relatives, and were paid with money. Wailing included phrases like, "Oh, why did this good man die? Why was it not a mean, good-for-nothing person?"[12] After the ceremony, the wailers washed out their mouths with salt water, telling the sorrow to leave them. They would put red paint back on their faces and join the relatives of the family for a few more days before returning to their homes.

A potlatch was expected soon after the burial and at the first anniversary of the death, or on the occasion of a reburial. Gifts would be given to help participants satisfy their grief. A personal possession of the dead person would be shown to guests at the first potlatch, then burned. Relatives fasted and cut their hair to a little shorter than shoulder length to leave less room for sorrow. They might blacken their faces for some time. The name of the deceased or any word that sounded like their name would not be used for many years. To mention

life spirit
shəyí

die
q'ʷúy; xʷə́y

bury a corpse
məq'ʷéət

43

The Native American Graves Protection and Repatriation Act

Native American Indians have a great respect and honor for their ancestors. The desecrations of Native American Indian gravesites, the removal of remains and artifacts to be placed in museums far from Tribal territories has been heart breaking. For centuries the voice of the Native American Indians fell on deaf ears when telling Euro-Americans to leave our ancestors in peace. Our people were forced to stand by in silence, fully aware, as sacred remains and artifacts were confiscated.

Passed in 1990, the Native American Graves Protection and Repatriation Act (NAGPRA) is a human rights law that, for the first time, requires that Native American graves on federal and native lands be given the same respect that has always been accorded Euro-American graves. Theft or the selling of objects from graves or sacred sites is prosecuted under the NAGPRA law.

NAGPRA affects any museum, federal agency, or institution that receives federal funds, in the form of research grants, direct allocation, student financial aid, and so forth. For example, if a museum is part of a university that receives federal funds, then the museum would be subject to NAGPRA. It only covers federally recognized Tribes.

NAGPRA makes it possible for the Jamestown S'Klallam Tribe to bring home our ancestors.

A number of museums are happy to cooperate, as these ancestral remains have been stored and neglected on shelves for decades. NAGPRA has created a positive dialogue among Tribes and the federal agencies and museums that hold artifacts and remains. The shared knowledge has benefited both Tribes and museums. Of course, as with all new laws and regulations, things are not always smooth nor do all see NAGPRA as a good thing. A recent court case used the remains of Kennewick Man to bring into question NAGPRA and the rights of Native Americans to recover ancient human remains within their traditional territory.

NAGPRA has not given Tribes a wholesale right to strip museums. The law defines what objects may be returned to Tribes: human remains, sacred objects, and objects of cultural patrimony. Tribes and museums engage in a consulting process to determine if the objects being claimed are going to the appropriate Tribe. This may be very difficult with Tribes that were removed from their native territories and passed through another Tribe's territory before arriving at the area assigned by the federal government. Some of these removals were across several states and the territories of several different Tribes.

NAGPRA places burdens on both Tribes and museums. The museums and federal agencies must supply an inventory of human remains and a survey of all objects in their collections to affiliated Tribes. If a Tribe believes an object or human remain belongs to their Tribe or a citizen of the Tribe, then a written request for return may be made. It is the responsibility of the Tribe to provide information to support its claim. NAGPRA gives equal status to Tribal oral traditions and history as to the written word. Tribal oral traditions and history have a valid voice in the request for information related to artifacts and human remains.

If the museum agrees with the claim, then all the information is sent to the NAGPRA office (a part of the Interior Department assigned to the National Park Service office). NAGPRA staff review the information to determine if it is correct. Once the review is complete, and if there are no problems, a notice is published in the Federal Register with a thirty day waiting period before a Tribe may retrieve their claim. This thirty-day waiting period is intended to give notice and an opportunity for counter claims.

The NAGPRA review committee has seven citizens: Museum professionals select three citizens; federally recognized Tribes select three citizens; and these six citizens on the committee select the seventh person. If there is a dispute, either between the museum and Tribe or between two different Tribes making counter claims, then the NAGPRA review committee will listen to the dispute and make a recommendation. If all parties do not accept the recommendation that is given by the NAGPRA review committee, then the only other recourse is to take the claim to court.

NAGPRA is another important step in affirming the sovereignty of Native American Tribes.

—Tribal Citizen Kathleen Duncan

a dead person's name was a very serious social infraction. The dead person's house was left vacant for at least a month or longer because the spirit of the deceased, in ghostlike form, was thought to be nearby, trying to take his relatives with him to the land of the dead. A shaman could be paid to cleanse the house and village.

The traditional S'Klallam way of life patterned all the human life cycles, from birth and coming of age to passing on. As with other native Tribes, their way of life was woven into the fabric of the land and the resources provided by that environment. Lodging, clothing, and the different work required by men and women were dictated by sea and land resources, seasonal harvesting, and cultural beliefs. These sometimes dictated great hardship, as with the sacrifices a S'Klallam woman gladly endured to produce a large, healthy baby. Tremendous knowledge and skill was necessary in the identifying, acquiring, preserving, and preparing food, the carving of a canoe, or the building of a longhouse. Hard work and ambition, along with all the other traits of a good man, and the help of the right guardian spirits made a community leader and thus made that person eligible for a marriage of prestige or alliance. The S'Klallam men and women of traditional times knew the importance of learning and practicing to the best of their abilities their way of life.

> Relatives fasted and cut their hair to a little shorter than shoulder length to leave less room for sorrow.

Making a Living in the Late Nineteenth Century

The 1880 S'Klallam census sheets, enumerated by agent Edwin Eells, provide an interesting occupational snapshot a quarter century after the signing of the Point-No-Point Treaty.

By far, the vast majority of S'Klallam men reported that they were fishermen, sealers, and medicine men, while S'Klallam women reported mat and basket maker as their main occupation. The next largest category for men was laborer/wood chopper/saw mill employee. For women, it was washerwoman. A significant number of men reported two occupational categories, such as laborer and fisherman (or farmer); canoe maker and medicine man; or fisherman and hunter. Women did not report multiple occupations. Two Indian policemen showed up in the 1880 census. It is interesting to note that a significant number of hunters are identified in this first census. For quite some time, anthropologists have maintained that the S'Klallam lived on fishing and shellfishing, and only one or two hunters from each of the villages ventured into the forests and foothills of the Olympics. The Elwha S'Klallam, given their location up the river, were sometimes cited as an exception. Occupational data from the first census, recent archaeological evidence in and near the Olympic National Park, as well as oral history provide convincing evidence that elk, deer, bear, and other land animals were a regular part of the S'Klallam diet and ceremonial life.

Contemporary Ways

So many aspects of change affected S'Klallam villagers that it is difficult to identify areas where ways of life remained constant. However, it is clear that the once large, feared, and respected S'Klallam were marginalized by the dominant society in a relatively short period of time. Fishing and shellfishing changed dramatically when settlers took over the best fishing stations and, by the early 1900s, began to ban net fishing and regulate salmon fishing to benefit non-native commercial and sports fishermen. Still, after 1900, Jamestown villagers carved out an existence by fishing, crabbing, clamming (selling locally and as far away as Seattle), and with supplemental wage-labor jobs on farms, in canneries, and in lumber mills. Individual gardens became commonplace with potatoes, corn, peas, beans, onions, tomatoes, squash, and a wide variety of foods. Wild berries still predominated in this rich diet.

In the late 1800s, salmon began to be salted as much as smoked, and sugar, coffee, butter or lard, as well as spices, became indispensable. Still, canoes, traditional fishing gear, and digging sticks were just as efficient and used just as widely. The large potlatch and feast, including secret society initiations, were held as late as 1878. Over the next seven decades, however, the S'Klallam were increasingly recognized for their adoption of non-native ways, good relations with neighbors (despite attempts to force them onto the Skokomish Reservation), and, overall, economic well-being.

After the Great Depression, as the United States became industrialized and the Pacific Northwest gave way to the powers of corporations, government bureaucracies, and larger cities, the S'Klallam, along with other Indian groups, faced increasing marginalization. When the post-war economy took off, they were left behind.

The real blow to the S'Klallam way of life was the disintegration of inherited or acquired status and wealth. In addition, the prohibitions against "Indian medicine," spirit helpers, secret societies, spirit dancing, and potlatching or feasting never fully extinguished these pillars of society but significantly ruptured family and community. Proper training, language, oral stories, and ceremonial and social ways began to disappear.

While it is evident that the S'Klallam adopted and adapted contemporary ways of life, the direct connection to traditional ways is striking. Where gender roles, housing, clothing, transportation, food production and use, and marriage practices have given way to white intrusion, the ideals of S'Klallam character, community self-sufficiency, political leadership in the region, and maintenance of the environment have never wavered and are directly tied to contemporary strategies for economic development.

The major economic development goals of the Jamestown

S'Klallam Tribe have not changed over time. The Tribe has
consistently worked toward achieving self-sufficiency by developing
an asset base, producing income from for-profit businesses, and
creating increased employment opportunities. The major challenges
have been to respond to a rapidly shifting local economy and changes
in funding opportunities provided by federal programs.[13]

Business Ventures

The Jamestown Tribe has been involved in a significant number of
economic development projects, including a casino, three art galleries,
an oyster farm, a seasonal fireworks business, several apartment
complexes, and a commercial industrial building.

In 1983, the Tribe created JKT Development as a corporate
arm. JKT spun off corporate entities with advisory boards for each
economic enterprise. This strategy was employed for several reasons.
Each board is directly accountable to the Tribal Council, and the
Tribe has limited liability because each enterprise is responsible for
its own actions and assets. This multilayered corporate structure is
very familiar to the non-Indian world, which is a plus when dealing
with others. However, there are costs associated with this model, such
as increased administrative support, differing policies, audit costs,
and varied reporting methods. There is also an unresolved question
surrounding federal corporate taxes being charged to profits from
Tribally charted corporate entities. This incubator model, which the
economic development division has used successfully for over fifteen
years, may need to change in the future. The Tribe has a long-range
strategic plan that prepares them to deal effectively with such issues.

Indian Gaming

By far the largest and riskiest economic development venture for the
Jamestown S'Klallam Tribe was the 7 Cedars Casino, a 54,000-square-
foot gaming complex located about two miles from Tribal offices in
Blyn, Washington. Although most non- Indians see Indian gaming
as an easy, sure-fire, and lucrative enterprise, the truth is, a very small
number of the more than 350 Indian gaming facilities in the United
States make significant profits. Many Indian casinos barely make
payroll, some are in debt, and some have already closed. Gaming is
a risky business The Indian casinos enjoying the greatest success are
located near large metropolitan areas and have no nearby competition.

Indian gaming was not a new idea to the S'Klallam. A significant
written and oral history surrounds traditional bone and disk games,
as well as canoe and horse races (see pages 108-109 for more
information on these traditional games). Gaming as a Tribally
operated business was considered as early as 1985. At first, the Tribe
considered building a bingo hall. This idea was less economically
feasible than a fully developed gaming facility. The S'Klallam, funded

Front and side views of the 7 Cedars Casino (Photographs courtesy of the Jamestown Tribe photo collection).

by a three-year grant from the Administration for Native Americans, began the formal plans for a gaming operation in 1992.

The largest entertainment facility on the Olympic Peninsula, the 7 Cedars Casino, opened in February of 1995. A six hundred–seat bingo hall was included, along with space for blackjack, keno, craps, roulette, poker, and pull-tab machines. The casino, with its beautiful, award-winning design, also offers the Salish Room restaurant, the Totem Lounge, the Northwest Native Expressions Gallery and Gift Shop, and the Bingo Bay Deli. The casino highlights the uniqueness of the Tribe with totems and a Northwest Indian interior and also provides Las Vegas-style entertainment for the Olympic Peninsula.

All of this belies the casino's difficult beginning. The 1995 summer season did not bring the planned increase in tourist trade. Instead, temporary closures of the Hood Canal Bridge decreased ferry service to Port Townsend, and a large number of the visitors who did come preferred camping and hiking to casino entertainment. Initially, this resulted in the Tribe losing money. Original staffing levels of five hundred employees were reduced to two hundred by February of 1996, before the casino was able to finally break even by 1997. While a significant debt balance remained on the facility, the Tribe paid it and now owns the casino outright. The market value of any casino, given this unique business, is not easy to judge, but the worth is between six and twelve million dollars.

One of the truly significant aspects of Tribal self-determination and self-governance is the ability to take risks, fail, and learn from mistakes. This experience is not new to non-Indian governments and corporations but is only several decades old for Tribes. The 7 Cedars Casino was a valuable learning experience. The Tribe found that given restrictions on the type of slot machines used, casino gaming was not an instant success. The Tribe had moved from managing smaller businesses to running a large operation, which made the casino a more challenging economic development venture than anticipated.

The casino has struggled to maintain operations in a difficult state gaming climate. The Washington gaming industry will not take a significant upturn without the introduction of slot machines that return coins, the backbone of all successful Las Vegas–type operations. A statewide referendum to allow slot machines has twice failed to gain voter approval, but there are continuing efforts by all Washington gaming Tribes to deal with this issue. A significant increase in revenue was realized in July 1999 when a new type of machine was introduced that used tickets.

The Jamestown Tribe will not be able to significantly change things without attracting an increased number of tourists to the casino. This means developing additional attractions and risking additional

49

investment capital. The Jamestown economic development staff, using recent market surveys, estimates that about 1.75 million people annually visit the Olympic Peninsula and spend over $200 million in Clallam and Jefferson counties.

Forecasted competition from other Tribes, who are planning gaming facilities on the peninsula, also suggests that the Jamestown Tribe will have to enhance its casino operation. The destination tourist market is still largely underdeveloped and the future for gaming and related tourist activities looks very promising for the Tribe.

Galleries

The Jamestown S'Klallam Tribe has always been committed to pursuing business opportunities that build on traditional values, skills, and practices. One of its first endeavors, the creation and publication of limited edition Northwest art prints, led to the opening of its first gallery in 1993 at the Tribal offices complex. In 2001, there are three Northwest Native Expressions galleries. The other two are in the casino and in Port Townsend.

The opening of the first gallery was a resounding success, significantly exceeding the first year's profit estimates. The Port Townsend gallery was opened in 1993 and was also very successful. In planning the casino, the Tribe decided to open a gift shop and gallery that would be the focal point of the main entrance and that would highlight Northwest Indian culture. While a sound aesthetic and cultural decision, it proved to be a disaster for the gallery business. A major problem was that the gallery had to be open seven days a week from 10 A. M. to 10 P. M. to coincide with the gaming hours. The cost for staff over long hours was not profitable. In addition, the casino gallery's close proximity to the gallery at Tribal offices cut into sales for both galleries. To cut down on staffing needs, the casino gallery eventually had to be combined with the gift shop.

oyster
λə́x̌ʷλ'ə́x̌ʷ

This venture proved to be another learning experience for the Tribe. The challenge was to balance a desire for selling culturally appropriate items while finding a mix of products that appealed to the general public. Overall, though, the galleries have been a tremendous success. The long-term future will be particularly beneficial to Tribal citizens who carve, paint, weave, or engage in any of the other traditional crafts because interest in Pacific Northwest native art is still increasing. Competition in the United States is much lower than in Canada, and it is projected as a growing market.

catch, harvest
sqə́čəʔ

rope
x̌ʷéʔɬəm

Commercial Fishing

No other traditional area is more important today to the Jamestown S'Klallam people than fishing and gathering shellfish. The Tribe is committed not only to restoration and preservation of fish and shellfish, but also to making it a viable business alternative for the

Tribe. In 1986, the Tribe became actively involved in two traditional enterprises, salmon and oysters. Since then, they have expanded to include Dungeness crab and other seafood resources.

The goal of developing a fish farm in Discovery Bay began with several years of careful planning by aquaculture staff. As often happens with planning efforts, in the time between 1986 and 1991 while seeking enterprise partners, testing fish farm methods, acquiring permits, and seeking funds, the market changed. Prices for farm-reared fish dropped from $10 a pound to $4 a pound. Several similar farms had failed, so venture capital was scarce. The Tribe still managed to pull together an experimental partnership, located at Whiskey Creek, to determine the viability of rearing Atlantic salmon in uniquely designed cages in the fast-flowing waters of the Strait of Juan de Fuca. The experiment was successful but, ultimately, the business was not profitable enough to attract needed partners, and operations closed February 1994.

The Tribe learned a lot about the fish farm business from this endeavor. The offshore experimental site resulted in much greater growth rates for fish. However, it was harder on the smelts, so they had to be introduced later in their life cycle to make this business work. The cage design worked and was improved upon. At this point, the Tribe does not know if or when it will re-enter the salmon farming business, but there is still a potential for lease income from the farm sites.

Shell Fishing

The Pacific oyster is a $40 million industry in Washington. In 1988, the S'Klallam Tribe entered into a partnership with a small oyster company on Dungeness Bay. By 1990, the Tribe had purchased the Dungeness Oyster House, which had been farming since 1963, along with a lease to acquire additional tidelands in Sequim Bay. Sales increased sevenfold in two years, and the Tribe developed a dilapidated family oyster farm into a profitable business, ranking in the top 30 percent of producers in the Pacific Northwest.

In the years between 1990 and 1994, the Tribe faced many challenges with oyster farming. The main beds were subject to flooding, and twice, significant tidelands acreage was lost. The beds are now located where flooding will not occur. Oyster-rearing techniques abound, and the Tribe discovered that while individuals might be successful using, say, a rack-and-bag method, that is not the same thing as using that technique to turn a profit in a large-scale farm. Other challenges revolved around developing increasingly productive beds.

Both the cold Pacific Ocean water and the icy Dungeness River water from the Olympic peaks guarantee year-round oyster farming for the Tribe. After up to five years of care, the oysters are harvested at low tide, washed, sorted, and graded by shape and weight. They are then marketed throughout the United States and across the Pacific

Rim. Long-term potential in this arena is extremely encouraging.

The JKT Oyster Farm sells two products, live on-the-shell single oysters and clusters of live oysters. The two products complement each other by taking advantage of different growing conditions on tidelands and different market niches.

The Sequim Bay tidelands are not currently used because of high mortality rates. A combination of factors made this location commercially impractical, including a shallow bay, low flow, and low-oxygenated water. The market can also be quite volatile given public perceptions of safety, such as the

The Tribal oyster farm (Photographs courtesy of the Jamestown Tribe photo collection).

presence of red tide. However, the problems in one area of the country can translate to increased production from oyster beds untouched by contamination. The Dungeness Oyster House label stands for pristine quality, and the future market looks very good. Thus, the oyster farm business has been both extremely challenging and successful for the Tribe. They have taken a traditional natural resource and transformed it into a modern business.

Oysters are only a small part of a large and varied worldwide seafood market. Steamer clams, shrimp, and crab are dominated by

Oyster-Farming Methods

The Tribe uses three different methods at Dungeness Bay to grow oysters:
1.The **bottom-culture method** involves growing oysters on the intertidal substrate and periodically raking it so they won't sink into the mud or clump together.
2. The **long-line method** involves stringing shells,which are seeded with spat (young oysters), on a rope. The labor is minimal and simply involves making sure the lines are taut. This method can be used in normally unsuitable water that might have too muddy a bottom or that is home to too many predators.
3.The **rack-and-bag method**, using a rack and bag with submerged nursery trays, is very labor intensive. Clumping is a severe problem with this method.

well-established wild-harvest suppliers. These markets, particularly the Manila clam market, hold promise for farming. In the long run, the Tribe plans to expand the oyster farm to meet new market demands.

Seafood lovers around the world recognize the Dungeness crab. It derives its name from the Dungeness Spit but can be harvested at Cook Inlet in Alaska and down into northern California. The crab, which is smaller than the famous king crab, can be identified because of the lack of spines on the top of its shell and its shorter legs. They are caught live from small boats using squid, clam, or fish bait. Technological innovations have replaced the old crab baskets made of wood. The new circular pots are built out of steel with rubber wraps and wire mesh.

Thus, the oyster farm business has been both extremely challenging and successful for the Tribe. They have taken a traditional natural resource and transformed it into a modern business.

The Tribe harvests only males with a shell six and a quarter inches or wider to ensure a renewable resource. New technology also ensures the fresh catch reaches the market in a timely manner. The caught crabs are immediately cooled with ice to keep them in a "sleep" and relatively inactive. When they are ready for shipment, a gel ice and an atmosphere that is supersaturated with oxygen guarantee freshness.

One tremendous success story has been the geoduck market. Most people unfamiliar with the Pacific Northwest think you are pulling their leg when you tell them about the geoduck, pronounced "gweduck." These huge mollusks can weigh ten pounds and have a shell that measures nine inches across. The geoduck is the largest burrowing clam in the world. On a really low tide, two recreational clam diggers, one to dig a four-by-four hole and the other to hold onto the neck of the geoduck, can bag this amazing catch. These clams cannot burrow as fast as the speedy razor clams on the coast, but if they withdraw their siphon, they are hard to find. It is this two-foot-long neck that is the real treat. It is cut, ground up or minced into patties, or used for sushi.

The primary market is in China. To turn a profit with this delicacy,

Dungeness crab
ʔáʔčx

crab trap
sxʷʔačx̣áy

clam shell
kʷʷáʔŋən

53

A commercial Tribal diver emerges from the water displaying a harvested geoduck. (Photograph courtesy of the Jamestown Tribe photo collection)

divers work with high pressure water picks at a depth of forty to seventy feet near tidal channels, mud floats, muddy or sand-gravel beaches, and in eelgrass on sheltered coastline throughout the Puget Sound and in the Strait of Juan de Fuca, all the way to Alaska. United States Navy divers discovered this method accidentally. Wet suits, air pumped from a compressor on board the boat, and weights enable divers to walk along the bottom, looking for a "show," or dimple left in the sand from a retracted siphon. Geoduck harvesters are expert "show readers."

By 2001, Jamestown Seafood was harvesting and shipping three to four hundred thousand pounds of geoduck each year. The clams are in the air to customers within twelve to eighteen hours after divers bring them up. The Tribe's harvest program began in 1990 and was commercially viable in 1995. By 1998, the Tribe took over its own marketing and shipping direct to customers.

Tribal divers landed a total of 201,910 pounds of geoduck in 1999 and 273,845 pounds in 2001; however, divers harvested only 157,695 pounds in 2000 because of red tide and paralytic shellfish poison (PSP). Treaty council enforcement officers test the levels of PSP regularly. They also check and reset buoys to mark harvest tracts and check divers to ensure geoducks are graded accurately to maintain high quality for the market.

The Tribe's success was highlighted in a 1999 issue of AgExporter, a United States Department of Agriculture magazine: "According to John Robben, President of Jamestown Seafood, 'We had been exporting geoducks indirectly through another company for several years. Then two years ago we went to the International Seafood Exhibition in Dalian, China, for the first time. We made some contacts there and returned to the exhibition last year. In January 1998 we began exporting geoducks to China ourselves.' Last year Jamestown Seafood exported 100,000 pounds of geoducks to Asia valued at $600,000, about one-half the value of total geoduck sales worldwide."[14]

Challenges that continue within the industry include occasional red-tide closures, weather conditions, and interTribal negotiations over harvest shares. As in most of its business enterprises, the Tribe has a lot to learn. The Tribe visited China to market the product and then representatives came to Jamestown to see the harvesting and packing process. Issues of price and in what condition the product arrived had to be worked out in the early stages, but the enterprise continues to grow and is yet another successful economic enterprise for the Tribe.

Other Shellfish Harvest (Except Oysters) in Pounds[15]

	1999	2000	2001
Dungeness Crab	37,014	71,675	78,569
Cockles	---	23	20
Green sea urchin	2,044	4,141	992
Red sea urchin	---	---	498
Horse clams	294	24	73
Manila clams	12,982	6,886	3,100
Native little neck clams	13,084	8,951	4,815
Pacific oysters (dozens)	1,992	1,774	6,892
Spot shrimp	3,342	4,121	2,203
Butter clams	---	708	825
Mussels	---	40	---

Dungeness Bay Coho Salmon Harvest (Number of Fish)

Location	1999	2000	2001
Jamestown	800	3,589	4,080
Lower Elwha	6	373	499
Port Gamble	---	417	---
Non-Treaty	718	3,547	4,993

Fireworks, Property Acquisition, and Other Economic Enterprises

JKT fireworks stands have been a good seasonal business for the Tribe since 1985. Because the Tribe is not subject to county prohibitions for sale of certain types of fireworks, it has developed a market niche and is recognized locally as a successful business. This business has provided funds for Tribal governmental and administrative activities, as well as training for Tribal youth in entry-level retail jobs.

The Tribe also tried, unsuccessfully, to enter the computer system industry. U.S. Department of Housing and Urban Development funding available to the Tribe in 1986 was only available for the development of a business. Using these federal funds, the Jamestown Tribe was able to purchase an industrial complex and a computer systems business at the same time. The computer firm specialized in DEC equipment servicing and the Tribe expanded it to include industrial computer component design and manufacturing. The business tried increased marketing through mailers, hiring direct sales representatives, and pursuing government contracts. Ultimately, the shift to PC systems and away from CPM to DOS resulted in the decision to sell the business. The Bainbridge Island Industrial Building was recently sold for a modest gain.

In fact, property acquisition has been a major success story for the Tribe. Acquisitions included twenty-one acres for the casino, twenty-nine acres for future development, nine acres on Highway 101 across from the casino, and ninety acres at the very east end of Clallam County on Highway 101, which has potential for a major tourist attraction.

From a modest beginning with the purchase of two small apartment complexes (thirty-eight units and twenty-eight units) in Port Angeles, property acquisition has been a mainstay of economic development for the Jamestown S'Klallam Tribe. They have competed for and acquired over $4 million in grants from federal and state resources for economic development over the past seventeen years. Over that same period, the business asset base of the Tribe has increased from zero to over $16 million. This is a remarkable record in today's challenging financial world.

> The business asset base of the Tribe has increased from zero to over $16 million.

Planning for the Future

A long-term strategy, characterized by conservative asset development and, in sharp contrast, the willingness to take business risks and learn through mistakes, has paid off for the Jamestown S'Klallam Tribe over the past fifteen years. There is no reason to believe it won't work in the future. The major economic development goal of the Tribe is to reduce reliance on governmental funding. The Tribe will continue

56

to invest in real property to develop its asset base, develop current businesses to a position where they can support other Tribal needs, provide start-up capital for new businesses, and maintain employment opportunities for Tribal citizens, with a special emphasis on creating more diverse, high-quality jobs.

The Jamestown S'Klallam Tribe has entered into an agreement with the Peninsula (Community) College to develop a Computer Technology Center (CTC). With a focus on providing a variety of computer networking, database management, and hardware skills training to Tribal citizens and families, the CTC will become the backbone of future high-tech business ventures for the Tribe and Tribal citizens.

Currently, the S'Klallam Tribe has launched market investigations and feasibility studies for a major new tourist attraction, including a resort hotel and conference center adjacent to the casino. Another idea under consideration is an eighteen-hole championship golf course if adequate land can be acquired. A gas station with convenience store has great potential, particularly in conjunction with a destination hotel/conference center or RV campground. Several other current businesses are under study for possible acquisition, and the Tribe is currently looking for a joint-venture partner to build single-family residences, duplexes, and quadraplexes for both Tribal citizens and the public.

In 2000 and beyond, the Tribal strategic vision to move toward economic self-sufficiency is based on investment in and management of the following:
- assets that increase Tribal capacity to serve its citizenship and accelerate capital growth
- resources to generate operating income for Tribal government activities and business enterprises
- industries, technologies, and human resources that will provide diverse high-quality employment opportunities for Tribal citizens and other Native Americans

The contributions the Jamestown S'Klallam Tribe makes to Washington's economy are not clearly understood nor widely appreciated by state and local government officials or the general public. There has been little gathering of data or analysis of direct or indirect economic impacts. How much money the Tribe spends for goods and services or how many tourist dollars are attracted to the peninsula partly because of the presence of Indian Tribes and enterprises are completely unknown. A recent study on the economic contributions of all the Tribes in Washington does provide a broad picture of significant impacts. Washington has twenty-seven federally recognized Indian Tribes with a combined population of about 91,000, and they contribute $1 billion annually to the state's overall economy. Tribal enterprises in 1997 spent $865.8 million for supplies, equipment, and services and paid an estimated $51.3 million in federal employment and payroll-related taxes. The Tribes also paid an estimated $5.3 million in state employment and payroll- related taxes in 1997. In 2001, Tribal enterprises employed 14,375 Washington citizens full time, including nonTribal employees. More than half of these jobs are in the services sector. [16]

The economic success stories of this small Tribe are truly extraordinary. This is even more impressive in light of the delay in S'Klallam federal recognition. Several things set them apart from other Tribes across the country. Foremost is the visionary leadership of Chairman Allen and key council citizens and staff to set the Tribe on a course toward self-sufficiency rather than federal dependence. Equally important is that they recognized the need for, and created, a solid Tribal governmental organization to support their economic development ventures. They remained true to their traditions by preserving fishing, shellfishing, native arts, and gaming as key businesses, which were always integral to their culture. At the same time, they used assets from largely European ventures, like apartment complexes, to leverage funds for the more traditional pursuits. As we would expect, not all of their business efforts have succeeded. Regardless, the S'Klallam are in a strong economic position with a bright future.

The future of S'Klallam economic development lies with diversification and not simply gaming. The Tribe's past record and future plans will move it toward the goal of reducing its reliance on federal funds while also increasing its overall positive economic impact on the region and state.

Why S'Klallam Children Always Mind Their Mother

as told to the author by Elaine Grinnell, Jamestown Elder and storyteller

This is a little story. It is about this young couple who finally had a baby. They lived down at what we now know as Hood Canal. My, they waited a long time for that baby and, oh gee, the father was really happy when that baby was coming. And by the time that he arrived, and it was a son also, and mind you, the father happened to be the best hunter, the best fisher, and the best provider in the whole village. Of course he wanted a son to carry on all the things that he was doing, and he wanted a partner too. Yeah, the boy was born and that was the happiest day in his dad's life. He had a blanket all prepared. It was made out of a cedar bark and you know it was lined with fur so it was nice and warm. As soon as that baby was born, he took that baby, wrapped it up and he would just walk with it. He would tell stories of the area. He would tell about the four seasons and all the fish that came through, where you could hunt ducks, and where you could dig clams. Things that you really need to know in life. Well, every day he would say "Can I take him fishing with me?" And mother would say, "No, he's too little. You can't take him fishing." He sorta knew that's the response he would get. But every day he would carry the child all over and just talk and talk to him just as if he understood. This went on until the little boy was able to walk and he was about a year old. As soon as he was able to walk, then the father asked the mother,"Now can I take him fishing?" She said, "He's able to walk." She said, "OK, you can take him fishing." She knew she was going to have to let him go sometime or another. Oh, she didn't want him to go but she had to let go. He had to be taught.

So Father put him in the canoe the next morning. They caught the ebb tide. They no sooner left the beach and that cedar bark sail went up. There was a gentle breeze coming from the east. It caught the small canoe, Father and his son, and that square cedar–bark sail. In no time they were sailing around the point going to the west to the salmon grounds. On the way out there, of course, he was telling him all about the ducks that fly over here, the geese and when they fly and the widgen and the mallards and all those. Oh my, so many things to remember, the little boy thought. You can catch lingcod right here in this hole. You can catch skate over there in that hole, halibut over there. You can dig horse clams here and butter clams over there. Oh, he was going through all the clams. Finally, they got out to the fishing grounds and all the hooks were put in.

Oh, they had such a good day. Gee, they caught a lot of fish. As they did from then on. They made quite a pair.

Every night when they would come home, they'd come in on that high tide. They'd come floating in with that square cedar–bark sail. They were having a good time. Life was good.

Then the boy got sick when he was about nine years old. Mother says, "Now, you have to stay home and get well. Tomorrow or maybe the next day you can go fishing with Father again." Well, by this time the little boy had gone out so many times with his father that he really didn't know if his father could fish without him. He was feeling very self–confident about his fishing. So it was very sad for him to stand on the beach with his mother and watch his father go out without him. As soon as Father got into the canoe, he just went out a little ways and the cedarbark sail went up and the east wind filled the cedar–bark sail and away he went very quickly out around the point and off fishing. When he got out there, he wasn't watching the weather very closely. He was way too busy. He started putting in his hooks on one side. He got all that done and he put them in on the other side. He sat down to rest after all this and he looked back to the west. And then he saw, they're wind waves; that's a good indicator of a storm coming, one of those quick squalls that we get around here." So he thought, "I better get out of here. So he started pulling all of his lines back in, but by this time those jumpy little waves had gone on by him. That dark line had gone by him and now it was getting rougher. The wind was picking up and it was getting stronger and the waves were getting higher. He thought, "Well, I'm going to go right for the end of the spit." He thought, "Should I put the sail up?" He was thinking all of these things. It was really getting rough now and he thought,

father
cə́t

mother
tán

canoe
sn'əxʷɫ;
kʷəním

59

"I better not put the sail up, I'll lose control." He started paddling for the beach and he thought, "I'm going to go into the end of the spit. Nope, I better not. I better pull right across into the beach. If I have to, I can stay all night."

So that's what he did. He angled into the beach all right, but this great big wave came and it took him way up in the air and then just dropped out from under him and made him dive into the preceding wave, filled up the canoe and he turned over. Back in the village now everyone was experiencing the same storm. People were coming in from all over. The fishers, the hunters, and everyone was coming home. The little boy and his mother were just walking up and down the beach asking questions."Have you seen my father?" "Have you seen my husband?" "Oh no, no." Everybody started watching for him and he never did come back. The next day a search was organized. A few people went up this way, north, south, east, and west. They went along the beach and still they didn't find him. Finally, they said, "My, what are we going to do?" On the third day now, the searchers went out and they found his overturned canoe and, oh no, he wasn't in it. So they brought his canoe back and then they had a burial for him. It went on for three days and three nights. That little boy just felt so bad thinking that if he had been there then he could have saved him. But you know, he must have known that he wasn't going to be with me very long. Maybe that's why he spent so much time with me, all that time that he was here. He was with me every day, every minute. He taught me so many things. Maybe that's the reason. He knew. Well, now I'm the man of the family. I'm only nine, but I'm the man of the family. So I'm going to have to provide for my family.

"Tomorrow, I'm going to go fishing," he told his mother.

And Mother says, "Oh no." He held up his hand and he said, "Tomorrow, I'm going to go fishing. I'm the man of the house now and I will provide the food." Just the way he said that, she knew that he had his mind made up and his father would have been proud.

So the next morning, indeed, he jumped in his canoe and said he'd be back later. No sooner had he left the beach and up went that square cedar–bark sail. The east wind picked up that sail and away he went, disappearing around the spit. Sure enough he came back and, oh my, he had a lot of fish, especially for a nine–year–old. His dad had taught him well. The little boy was quite proud too, but of course he didn't say anything. Mother and grandmother and everybody else did all the bragging. This went on for several days. Finally, the little boy had done so well during one day, that in the evening when he came home early, no one was home. Usually the food is all on the table, anyway, she must be out pulling cedar for hats, skirts, whatever. I'm going to put my canoe up on the beach and I'm going to go down to the point. I haven't been down there in quite a long time. He went down to the beach. He jumped on the half buried logs, in the sand, just like kids do when they go down to the beach. He would run on one for as long as he could and then he would jump to another, fall off, get back on laughing, and just go right on down the beach until he finally got down to the point. There was a great big log down there, must have been washed in by the winter tide.

Yes, the storms and everything must have brought that one in. And so he climbed right up on it, and oh, there was a lake on the other side, it was a small lake. So he jumped off that log and he went on the other side and he reached down and touched it. He thought, I'm going to go swimming.

He reached out and touched it and he tasted it. It tasted like drinking water, not like the water out there where he catches all the fish. So, I think I'm going to go swimming. He started taking his clothes off and he looked around, and, oh, the sun's going down. I better come back tomorrow, yeah, that's what I'll do. I'll come back tomorrow and I'll go swimming. That water was nice and warm because the lake wasn't very big. The sun shined on it all day long and it was warm. He was kind of excited about his idea. So he jumped on the logs and he ran on home.

By the time he got home, well, then his mother and the extended family were there too and they were all talking about what had happened during the day. Finally, it came to his turn and he started telling them about going down to the point and he saw this lake and tomorrow he was going to go back and go swimming. His mother quit smiling and she looked at him and said, "What did you say?" And so he told her of his trip down there to the point. There's a small lake and that he's gonna go swimming in it tomorrow. She looked at him and she got really serious. She says, "Don't go down there." He said, "Why?"

"Because there's evil spirits there.""Evil spirits?!" She was very serious, "Don't go down there because there's evil spirits." So he knew better than to argue, so he just dropped the subject. But he kept thinking as he was fishing the next day, I wonder what evil spirits look like? Was she teasing? I wonder what evil spirits look like? Well, I know that you would never do this. But, during the day he couldn't stand it anymore. He was way too curious. And so he went down to the point, but he was no longer running on the logs. He was hiding behind them in that grass that grows on the beach. He was hiding. He'd look up every once in a while to see if there was any evil spirits. He'd run and hide behind the logs and the grass and the small bushes. He finally got down to that big log. Oh, and so he kind of peaked over that big log. He looked out, this way and that way. No evil spirits. He crawled up on it. He looked way down deep into the water. The water was so clear he could see all the way down, way out there. He didn't see any evil spirits. Hmm, he saw a school of fish, but they were just little short ones; they weren't very big at all. He's used to catching those real big ones out on the saltwater, so he surely wasn't afraid of little fish like that. So he went out and he started swimming. He just dropped his clothes and ran to the edge. There was nobody around. He dropped them right there. And he went out and started swimming back and forth, back and forth, back and forth, back and forth. Then he stopped right out in the center and he thought, I wonder if there are any evil spirits.

No evil spirits. He started swimming back and forth, back and forth, back and forth, back and forth. Oh, it was so good, now he realized that the small school of fish had just kind of surrounded him. They were small ones though.

He figured they must be lonesome because nobody ever went down there to swim with them. They followed him back and forth, back and forth. He stopped right out in the middle and he thought, Oh, I'm hungry, I'm hungry. He reached right out and he grabbed one of those fish and it just wiggled in his hand like this. He thought, Well, it's a fish. It looks a little bit different than what I catch out there, but it's a fish. And it was just wiggling in his hand and he thought, I'm gonna cook it.

So he swam back to the beach and he built just a little fire because, you see, he just had a little fish. He got a branch and he impaled that fish. He pushed that branch into the sand right alongside the fire. He leaned it over the fire and let it start cooking. And while he was letting that fish cook, he just kind of walked over to that great big ol' log. He sat down right alongside of it. You know it had been sitting out in the sun all day long. Oh, it was nice on his little, cold body and he wiggled down in the sand to get warm. He leaned up against that log and raised his little face to the sunshine, closed his eyes. He reached out with his one hand, cupped it and he filled it full of sand. He let it run through his hands. He did that over and over again.

This is a good day. This is a good day. This is a good day. This is a good day. The only thing that he could hear was the sand running through his hands and his heart beating. Oh, this is a good day. And then he took a real deep breath. You know when you've cooked fish on the beach as many times as he had, you know when the fish is done and ready to eat. Yes, it was ready. He reached out and he grabbed that fish, that stick. And he started eating the fish. He ate and he ate. He looked around for evil spirits and he didn't see anything. In fact, his mother must have been teasing. I'll have to go home and tell her I was down here and there's no evil spirits. He kept eating and eating, looking around just in case. The last bite he thought, I better get home and tell Mother what I've done and there's no evil spirits down here.

And so he started getting up now, and then out comes this really strange voice out of his throat— "oooooooh."He jumped up and he looked at his arms— they were black and feathered. Oh no, he looked at his body and it was black and feathered and his feet were even webbed. Oh no, he didn't realize it but the evil spirit was in the body of that fish. And now look at him, he's trapped in the body of a loon. Oh, I've got to go tell my mother what I've done. I've disobeyed her and now look at me, I'm trapped in the body of a loon. So he started flying and flying. He flew and he flew.

And finally when he came to his home, he looked down and there was his mother working in the garden with her great big long garden stick. Pretty soon she was aware of all this squawking and screaming going on overhead.

She looked up and here was this otherwise very shy bird. Usually, the loon will stay way out in the water but this one was flying right over her head in a tight circle.

"Get away from me you crazy loon! Get away from me."

And she took her garden stick and she struck out into the air. "Get away from me." And he was just telling his mother.

"It's just me, your son, and I'm so sorry that I disobeyed you."

"Get away from me you crazy loon." All at once she took a great big healthy swing and she hit him right here on the wing and, oh, down he went, nearly hitting the ground. Oh, if I stay here she's gonna kill me. So I have to go back to that lake. So that's what he did. And you know if you go down to a body of water really early in the morning or real late in the evening and you listen real carefully you can hear that long mournful call of that little boy that's still stuck in the body of a loon, "ooooooooh," because he didn't mind his mother.

3

Community

Traditional Ways

The stories and descriptions in this chapter are only a small slice of the traditional village life of the S'Klallam. They provide a glimpse into selected aspects of a rich, complex, and meaningful system of thought and tradition. One of the primary benefits of these stories is that they can provide a path to discovering and understanding contemporary S'Klallam lifestyles.

Origins

The term "myth" carries much cultural baggage. "Myth" is not commonly used to refer to the Judeo-Christian origin story but is all too often used to label indigenous origin stories. A myth is simply a story that has some basis in truth and reality for the group that first told it. Of course, over time it changed, and when portions of the story recount adventures that defy principles of natural science, it becomes less believable for some. The tendency for proponents of western science to insist everything can and should be explained is extremely problematic, not only for creation and origin stories but also simply for the sake of common sense.

Erna Gunther collected three different versions of a S'Klallam origin story. All three are similar to stories (although not usually as origin stories) existing in more than forty-five other Tribes both throughout the Pacific Northwest and as far away as the lands of the Cheyenne, Arapaho, Assiniboin, and Blackfoot.[1] She assumes that this story was passed on to the S'Klallam and is not S'Klallam in origin. This line of reasoning mirrors the obvious misconception by anthropologists and others that richer ceremonial and cultural ways were to be found to the north of the S'Klallam and that anything similar in an origin story or spirit dancing ceremony must have been borrowed from groups studied by "famous" anthropologists. This assertion has not stood the test of time.

Villages and leaders, in particular, forged alliances through ceremony, potlatching, and intermarriage. Slaves brought new knowledge, as did the extensive trading network. No one knows the origin of creation stories, any more than one knows which direction sharing and innovation traveled, whether south to north or circular. The question is not important or even appropriate to the S'Klallam or other native groups. The myths surrounding the stories about Judeo-Christian gods are equally clouded by questions of origin and diffusion. However, a belief in creation is, at least, one common denominator.

Each traditional S'Klallam village had a rich system of knowledge to pass on through generations, explaining who they were, how they were different from others, and why and how the special place in which they lived could provide for them.

Each traditional S'Klallam village had a rich system of knowledge to pass on through generations, explaining who they were, how they were different from others, and why and how the special place in which they lived could provide for them. The following village origin story, written by Gunther as she understood it from her informant, portrays S'Klallam origins from the union of a stranger and a woman, which produced wolves who were really humans.

couple
ta?yús

dog
sqáx̣e?;
sqməy'

young boy
swi?qú?i⁴

young girl
⁴na?čú?i⁴

There was a young woman who fell in love with a stranger. He looked so fine that she could not help loving him although she did not know who he was. She thought that he came from a neighboring village but she really could not tell because she saw him only at night. Sometimes she asked him who he was but he would never tell her. For a long time they met this way, and at last she realized that she was pregnant. She wanted the young man to stay with her people so she began to let her parents know that she would like to marry him. Her parents found out that she was pregnant and said, "You are pregnant, we cannot say anything, it is for you to decide. If you want him and he will have you, he can come and be one of our family." The young man never came again.

Now the girl gave birth to six little dogs, five male and one female. When this happened, her people left her, they were so ashamed. They went to the other side of Sequim Bay to live. The girl was left alone. She struggled to get enough food for the little dogs. She always went down to the beach when the tide was out to dig clams. The little dogs grew very rapidly.

Later when she went out digging clams, she would hear singing and dancing. When they danced while their mother was away, the little female dog would watch at the door so that they would not be taken unaware. When the mother started home, the little female dog told her brothers, who had taken off their dogskins and danced as human beings, that it was time to dress again. They put on the skins and lay down by the fire as dogs. When the mother bought home the clams, she opened them and fed them raw to the dogs. She kept on doing this because it was the only kind of food she could get.

The mother suspected that something strange went on while she was away, so she planned to surprise them. When she went to the beach again, she carried a small piece of rush mat. She stuck her digging stick in the ground and put the mat over it so it would look like a person bending over. She built a fire beside it. She started to work in the shadow of the mat. When she heard the dogs dancing, she stole carefully up to the house. The little female was taken by surprise, for seeing the fire on the beach, she thought her mother was there digging clams. The mother rushed up to the door and pushed the little dog aside. She entered and, seeing her children as human beings, said, "Here you are human beings and you made me suffer all the time. "They all sat down and hung their heads in shame. They said nothing for a long time. The mother saw their dogskins piled up, so she took them and threw them into the fire. Then the oldest boy talked. He told his brothers, "I am going to be a whaler, killing whales. "And the next one said that he was going to kill sea mammals smaller than whales—porpoises and seals. And another said that he would be a fisherman. The next one said that he would be a canoe maker. Another said he would be a hunter in the woods.

The mother said she would never forgive the little girl: she wanted to kill her. She prepared a place in the ground with hot ashes and covered the girl with them. But the child always came up again out of the ground just beyond the fire. The mother tried many times to burn her but every time she came out at a different place. They never knew what the mother finally did with her.

This happened at Washington Harbor and it is a true story. These boys were wolves instead of dogs but they did not find that out until they grew up.

When the boys had everything ready for their hunting, they started out in various directions. They brought home all kinds of food. Each brought home what he had promised to get. So their mother had a fine family and was well supplied. They had many fires burning to smoke all the food for winter use. When the people who had moved away saw the smoke, some came back to find out what had happened to the girl.

They found that she had a very nice family who were supplying her with everything. So they went back to tell others of her good fortune and all prepared to return. They bought food from her because she had so much, and through her trading, she became the richest and highest person in the village.

This must have happened here at Washington Harbor, because

the people used to believe that the wolves were their friends. The people living here used to make little wolf's heads, which the young boys wore during a potlatch. They crawled around squealing and pretending to be wolves, while the older people played on little whistles made of cedar and wound with cherry bark. So we believe that we are from the wolf children. There is no other Tribe about the Sound who can do this and use the wolf mask.[2]

There is no one agreed-upon origin story for all S'Klallam. However, there are many stories that place the S'Klallam people in their contemporary homeland and provide the foundation of their interaction with their environment. Other S'Klallam village origin stories were not recorded by anthropologists or others and have not yet resurfaced in oral tradition at Jamestown.

Class Distinctions

Any traditional S'Klallam had the potential to earn a reputation as a real man or to attain high rank. The basic and necessary ingredient was to be talked about by others in your village as someone who was a hard worker, was generous, and was serious about getting ahead in life. To attain high rank, you must also possess strong guardian spirits and become a member of the secret society. It also helped to be the best hunter of land animals in the village or among the best fishermen.

The sharp and distinct dividing line between real men and those of high rank revolved around whether you were known and how you were talked about by the people from other villages.

Thus, inherited names, songs, powerful spirits, and wealth would assure being known as an important man. Then, it was up to the individual to live up to this reputation and to acclaim any inherited rights while giving as many great potlatches as possible.

These events had to include important people from other villages and Tribes as well. Other speakers were necessary to proclaim your high status because modesty and dignity were equally important values.

Gamblers or shamans might be known by other villagers and even by people in other Tribes, but their reputation would revolve around cunning or fear. They might acquire considerable wealth and would have powerful guardian spirits. Others would name them as important men but, without the necessary moral reputation of a real man or the potlatches to proclaim their status, they would never be compared to a high status community leader.

While the divisions among the upper class, commoners, and slaves had some fluidity, particularly over time, the genetic dividing line was socially active well into the late 1800s. When federal officials began naming chiefs and the potlatch was driven underground, along with spirit dancing, social standing shifted toward areas such as participation in the Indian Shaker Church; service in the military; educational, athletic, and occupational achievements; and keeping family and community together.

When S'Klallam meet each other, the question of who you are is really directed toward finding out to what family you are related. Kinship lines are traced to the great-great-great-great-grandparent and but can take into consideration the most remote ancestors that are known.

Although rigid class distinctions have disappeared, family names and reputations are still important. Rank and status have disappeared, but the character and values of a real man are still woven into the fabric of contemporary S'Klallam ways of life.

Community Leaders

S'Klallam community leaders, who later became known as "chiefs," just like their other Pacific Northwest counterparts were at the top of the social hierarchy. By the end of the nineteenth century, a person of wealth and good S'Klallam character might be recognized as a leader by many, but formal centralized authority was the creation of the federal government. In the traditional S'Klallam language, a leader held in high esteem was distinguished from others by drawing out the initial sound in the word that recognized his standing. Wealth and, in particular, the number of major potlatches he gave during his lifetime largely determined his reputation.

The eldest son had the right, regardless of age, to succeed his father as headman. Women could never inherit this right, and if there were no sons, the line would move to a grandson or, in some cases, a younger brother. The story of how James Balch became recognized as "Chief" of the S'Klallam illustrates both the influence of the agent and the tradition of inheritance.

When Lord Jim from Dungeness died, he was recognized as Chief of the S'Klallam, as his father and grandfather had been before him. When the S'Klallam gathered on the Skokomish reservation for their annuity, the agent asked them who should be named chief. A wealthy Dungeness man, whose English name was Sam Johnson, said he should be chief because of the great number of potlatches he had given.

When the agent asked if Johnson was in line to inherit the position, he was told by others that James Balch, the chief's grandson, should be named chief. However, Balch was very young and so, when the agent told everyone to stand either with Johnson or Balch, all the men from Dungeness stood by Johnson. An Elder rose and spoke to all the people who had not chosen. She identified each by their village or Tribe and chided them, reminding them that Balch was Lord Jim's grandson, saying, "He is your own child." All of the people whom she spoke to stood behind James Balch, who was then "elected." Everyone there participated, whether they were officially listed as S'Klallam or not, because the S'Klallam had so many ties to the other Tribes through marriage that the other Tribespeople there had a right to vote.

A S'Klallam leader had important responsibilities beyond potlatching. In particular, he would be called upon and expected to settle differences between married couples, among family members, or between different village members. Beyond offering sound advice, he could threaten retribution by relatives of a wronged person. Fines, for beating a wife for example, were commonly assessed to be paid to the immediate relatives of the wronged person. If the fine was not paid, the relative could punish the wrongdoer with the leader's permission. In addition, the leader handled all blood money transactions between villages. The process did not always work if, for example, the price was too high. In these cases, it then fell to the leader to organize resources for a fight. The S'Klallam always had a widespread reputation among other Tribes as well as European Americans for being dangerous warriors. They were known for beheading their enemies and displaying the heads on poles for everyone to see. Men would dance and women would sing each day of the display, up to a week. However, the village leader was not ordinarily the leader of a fighting group, and if he went along to try to collect blood money from another village, he would not enter the village but would send speakers to them with his negotiations.

Trouble between S'Klallam villagers could, more often than not, result in immediate retribution. For example, annoying girls or women or using another's fish weir or duck net without permission would necessitate being ready for a fight.

When one S'Klallam village invited another to join them in a fight, a meeting was called where speakers and village leaders from both the visiting group and those being recruited would give their views of the proposal. If there was no consensus, each person would be pointed to and asked for an opinion.

Today, the Jamestown S'Klallam Tribal Council sets Tribal policy. Tribal leaders have continued to provide wise counsel in disputes between citizens, but the European American justice system has intervened in the process of settling intertribal conflicts.

War Spirit Power

The following story tells of how the S'Klallam discovered a special spirit power that made the enemy weak and limp so they were unable to defend themselves. It also tells why the S'Klallam travel in a line of canoes led by a dancer with eagletail fans. The special power received after bathing and fasting made enemies faint and weak so the S'Klallam could raid for the best stock of slaves or future wives with high standing without resorting to killing. This power also explains why,

Blood Money

The demand for blood money to right a perceived wrong, usually the death of someone, was the main reason to put together a raiding party. The fights were sometimes between S'Klallam villages, but more often they were with other villages and Tribes. If another of high status killed an upper-class person, then the victim's Tribe demanded blood money. Regardless of who was right or wrong, the demand was usually initially refused. The entire process could take a long time. Two messengers canoed back and forth between villages, and after each new message, the entire village would have to meet and consider the proposal. If a family could not raise the blood money price agreed upon, the community leader could get others to help pay it if they wanted to avoid a fight.

when invited to a potlatch, the S'Klallam would land dancing from the bow of a canoe. The power showed the strength of the S'Klallam and the weakness of other people. The special place that whales, lightning, dreams, and songs held for the S'Klallam come together in this story.

Two men were out trolling off the spit off Dungeness when they saw lightning coming down into the water—flashes of lightning hitting the water. And then one of them shouted, "Look! A whale over there!" And there was something like a wounded whale there in the water where the lightning had struck. They paddled over to the wounded whale, but then they saw that thing giving off flashes in the water, the water was all full of lightning, where it had come down. And their hands were wet where they held the paddles and they started getting numb from that thing in the water, their hands started getting numb! So one of the men shouted, "Keep away! Let's get away from it!" Then they paddled off a way and they saw the whale making for shore, with lightning coming out of him.

whale
čxʷáyu

They saw him go up on shore and into the woods, breaking down trees. He went up into the woods and away west from Dungeness Spit to where there is a little lake . . . where he lives. One of the fishermen went and bathed, bathed all the time and scrubbed himself with cedar boughs. And he fasted, one of the fishermen that saw that č'i·'nakʷ'. For two or three months he did this. And when he was all clean he went up to [the lake] where the č'i·'nakʷ' was and crawled up to the lake. He went cautiously, to see the č'i·'nakʷ'. As soon as he got close to the little lake he saw that thing like a whale's back and all the water full of little sparks. As soon as he saw

spiritual power
ɬq'íyən

power to kill
x̣ťáyu

that he went to sleep. And the č'i·'nakʷ' came and told him, "Here's what I'll give you. When you go to another country you use my name .Call me by my name, č'i·'nakʷ'. And that will make all the people there weak .They will be weak when they hear my name. "That's what the č'i·'nakʷ' said to that man. That was power he was getting now.

spirit dance
syəwən;
čiyáʔwən

This man came to and got up and looked around. He had the

č'i·'nakʷ' power now. He wasn't afraid now, he looked around and that little lake was full of water now! He went home. When he got home he told his people, "I've got that power now, that č'i·'nakʷ'. And when the warriors are going anywhere, they will take me along and I'll sing for them and we will make the people weak where we are going."

So now, whenever the people go anywhere, to potlatch, anywhere, they go one canoe after another in a line, with this man up in the bow of the leading canoe. He has eagletail fans in each hand and stands up and dances, waving the eagle feathers and singing: "haha' haha'/ ha č'i·'nakʷ'ha č'i·'nakʷ'."

When they go to war, a man with this power goes in the front of the head canoe and sings this to make the enemy people weak. He uses his power to weaken them. The Dungeness people could take a man with this power along to make the enemy weak. But it doesn't make him a warrior. It doesn't give him power for fighting.

Now [he] says, "Let's go to [Kyuquot] to try this power on those people there. "So they got ready and went to try the power of this man who had č'i·'nakʷ'. So they went to Kyuquot. [The man with the power] says, "We'll keep singing and land right in front of those [Kyuquot] people. We won't be afraid." So they landed at the village, the č'i·'nakʷ' man in the bow singing. And all the [Kyuquot] people were faint and weak. "What's this,we have no life at all!" The Dungeness men went into the village, and sure enough the people were all sitting limp, as if they had no life in them. They picked out good strong-looking people, goodlooking women, strong young men."Here, you come to the canoe. "The [Kyuquot] people would get up and stagger to the Klallam canoes, and they put them in and paddled off.

They went off with the slaves they had taken.[3]

Men with a thunder or rain guardian spirit were respected warriors, but each warrior did not need a special power related to fighting in order to participate, though it was a desirable thing to have. A well-known story illustrates the importance of being able to call upon spirit powers during a conflict: When some S'Klallam were canoeing to Vancouver Island, they saw another group outfitted and dressed for a fight, heading for S'Klallam territory. A warrior with the thunder spirit caused it to thunder and rain so hard that the other warriors beached their canoes, turned them upside down, and crawled under them for safety. They were easy prey for the S'Klallam.

S'Klallam would toss burning mats or torches on and over the walls of enemy stockaded positions. They would kill and decapitate men, and take women and children as slaves for labor and future trade. There is evidence that usually a fight would end when one or two warriors from either side were killed. However, in rare instances, an entire village would be taken over and burned to the ground.

The Secret Society

The origin of the secret society is not well documented. The ceremony was labeled a secret society by later observers because only high class initiates and their families were allowed to participate.

The S'Klallam and some other Northwest groups used the term "growling" to represent fierce or watchful, to describe secret society members. The major role of the group seemed to be a way to maintain status distinctions among families. The upper class, who had the resources, would pay to have their children initiated; however, the basis for the society was derived from everyday practices based on guardian spirit beliefs. While the secret society came and went, spirit dancing was revived throughout the Pacific Northwest in the twentieth century. After 1950, both U.S. and Canadian government restrictions on potlatching and other traditional ceremonies were eased, and within three decades new potlatch or longhouse structures to host inter Tribal events began to spring up throughout the area.[4]

Robert Collier from Jamestown told Gunther about his secret society initiation in her visits with him in 1924 and 1925. He joined the society after his family paid three hundred dollars to the members of the society. Men or women could be initiated, but usually children were taken into the society during adolescence, as was the case with Robert Collier: "When I joined there were ten of us joining, two of [Xateenim]'s boys, the two La Hash boys, Jimmie Dick, Edward Shanks, Nancy Howe, Richard Wood, a sister of Henry Allen and myself. Our old people asked us to join. My people wanted me in the [secret society] because membership shows that you are of high class. . . . When I joined, the initiation was at [Xateenim]'s potlatch."[5]

Robert's family asked relatives (particularly any uncles) and their friends from Port Gamble to come and sing and dance at his initiation. A S'Klallam uncle has a special relationship with his nephew. He is expected to give his nephew advice and always watch out for his welfare. The uncle would, for example, pay to have his nephew initiated into the secret society if the parents could not.

A group of members was assigned to each child, and although the Port Gamble members told Robert that he was not going to be killed, he believed they could kill children and bring them back to life. When the Port Gamble people came, tied their canoes together, and began to sing, Robert's family hid him in his house. The members kicked the door open and rushed in. One was bleeding at the mouth and was held back by a rope around his waist. Robert was carried in a blanket and taken to a screened-off corner of the potlatch house, where he was glad to see the other initiates. Songs were sung, but not in S'Klallam.

The words did not mean anything. They stayed there for a week with little to eat. What they got was smuggled in by women who were members. Anyone who was not a member thought they were dead. A member watched them all the time and sang to cover up any noise they made.

All week was set aside for the potlatch, and members danced after each meal in front of the screened area as an important part of the ceremony. The leader of a dance held a fan made of eagletail feathers. There were many different dances. During the women's dance, the leader would be in the middle of a circle.

The women would move their arms, hands out with palms forward, up and down. They danced forward, then danced back to the starting point and continued dancing in place. Sometimes all the young women who were members danced to certain songs with one hand at the shoulder, palm forward, and the other arm fully extended. Each hand exchanged places in time with the music. When men danced in certain songs they held both arms out all the way, palms forward, and moved them up and down with the music.

They danced in about fifteen-foot areas, but men and women were in separate circles. The leader was in the space between them, and he started the songs. Some women would move their heads forward and backward but not the men. Due to such intricacies, it was important that everyone practiced dancing at home before a potlatch.

The headdresses were particularly important and decorative at these dances: "For the headdresses they used brown and black wing feathers of the eagle. Each headdress had seven feathers, two in front, two on each side, and one in the back. At the top of each feather, they tied a strip of cedar bark painted red. It was six inches long. Later in my day, they used pieces of red flannel or ribbon. For all these dances their faces were painted black."[6]

A S'Klallam uncle has a special relationship with his nephew. He is expected to give his nephew advice and always watch out for his welfare.

After four days, Robert and the other initiates were taken out at night and taught how to dance and sing, and the story of the society was given to them with the threat of death if they ever told others or made fun of it.

On the last night of the potlatch, nonmembers were moved away where they could watch from a distance. Some of the young initiates would be brave enough to cut their tongues and they would smear their blood on those who could not. At this point, they were still considered dead, so they would be carried outside either naked or, in the case of girls and older men, clothed only in aprons. They would be lifted three times into the air, and the third time they were lifted, they would come back to life and be taken to put on their dancing clothes. The powers that participants received varied, and cedar fans or headdresses proclaimed both rank and the strength of one's spirit: "At Washington Harbor, they always dressed the children near the lagoon. When they had run each of us to the lagoon we had gotten our power. We all received something to show for this. I got a bow and arrow my uncle made for me. Some of the others got fans of cedar with strips of red flannel hanging from them. These fans showed that the children belong to a high class. Edward Shanks danced alone for he had a brave spirit. They put a point like a crane's beak on the front of his headdress."[7]

The power would be taken out of the initiates with song and dance. They were taken by the arms by two members and returned to the potlatch house where they were laid on mats. They had been told to groan and turn their faces. Any member could dance to get the power out, and when it happened, they took the power and members would have to run after the dancer to quiet him or her down.

The potlatch gifts were given out the next day and each new member's family gave money to the secret society's highest members. This was in addition to the original three hundred dollars already given members. For a month after his initiation, Robert was not in his right mind. His father made him a six-inch-long ironwood stick that he carried tied to his wrist. He was to use it when children who were not members questioned him or made fun of him. He recalls that some girls laughed at him, so when they came close, he hit them and they ran away.

Shamans

Usually men were shamans; only a few women have been known to receive such power. S'Klallam informants told Gunther about a place under this world where day and night and all the seasons are reversed. This place is the land of the dead, and it is where ghosts happily live, since retribution is not part of that world. Ghosts were known to linger around the house and possibly take other relatives with them, so after a death, shamans were hired to watch and keep this from happening.

The most important and powerful thing a shaman could do was journey to the land of the dead and bring back a lost life. There were

Bringing Back the Dead

Witsakxu from Port Discovery was known for the power to bring back lost lives. He would sing his song until he came to the land of the dead. His face would be painted white and his hair was made to stand out all over his head. Then he spoke a different language and crawled on the floor acting crazy. He fought with ghosts who chased him. He threw small sticks at them, and if he picked up a large stick, a member of the audience would have to wrestle it away from him before he hurt someone. He was blind and possessed of his power during his journey and only became sober when he returned, after washing the life in warm water and telling the audience his journey had been successful. Once, when he recovered the lives of a large group, just before he reached the land of the dead, he walked around the room and asked each person his or her name. After he found each person's life, he took that person's hand and added him or her to a human chain. When he had them all, he put them back without washing them because there were so many. He returned each life by cupping his hands and putting them on the head of each individual. He was paid a canoe, a blanket, and about thirty dollars.

only a few who were known for this, and they performed this feat if a person's life was captured by ghosts or had wandered off to the land of the dead. When a special kind of illness came over people, they knew that their life had been captured, and, if they could afford it, they would hire a shaman to return their life to them.

S'Klallam shamans also cured those who called them with certain illnesses, found lost articles, and displayed their powers at potlatches. A shaman had only certain powers and would not accept an invitation unless it was for a cure he had experience with and could be assured of success. A shaman's reputation was his stock in trade, and repeated failures would lead to ridicule and loss of his livelihood.

For physical illness a shaman sang while rubbing and or sucking the afflicted parts of the body, as in the following case: "When Tom was about fourteen years old he cut a ligament in his knee. . . . After two years on crutches, his grandmother took him to Hood Canal to Crow, a shaman. Crow felt the knee and said he could suck the bad matter out of it. He started sucking on it and Tom fainted. He tried it five times; then he cut a hole in the skin and sucked out lumps of bad matter. After six months Tom could walk. The shaman received ten dollars for his services."[8] In another instance, a shaman's rubbing cured a twelve-year-old boy. The shaman rubbed a sickness out of the boy that was about an inch long and looked like a flounder. When he put it on a flat stone, it split the rock in two. He then wrapped it in shredded cedar, chewed on it, and put it in a fire. The boy was cured.

A S'Klallam shaman could also cure by taking water in his hands, blowing on it, and throwing it on the body. Water is an important purifying agent in many ceremonies. Water could also reveal lost articles or people. A shaman named Dr. Bill had a dog as his spirit, and he could find lost persons. Once, he found a lost child at Beecher Bay. He sat on the floor of the child's house next to water in a bowl. Everyone helped by beating sticks on boards while Dr. Bill sang and called on his dog powers. He had a vision and led everyone to a place where they found the child's basket with salalberries. He then led them to a yew tree where they found the child's body. From his vision, Dr. Bill knew the man who was responsible, and years later the man was killed, everyone believed, by the child's uncle.

seek spirit power
kʷaʔčáct

put a spell on
nahústəŋ

cure
ɬə́ʔkʷt

Water is an important purifying agent in many ceremonies. Water could also reveal lost articles or people.

If an evil spirit was shot into you, a shaman would have to be hired with stronger powers than the one who committed the act. One story tells of a woman who had been shot by a shaman. She was cured by a stronger one, who said that the evil shaman would die in the same way as he took the evil spirit out of her. He burned the spirit he took from her body, and when a blue smoke rose up, he shot it with a gun. According to the tale, the evil shaman was subsequently shot in a quarrel, and when he fell into a fire, he burned to death.

Some shamans could control the weather. A S'Klallam received this power when he was chased by a mountain lion onto a beach near Blyn. He received the thunder spirit, and when he sang, observers could hear thunder. On one occasion, he caused it to rain when some white people who had heard of his power asked him to. Another time, he made it stop snowing while other Indians watched.

A fourteen-year-old boy was visited by a person with deer hooves rattling on his forehead. The boy could not talk and was bleeding from the nose and mouth. When his uncle, a shaman, was called to treat him, he recognized the power that the boy had received and helped him recover. Later, there was a great potlatch at Dungeness where the shamans were showing their powers. Gunther was told that "they would take out whatever power they had and let it on the ground or in the water. A snake, a bird, or a devil fish were all alive there for the people to see."[9] The shamans tested each other's powers by attempting to pull a limb out of a tree that had recently fallen and was still green. None there could do it. The boy had not yet shown his power, and his uncle, who had treated him, urged him to join in. He resisted and then finally knelt down next to the tree and let his power into it. He took hold of the limb and pulled it off and from then on was called to cure people, even at his early age.

Guardian Spirits

When Gunther talked to her informants in the mid-1920s, she reported a resistance in talking to her about what she called the "old religion." She attributed this to the fact that most of the older S'Klallam had converted to the Indian Shaker Church. She was convinced that there were many stories that had already been forgotten or were not attainable because of religious conversion. She did record considerable material on how individuals acquired and used their guardian spirits. She referred to individual prayers being offered to the earth (as a woman) and questioned Eells's assertion that in much earlier times the S'Klallam had worshipped the sun. She argued that Eells misunderstood the S'Klallam word, which could mean earth, sky, or dawn.[10] Both missionaries and anthropologists, because of their own beliefs, religions, or training, were constantly looking for any hint of a native group worshipping a deity, particularly a single god. Traditionally, while prayers were offered by the S'Klallam to the sun, earth, sky, dawn, dusk, or related natural phenomena, these were of secondary importance to guardian spirits and the acquisition of spirit powers, which guided people through everyday life.

Although a S'Klallam guardian spirit could come at any time, children were usually sent out to seek their vision during puberty. During the winter, particularly in a storm, was considered the best time because one would be forced to really test oneself against the elements.

earth, land
sčtə́ŋxʷən

How long a boy or girl lived alone outside depended on how powerful the spirit was that entered him or her and how long it took to bring the power under control. Children could feel the wrath of a digging stick if they hesitated to take the opportunity to seek a vision. A woman's menstrual period was a powerful counterbalance to acquiring and controlling one's power. For example, a piece of clothing from a menstruating woman would be needed to rub on the body if one acquired the very powerful thunder spirit.

One could dance at the next potlatch and reveal the spirit power; however, sometimes people waited for years because the guardian spirit could be rendered useless if it were revealed at the wrong time. At the potlatch, one could dance with those who had the same power, but each initiation song would be different. As you might imagine, jealousy sometimes arose between people with the same power.

Some guardian spirits were more useful or powerful than others. Some only provided people with songs to dance at potlatches, but others made individuals wealthy so they could give a large number of potlatches or made them great hunters or powerful in war.

Winter Illness

Each winter individuals might become ill, and that would be a sign that their spirit guardians were with them. They could sing at a potlatch or invite friends and relatives who had different spirits than theirs to sing for several days. The ill person started the songs because they were his or her own, then others could join in. The host would feed everyone each day and provide gifts when well again.

type of invisible power
qʼʷéxqs

Indian doctor, shaman
sxʷnáʔəm

seer; forecast the future
syə́w'ə

get power
ƛ̓kʷʷnáxʷ
cəskʷáŋəɬ

The power received was related to the hardships endured while seeking one's vision. If, in the dark one felt a spider web over his or her face, this would mean great luck in life. A more powerful spirit that came from way out on the water or from the north over the water made a person a clever trader and guaranteed the acquisition of wealth for potlatches. When a S'Klallam at Washington Harbor received this spirit, he also had a vision that told him he would give ten potlatches. He went against this vision and betrayed his power by giving eleven potlatches. Because of this, he died right after the eleventh potlatch.

One of Gunther's informants had a vision that would have given him the power to see things far away through a hole in the palm of his hand. The vision came when he was thirteen in the form of a woman who was very dark, with a purple forehead and large eyes with white eyelashes. He was afraid and did not accept the power even though his family and relatives begged him not to be afraid. The acquisition of power could be frightening and was not always embraced by the recipient. Sometimes the individual might not recognize the mistake until later in life, when it was too late do anything about it.

The paternal great-grandfather of Mrs. Robbie Davis at Esquimalt received a wealth power with the promise of enough wealth to support eighty wives. When he revealed his power, parents from all over sent him their daughters and he fulfilled his vision. He also received a harpoon and killed a whale, which was another part of the vision. He received these powers from a house full of people when he entered through a smoke hole. The house was underwater and he followed a skate to it. The skate was the door to the sun's house. When he went outside the house, he found his dead body in the water surrounded by blood and vomit. Thus, he realized that his body had not entered the house, only his life had. It took five days to control his power before he could get up and sing. Obviously, wealth power was a highly sought-after guardian spirit.

There were many other spirits. Some brought luck in fishing and hunting. Another spirit gave the power to kill game by pointing. Still another helped if the hunter were specifically after duck, elk, or deer. This same spirit helped women when they dug clams or fished. A hunting spirit, for example, was the herring, who appeared to one person wearing a cedar bark apron, feathers in his hair, and with red and black paint on his face. The man rejected this spirit by putting the herring he had found in a rotten log. He had been told how to do this and felt that because of its appearance, if it did not disappear immediately, he would fall dead. When he looked for it after he had backed away, it was gone. The herring spirit appeared to him later in his dreams and spoke in S'Klallam telling him he was a coward and that he could have been powerful.

The wolf spirit was powerful both in hunting and war. Wolves would test a boy's bravery and cut his joints so he was more limber than others and could run faster. In war, individuals with this power could outrun everyone chasing them. In raiding and facing the enemy, guardian spirits brought by a wolf, or the very powerful thunder power, could aid even women in battle. Such women would be allowed to join raiding parties. Indeed, the thunder power was so powerful that if it was shot into another person, no shaman could extract it.

An important power was the ability to make a large number of fish gather in one place or, in the case of another spirit, make them come near the shore. These powers would come alive in two boards, which were about two feet long and oval with holes in the sides to hold on to, and which contained a design reflective of the spirit received. Some were in the shape of a dogfish, salmon, or halibut. The boards were very powerful and, when they came alive, could result in death if they were in the hands of someone whom the owner did not approve. A story is told of a man from Port Discovery in the mid-1920s who did not believe in the power. The owner sang and called on the man to take the boards. When the man grabbed them, the boards came alive and moved him all around the house. When he fell down, he was dragged out of the house and into the water, where he drowned.

The Indian Shaker Church

The Indian Shaker Church was an important community institution that provided social and political stability for the Jamestown S'Klallam during the late nineteenth and early twentieth centuries. Early attempts of missionaries from various faiths had largely failed to convert the S'Klallam, as well as other Northwest Coast Indians, to Christianity. Contrary to this, the Indian Shaker Church was a magnet for many Indians and enjoyed widespread participation. This church had no relationship with other shaker religions in the United States. John Slocum, a Sehewamish Indian from the Hammersley Inlet on the Puget Sound, had a near-death experience in 1882 that marked the beginning of the church. His wife, Mary Thompson, about a year later revived John, again, from a severe illness by shaking over him. The church was not formally organized until 1892, but the hallmarks of shaking and healing drew large numbers of Indians to this new religion. Federal authorities tried to stop the practice but were unsuccessful. Several aspects of the church, such as a fierce condemnation of alcohol and the liberal use of Christian teachings and symbols, led some missionaries and Indian agents to take an ambivalent position regarding the Shakers. It was only when authorities felt too much of the old ways, or what was called spirit dancing, were being used that the religion was seen as a threat to civilizing the Indian peoples of the region.

It is difficult to overstate the importance of the Indian Shaker Church to the S'Klallam, and especially to the Jamestown community. Roman Catholic and Protestant ministers were in keen competition for Indian souls but they never had the same success as the Indian Shakers movement. Indian agents had driven shamans and what was popularly called "Indian doctoring" underground by the 1870s, and this new Indian (not European) church combined Christian elements with more traditional and familiar practices.

Early church services were held in various native languages, supplemented by Chinook jargon and English. The success of the church was in the belief, just as with shamans who could cure an illness, that shaking led to healing. More important, spirit guardians, a traditional religious hallmark, were still available to everyone in the Shaker Church, only now they manifested themselves in the shake.

This new church movement continued the process of undermining the usefulness of shamans or Indian doctors because now all parishioners were curers who were able to see the "dark spot," or evil, in a person and help throw it away out a window or door. Shamans lived by receiving goods and, later, charging fees for their services. The new church eroded a major support system for them.

Church healers brushed their hands over the affected part of the body while others rang bells and chanted using the same words that shamans had used in earlier times. A cross and candlestick joined religious pictures behind a pulpit. The church leader, who is respected for his ability to pray, is assisted by parishioners who kneel with lit candles held aloft in each hand. Bell ringing, brushing, circling around those who are ill, singing, chanting, and praying can last for hours at a time. Songs were sometimes the property of individuals just as in precontact times.

While Indian agents and missionaries initially saw the Shaker Church in a negative light, gradually they softened their stance because of the church's policy of abstinence. Reverend Myron Eells, who was a frequent visitor to the Jamestown Shaker Church, wrote down the following speeches in July 1877. They both focused on a major life change wrought by joining the church:

By Lord Jim Balch, head chief:

I thank God that he has helped you to give me a good heart. God taught you, and so you have come to teach us. Truly we were bad formerly. Formerly we asked,
"Where is our Agent?" Perhaps there was none (i.e., there was none to us, he took no notice of us). Hence, formerly we drank very much whiskey. We knew about the Agent at Skokomish only what the Port Gamble Indians told us. Formerly the Port Gamble Indians and Skokomish Indians alone received annuities from the Agent, and we only knew of him by hearsay. Formerly we heard that there was a Minister at Skokomish, but we knew nothing of what he said. No Minister came here when I was a boy, so we knew not what God thought was bad. Formerly we drank whiskey, probably because there was no Agent like Mr. Eells, who took care of us. So we all knew how to drink whiskey. I will not conceal our former wickedness. What does a child do? Always the same as his father. My father formerly drank whiskey. If my father had had any Agent like Mr. Eells, he would have done better, and then I would have done better also. By and by, as my children grow up, they will see that I am trying to be good, and they will become good. As you often come here, and the people do not improve very fast, it shows that formerly they were bad and hard. Now we are improving. So I thank you. I am done.

By Cook House Billy, the acting minister:

I thank God that he has given you instruction, so that you have been able to teach me. I acknowledge that formerly I drank whiskey. Now as you have come this time to see us, I intend to abandon all my evil ways. I will not say that I have always been good. God saw me do wrong, and perhaps Jesus put it down in his book. I am afraid to say that I did not do wrong formerly, for

Jesus knows I did, and hence I will not conceal it. Formerly when I drank whiskey I may have told lies. Now I wish to stop this lying. Perhaps when I drank I stole, but when not drunk I did not steal. I think Jesus knows all about it, but now I wish to stop all this wicked conduct. I am afraid of hell for now I know about it. I know that when the wicked die, they go to hell; but if a person does no wrong he will go to God.

What does one gain by drinking? Nothing but sorrow.

When formerly I worked for white men, I received one dollar a day, three dollars for three days, and then I paid it out for whiskey, at the rate of one dollar a bottle, and the whiskey quickly ate up all my money. So now I intend to stop drinking, and have a strong mind.

When I drank I spent my money for liquor. I slept, I woke up, my money was gone. What did I have for my money? Now you may open your ears, when you get to Skokomish about my drinking. Heretofore, when you have come, I spoke not as I do now. You never talk bad when you come here, but always good, so I thank you for coming. It is as if you were in a bad place, and you were leading us in a good way. So I thank you. I am done.[11]

Lord Jim Balch is identified by Eells here as "head chief." In 1877 the Jamestown S'Klallam were not federally recognized, they had not moved to the Skokomish Reservation where Eells lives, but they were receiving services and both Reverend Eells and his brother, the Indian agent to whom Balch refers to in his speech, apparently recognized and verified the Tribal status of the community.

Each of these orators began, as was the practice, by thanking God and then referring to how bad they had been before joining the church, particularly by drinking whiskey. Balch, who was chief, spoke for all Jamestown S'Klallam when he blamed their tendency to use whiskey on the lack of regular attention and annuities received from the agent. The acting minister, Cook House Billy, confessed not only to drinking but to telling lies and stealing, and he testified that he wanted to change his wicked ways so he would not go to hell, since he now knew about it. He provided insight into the destructive cycle of alcohol when he testified he was paid a dollar a day—the cost of a bottle of whiskey. He would work three days, buy three bottles, and wake up broke.

The broad appeal of the Indian Shaker Church because of its continued use of traditional ways is illustrated by the following story. Reverend William (James) Hall of the Jamestown Shaker Church was known to have cured a woman who "went out of her head." Reverend Hall put the intrusion he removed from her in a baking powder can and buried it. Several days later, the man who had supposedly become angry with the woman and caused her illness in the first place was caught trying to dig up the powder, which he said was his. He was ultimately thwarted in his efforts when he died after reaching the can.[12]

> By far the most current and comprehensive reference on the history of the Indian Shaker Church is found in Robert H. Ruby and John A. Brown's John Slocum and the Indian Shaker Church (Norman: University of Oklahoma Press, 1996).

These were far more than just hard times for the Jamestown people, and the Shaker Church helped hold them together politically, socially, and geographically. For some, the mixture of Christian and old Indian ways was what attracted them to the church. For others it was probably the church socials, fellowship, and sense of community. Regardless, the Shaker Church, unlike shamanism, served as a necessary touchstone and useful bridge between traditional and contemporary times for the Jamestown S'Klallam. Unfortunately, the church in Jamestown later burned down and there were not enough Shakers to rebuild it.

The Jamestown Shaker Church. Acting minister Billy Hall is sitting on the fence rail, hat in hand, on the far right of the group. (Photograph courtesy of the Bert Kellogg Collection of the North Olympic Library System)

Potlatches

The term "potlatch" comes from the Chinook jargon, a unique vocabulary of words based on Chinook and Nootka that developed into a language between traders and trappers and the language- diverse Pacific Northwest Tribes. The potlatch, as an inter Tribal mode of socialization, existed before European contact. The definition of potlatch in the Chinook jargon is "to give" or "a gift." The potlatch, as practiced by Northwest Tribes, is an important ceremony that is integral to the social status of individuals. To amass wealth and give it away at a potlatch is a traditional value. At such an event it was customary to provide good food, recognize individuals who deserved it, and give good advice.

> For information on the Chinook jargon, see Gill's <u>Dictionary of the Chinook Jargon</u>, 14th edition, by John Gill (Portland, Ore.: J. K. Gill Co., 1909). A more comprehensive work with a historical emphasis is Edward Harper Thomas's <u>Chinook: A History and Dictionary</u> (Portland, Ore.: Binfords & Mort, 1970).

In earlier times, the S'Klallam potlatch would last about a week, with constant visiting, games, eating (including two large meals a day), trading, and gambling. Visitors were housed in the larger potlatch house, with the overflow going to houses of the upper class, or relatives. A good host would tie up visitors' canoe paddles to signify they were welcome to stay a long time. Presents were expected to be exchanged every day. It took three to four years to acquire enough resources to host a large inter Tribal potlatch. Smaller potlatches or feasts would be called especially for a naming, puberty, or the anniversary of an important event, and they might involve only a single village or some close neighbors.

A S'Klallam leader with inherited status who gave a large potlatch would have a speaker who sang in a half-crying voice the inherited songs and proclamations of status, including what the community leader wanted to tell the invitees. These orations occurred between large gift distributions. Each type of song required a specific protocol. For example, only wealthy relatives could join in when a wealth song was offered. The S'Klallam lead singer might hold in his right hand, above the shoulder and slightly behind the head, a fan of cedar edged with mountain goat wool.[13]

The following potlatch story is specific to the Dungeness S'Klallam and highlights the traditional preparations and procedures for landing by canoe at a potlatch. To land dancing showed both proper respect for the invitation as well as the strength of one's family and village. The S'Klallam did not host this potlatch, so their responsibilities included the following:

- bringing adequate amounts of gifts for the village headman and honored guests
- ensuring their hosts knew when they would arrive
- approaching at the proper time with the correct protocol and dances and songs

- having an interpreter for those who did not understand the S'Klallam language

To land properly took much preparation and coordination for both the hosts and the invited guests. Protocol demanded that if you arrived late, you would land within sight and camp overnight. The next day you could prepare for a proper entrance. The canoes had to be tied together so dancers would have a platform. Gifts needed to be organized and special clothing and face paint readied for the landing. If you received the invitation, it was important that you bring all your relatives with you. This was a way of showing both respect for your hosts and your own high status in your community.

> For great detail about potlatches, see William W. Elmendorf, The Structure of Twana Culture (Pullman: Washington State University Press, 1992) and Twana Narratives: Native Historical Accounts of a Coast Salish Culture (Seattle: University of Washington Press, 1993).

Singing and dancing were integral to this ceremony. A large platform was created with planks the S'Klallam brought with them. Sometimes there were planks on one canoe, but more often two canoes were used. They tied two canoes toward the bow. The entire group was led by two sets of canoes, each with a dancer, and they approached in a line but came abreast of each other near the shore with everyone singing. At this particular potlatch, the Dungeness headman showed his bear mask to affirm his power, and the Skokomish were in awe because that was not their usual custom. Once the landing occurred, the invitees sang and danced in a zigzag line (as they did in their canoes when they first approached) and went directly to the potlatch house where their place of honor awaited them. They sang and danced before sitting down. People would sing so much, they might lose their voices.

This description notes white goose down from the dancer's hair, but other references cite white swan down as important to the S'Klallam in many ceremonies. It was carried in a deerskin pouch and tied around the neck.

This landing culminated in a feast, which the hosts started to prepare much earlier. The proper landing time was around noon. Regardless of the time of the landing, both sides knew it was proper to feed new guests. Frank James Allen, Elmendorf's informant, describes the potlatch.

And now the Klallam, from Dungeness, came and landed at təbaʼdas and got ready to land at the potlatch house the next morning. I was there to see my mother's people, and waxʷəlacuD told me they were going to land dancing čʼiʼnakʷʼ' and he asked me to help in one of the Klallam canoes. So the next morning I went with them. And first two canoes went out from təbaʼdas,

85

masked
dancer
sx̣ʷə́yx̣ʷi

Cowichan
qəwʔə́čən

a dance
(Indian)
qʷ(ə)yíəš ;
kʷənʔúcən

ahead of the others, to open a way for the č'i·ʼnakʷ'. And there was a young man on a platform in the bow of each canoe, dancing with eagletail fans. And those two canoes went up to stačəɲi'qʷ with everybody in them singing: aha' yaha' / ha č'i·ʼnakʷ'ha č'i·ʼnakʷ'. And then they came back to təba·das and went out again leading all the other Klallam canoes. And this time they came in to Enatai in a zigzag line, singing the č'i·ʼnakʷ'song, and they all lined up side-by-side facing the beach and came to land that way, bow first. Now xaqtə'' had an interpreter, and he wanted to give away property to the head men at the potlatch. So as the canoes came up one man wore xaqtə's stačəɲi'qʷ, he showed his bear-head mask, his power to give away property. Those masks are not a Skokomish custom. They are not tamánamis; they show them before they give away property. And some of the people on shore who were not tu'kʷałi people thought there was going to be tu'kʷałi right now, and they ran and hid. But xaqtəhollered through his speaker,"This is the way I am, this is my way in giving away property!" And now he called the men who were giving the potlatch to come down to the shore, and the interpreter threw blankets to each one from the canoe. And now the Klallam landed their canoes and went to the potlatch house. And they danced in, singing č'i·ʼnakʷ' with qua'łtəm leading them. Ahead of him went a Port Gamble man (čaćwi'qa) with a spear and another man (č'a'witən) in the rear with a gun. And they danced in a zigzag line and went around inside the house in a circle, this way (counterclockwise), with white goose down flying from their hair. And now they stop and they sit down in the place the potlatch people give them.[14]

At this same potlatch, the Dungeness S'Klallam joined other S'Klallam villages to give blankets to other important guests, honor agent Eells with a favorite food of his (dried halibut), sing a song demonstrating their strength (greatness), and finish with a song to make everyone laugh. The S'Klallam people, like all native people in the Northwest, entertained guests with humor. This characteristic is a mainstay of S'Klallam family and village life, both traditionally and today.

However, just as important were the powers they could also show. The S'Klallam used masks with mouths that moved, dramatically posed behind a curtain. They only showed a little of their power that night and they told the audience so. Men with guns patrolled the audience for anyone who did not take this seriously. Four men of high standing sang and danced with painted faces. Their song proclaimed the greatness of the S'Klallam people. The proper demonstration of these powers earned the respect of other Tribes.

> The S'Klallam people, like all native people in the Northwest, entertained guests with humor. This characteristic is a mainstay of S'Klallam family and village life, both traditionally and today.

And now the interpreters holler,"Klallam are going to play tonight! Dungeness, Klallam Bay, Port Gamble are all one tonight. . . . And now they put a curtain across one corner of the house and those men get ready behind it. And they take two young fellows in with them to wear xaqtə''s and wa'xʷəɬacuD's masks. And the Nisqually and lots of people in the house are afraid now, they're afraid those Klallam are going to show [masks]. But they're just going to show those faces. And wa'xʷəɬacuD stood out now. "I'm going to show my way tonight. You watch well, people."And then xaqtə' stood up. "Now I'm going to show my way tonight."And then wa'xʷəɬacuD spoke to ɬa'txcut and su'stx and they acted as speakers for him and for xaqtə'. And wa'xʷəɬacuD called men from other Tribes, not Klallam or any of the Skokomish, and gave them blankets. And xaqtə' did the same after wa'xʷəɬacuD was through. Just the big men of those Tribes they called, one by one. And now the blankets are done. And now su'stx got up with a big dried halibut and hollered,"Where are you, Edwin Eells? Come on, Edwin Eells! xaqtə' has this for you!" And the agent Edwin Eells came out and he took that big halibut and smiled and said,"Thank you, thank you!" And he started chewing on a piece of that halibut right there. He was a great man for eating dried fish. And now the interpreters holler,"You watch now, people! You watch the Klallam, what they're going to do tonight!" And now they're going to let the people see a little of what [tlu'quali] means, but they're not going to show it all. And those four high-up men stand outside that curtain, those four high-up men. And two men stand on either side of them with guns, watching for anyone to laugh. Those four don't have [tlu'quali] paint on; their faces are bare. They are showing who they are now. And now they pull the curtain aside and there behind the curtain is a long-haired woman sitting with a baby in her arms. And on either side of her are those two masks, opening and shutting their mouths. And they let the people see that for a minute and put the curtain back again. And now the Klallam get up to dance. And they sing: ["I am the great one, the Klallam"]. And now they finish dancing, and those four men sit down with the rest. They're done showing their way now.[15]

A humorous nighttime dance is the final performance for the S'Klallam. The informant, Frank Allen, uses the term "cootchy-cootchy" then "hootchy-cooch," which was undoubtedly an English reference he attached to the event. However, regardless of the name, the dance was known because as soon as it was announced, people in the audience laughed. Elmendorf refers to it as "night-work dance," which was his interpretation of Allen's story. Elmendorf thought it meant copulation and the English words reflect that rough translation.

And now the Klallam get ready for cootchy-cootchy. They are going to give their hootchy-cootch dance now. And one of the interpreters hollers, "Klallam are going to show us a thing now. A nighttime dance they give now." And some of the people that knew about it began to laugh. That dance is [nightwork dance], and it means "copulation." And now qa'ɬtəm and another Klallam man got up and they danced, singing: ["Move your stern! ha ha ha! / it is sweet! / ha ha ha)!]" And they jerked their hips at one another and danced around that way. And that agent laughed and laughed. And now the interpreters said, "And now the Klallam will show us č'iˑ'nakʷ'." And the Klallam get up and dance č'iˑ'nakʷ' in a zigzag line from one end of the house to the other, with qa'ɬtəm leading them again. And now the Klallam are done. They finish and sit down. [16]

The traditional potlatch included both serious displays of power, meant to gain respect, as well as humor and wellthought- out jokes. While it was not always proper to show up one's hosts, other Tribes invited to the potlatch were fair game. A description of another potlatch landing by the S'Klallam makes fun of the Cowichan.

Well, the year comes, the year the sux[t] are going to potlatch. So my uncle gathers all kinds of blankets and guns. He's going to show the Cowichan style, how they do at potlatch time. Now the su#x[t] are ready and they call people from all over. The Klallam get there last, they want to get there to the potlatch after the Cowichan come. . . . My uncle nayaxqénəm hollers for the Cowichan to come down to the water now, he's going to throw them those guns. His interpreter hollers, "nayaxqénəm wants you to be ready for these guns, you Cowichan!" and my uncle gives two guns to the interpreter and he hollers, "Ready now, Cowichan!" and throws the guns in the water. And the Cowichan wade out and dive for those guns in eight or ten feet of water. Now one Cowichan comes up with a gun. Now another gets one. And now my uncle throws three guns and all the Cowichan go bubbling under the water, looking for the guns. That's Cowichan-style my uncle is doing; he's making fun with the Cowichan. [17]

Gaming and Gambling

Gaming and gambling have a long and unbroken history of significant cultural and social impact among virtually all aboriginal peoples in both North and South America. Indians played a broad variety of physical games to develop skills and test strength as well as games of chance, which might be played for fun or for huge stakes. The breadth and depth of Indian games and gaming can hardly be captured in a brief way, but some common games were

- dice games
- stick games
- hand games
- archery
- hoop and pole
- shinny
- hand-and-foot ball
- stone throwing
- all manner of canoe, horse, and foot races

> There is a broad variety of sources on Indian gaming. See in particular Stewart Culin's Games of the North American Indians (New York: Dover Pub., 1975). For a Washington source, see Robin K. Wright, editor, A Time of Gathering (Seattle: University of Washington Press, 1991).

Serious Indian gambling in the Northwest took place between different villages or groups and were contests in which the winning team showed they had more power, as evidenced by the songs they sang and the words they spoke, to disrupt their opponents. The S'Klallam preferred to gamble with outsiders because they did not want to take each other's money. At S'Klallam potlatches large amounts of money and possessions traded hands. Gambling was the most important form of entertainment, especially when there were interruptions of feasting and dancing.

> The S'Klallam preferred to gamble with outsiders because they did not want to take each other's money.

A S'Klallam who was a professional gambler could have good social standing, especially if he had not been caught outright cheating. Such individuals were well known to everyone who played, and it was a challenge and great event to beat them. Gambling, though, did not fit with all posts of high standing. The story is told that when a S'Klallam gambler became a leader in his village, he gave up his profession.

A very powerful spirit for accumulating wealth was the sun spirit and this power could help in gambling. Gunther recounts the following stories of powers related to gambling.

> A man from Washington Harbor had gone over to Whidbey Island to gamble and had lost everything he took with him. He paddled home in the fog, drifting along without caring whether he lost his way or not. He struck a rock with his paddle and this became his power. After arriving home, he did not eat for many days. This made him an expert at the disk game.
> Another man secured success in playing the disk game for his whole Tribe. He was walking along the road at Jamestown when he heard a disk game song although there was nobody with him. It was a calm, windless day. He looked up and saw two cottonwood trees moving their top limbs just the way a player moves his arms in the disk game. From that time on the Klallam always won when they played the disk game during hop–picking season.[18]

Slahal

Slahal (the hand or bone game) was the game of choice and was played with carved bones or, in earlier times, with wooden sticks. The game is alive and well today. While some aspects of slahal varied, given its wide use among Northwest Tribes, the basics were pretty much the same. The game was played by two sides facing each other. One man on each team manipulated a pair of bones, one marked and one unmarked. Holders or hiders of the bones earned reputations for filled with a forest or animal depiction, to intricate carvings of personal importance to the player.

Reverend Eells described the bone game as involving carved pieces about two inches long and a half-inch in diameter. Sometimes the bones were larger or made of pieces of wood. In earlier times, individuals played a version of the game with one stick or bone, moving it rapidly from hand to hand and behind the back. Eells sometimes observed the entire Tribe involved in a game but generally counted six or eight who sat about six feet across from each other. He claimed he knew of a game played to a draw after four days and nights.[19]

Professional gamblers knew how to read the face, shoulders, and hand movements of opponents. Sometimes, even the observers surrounding the players would give away the position of the marked bones to the astute professional. Some professionals were well known

90

for the ability to switch the bones from hand to hand while in play. This did not occur often but was a way to show the power one held over opponents.

Fierce drumming, singing, shouts, and gestures toward the individual making the guess fueled the game's intensity. A board, elevated with rocks, was the traditional drum, but hide drums were also used later. Songs were sung to gain the assistance of supernatural powers. These songs were individually owned in the beginning but that gradually changed.

Hand signals were used to guess and collect all tally sticks, which determined the final winners. In longer games, tally sticks, either ten or twenty in number, were used to keep track of the game. In a large game, a side might have to win all the sticks twice. In some games end sticks were used instead of a large number of sticks. When all the center sticks were collected, one end stick would be won. There were some variations in hand signals, and these changed over time. In general, with two sets of bones in motion, the female bones could end up in four positions and if, for example, the female bones were both in the left hand of the hider (to the guesser's right as he faced him), he would gesture toward the right. The guess could be made by pointing the forefinger down, or as a variation, the left arm could be thrown across the chest to the right, with the fist closed and the index finger extended. These signal variations for the guess would have had no consequence, as long as all players understood the signals.

With every correct guess, the bones moved to the opposing team where the leader gave them to two teammates (usually on opposite sides of him) to shuffle and hide. In some games, you could put the bones under loose clothing or behind your back. The leader challenged the other team and directed his fellow players in song. Observers and supporters of each group stood behind the players.

Slahal was usually played outside in the summer but might also be played indoors or even outside in the winter. Games were often played all night, over several nights, or even for a week. The leader positioned himself in the center, and if the games did not go well, he might give

For a detailed description of the bone game, see Marian W. Smith's The Puyallup-Nisqually (New York: Columbia University Press, 1940), 207–21. As early as 1877, George Gibbs also described the bone games in Tribes of Western Washington and Northwestern Oregon (Washington, D. C.: Government Printing Office, 1877). Some brief material on gaming and gambling specific to the Central Coast Salish (and S'Klallam) is found in Wayne Suttles's "Central Coast Salish," on pages 469 and 472 in Handbook of North American Indians: Northwest Coast, edited by Wayne Suttles (Washington, D.C.: Smithsonian Institution Press, 1990). Several social scientists have captured the music and songs, which were such an important part of the bone game. For example, see Wendy Bross Stuart's "Gambling Music of the Coast Salish Indians," Mercury Series, Ethnology Division, no. 3 (Ottawa, Canada: National Museum of Man, 1972); Frances Densmore, "Music of the Indians of British Columbia," Anthropological Papers, no. 27, Bureau of American Ethnology Bulletin 136 (Washington D.C.: Smithsonian Institution, 1943).

up his position to someone else. A second sat next to the guesser and sometimes guessed, if asked. The second was often a powerful singer and that contribution was his primary duty.

Either a man or a woman could be hired by a gambler to be a wisher to help bring confusion to his opponents. Gunther reported that the wisher said the first name of the guesser on the other team, then said things like, "Your eyes are dull, your mind is dull, your guesses are wrong." Another aid for S'Klallam success was useful to the disk game gambler. He would mix the fungus from a bulrush or salmonberry bush with the cedar from his gaming outfit. Gamblers would also commonly pray to the earth for success.[20]

Disk Game

The disk game was also popular. Players hid disks in a bundle or wad of cedar bark fibers.[21] The bundle was rolled on a mat between the two sides, torn apart, and the guesser would try to guess where one marked disk ended up. Some Tribes used a polished stick instead of a disk. S'Klallam gamblers sometimes specialized in one game or the other.

Pacific Northwest Tribes played different types of disk games, some for gambling and others for ceremonial purposes. They played their games at night, and bet on a large scale (slaves, canoes, and so forth). The game was played with ten or twelve disks, and the male disk was all white or all black. A player would shake shredded bark bundle with the disks all rattling against each other. Then the player would pull the bundle apart so disks were in each bundle. The mat was then rotated. When the bundle was divided and the mat moved around, the opponent pointed to the half with the male in it. The player or holder with the bundle could move it back and forth, and around and around, and the guesser could change his mind until the holder was done shaking the bundles. While most games involved twenty tally sticks, there were fifty-eight tally sticks in ceremonial games, which meant that it could take more than a week to play. Only two men played against each other, but the crowd of watchers sang to encourage the player they favored. As you might guess, the results of some games could be hotly debated.

Gunther writes of one such game at a S'Klallam potlatch: "They were playing the disk game with dancing when one side had lost all but one counter. A new man came in and won back half the sticks. The losing side began to fight, the principal players wrestling with each other. The chief stopped the quarrel. The wrestlers were two well-known shamans."[22] The S'Klallam disk game attracted some professional gamblers who played on a rush mat pegged to the ground with pins. The mat is bunched in the center so the disks can be rolled against it, and during the game the spectators and bettors sing. Later in the nineteenth century, S'Klallam gambling songs were sung in Chinook jargon, sometimes with words from their relatives and friends on Vancouver Island:

k[t]ahxʷwyah mika staham
How good your guess

Maikʷa [tšipi] hai [iɬ hi]
Your mistake (syllables of derision)
Hai [ɬi hi] hai [ɬi hi][23]

S'Klallam professional gamblers inherited songs or gained them through a spiritual experience.

In the mid-nineteenth century, respected artist Paul Kane reported that he observed and sketched a gambling party inside the S'Klallam lodge across from Fort Victoria on Vancouver Island.[24] He had wandered into a disk game. Kane described the game as played with ten small circular pieces of wood (one black) and a bundle of frayed cedar bark. It was often played for two or three nights running. While there was increasing social pressure on headmen to give up gambling as European American influences began to take root, this didn't completely stop community leaders from participating. In 1845 a Cowichan chief, who was a well-known gambler, made the trip over to play with the S'Klallam. By the late 1800s, however, the disk game waned in popularity and eventually gave way to the hand or bone game.

Other Popular Games

During any summer, the S'Klallam shoreline was alive with villagers playing games like shinny, hoop and pole, tug of war, lifting and throwing large rocks, and archery. Canoe races with teams and individuals were a consistent and important part of social gatherings. S'Klallam men also played a version of tug of war with a stick held by the strongest on the team with teammates holding the waist of the man in front of them (a longer stick would serve the same purpose with both teams holding the stick) and trying to push the opponents back. Wrestlers, like professional gamblers, traveled to the potlatches or other large gatherings. Foot races were run on the beach or on shore for a distance of two or three hundred yards. Spectators often bet on wrestling, canoe races, and foot races.

S'Klallam canoe races, with specially made canoes that were about forty feet long and just wide enough for one person in a row (team courses one-and-a-half miles long. The first team up and back won the race. Other racing canoes were built wider so two paddlers could sit next to each other.

Other games that S'Klallam women and children played included the laughing game, shuttlecock, and hiding the ball. To play the laughing game, women sat in rows facing each other with a stick in the ground and a clamshell hanging on it. To win, one would have to retrieve the shell without laughing or even smiling. The real difficulty,

beat in a
contest
c̓ɬət

canoe race
táy

gamble;
slahal
sɬəhá;
miʔtáʔɬi

laugh
(group
of people)
niyaʔnə́yəŋ;
niʔnaʔčáxən

of course, were the songs, gestures, and personal remarks from the opposing team. Men who gambled faced this same gauntlet of insults and songs.

Only women played the game beaver tooth. It involved two contestants seated opposite each other with a dozen or more tally sticks. Carved wood teeth were thrown on the mat. A single male tooth was unmarked, and when it appeared, the point was lost.

Shinny, played on the beach by teams of S'Klallam men and boys, was a ball game in which scoring two consecutive goals won. Any number could play on the field, which was several hundred yards long but only a dozen yards wide. The ball was a knot of maple, and the shinny stick might be a fir limb. Each team needed good runners who tried to catch opponents and knock the ball out of their hands. The ball was hit with the shinny stick (which can also be used to trip an opponent) and everyone on both teams tried to move the ball over the opposing goal. Another version of shinny was played with even teams of eleven that could use shinny sticks to move the ball but could not pick it up.

In another game, a ball was tossed high in the air and everyone started in a close group, jumped for the ball to catch it, then ran. Everyone chased down the person who caught the ball, and whoever caught the person got to toss the ball next.

Only boys reportedly played hoop and pole, but girls probably also played this game. The winner could throw a pole through a rolling hoop made of bent twigs tied together. The opponent rolled the hoop and, if the thrower missed, got one counter. Whoever collected six counters won.

Contemporary Ways

Today's Jamestown community has inherited a rich array of traditional ways of life. While many traditions underwent significant changes, many are practiced today and will be passed on to future generations. Core traditional practices that have endured, for example, include gift giving, sharing, feasting, and potlatching. While the secret society has been given up and shamans are no longer practicing, the values of gift giving at important social occasions like an individual's naming or a longhouse dedication are still widely practiced and socially expected. An invitation to an Elder's home requires a gift exchange, and the value of giving and sharing is passed on to children and grandchildren. Today's inter Tribal social gatherings are an invitation to travel across the Northwest, especially for potlatching, feasting, and bone games.

Class distinctions were certainly more significant and valued in earlier times, particularly to the extremes of community leaders and slaves. Even today, Jamestown families know and pass along their genealogy and value their lineage in the face of an American dictum that values individual achievement over inherited rights.

When shaman practices were driven underground, they suffered, particularly when the Indian Shaker Church gained popularity. Secret society initiations were also nearly extinguished, but later experienced a revival of sorts only to disappear again. Guardian spirits continue to be important but vary widely given their personal use or rejection by individuals.

The potlatch was also severely restricted by Indian agents and missionaries, but its central importance in traditional S'Klallam life has likewise led to its revival and it currently plays a major role, thus maintaining dancing, singing, and humor at the core of contemporary S'Klallam life. As discussed in the last chapter, Indian gaming is alive and well. The bone game and other traditional games are robust today across the Pacific Northwest.

Both the basic fabric and future well-being of the Jamestown S'Klallam Tribe are intricately woven in family and community. This is as true today as it was thousands of years ago. As with all Indians, Jamestown family and community members have been under assault and severely affected by a wide variety of social and economic ills since the mid-1850s. Disease, alcoholism, unemployment, poor education, and a wide variety of other socioeconomic indicators all place Indians on the bottom of the American totem pole. The results at Jamestown have been disastrous.

According to the "1991 Tribal Demographics and Needs Assessment Survey," 30 percent of Jamestown S'Klallam Tribal citizens live on incomes below the poverty level, and one-third of all Tribal households exist on incomes below $10,000 a year.[25] The median Tribal household income was estimated at about $17,000 in 1991. A survey in May of 1996 showed that of the total Indian labor force of 246 in the Jamestown S'Klallam service area, 24 percent were unemployed.

The most helpful materials regarding Tribal family and community include " Tribal Strategic Plans" (1984 and 1994), the "Managed Care Feasibility Study Report" (1995), and various Tribal internal documents, including baseline measures reports and the "Jamestown S'Klallam Tribe: Cultural Resources and Needs Assessment Survey," final report to National Park Service, Historical Preservation Division, 14 October 1996. These documents are all on file at Jamestown S'Klallam Tribal offices in Blyn, Washington.

The demographic profile of Jamestown S'Klallam Tribal citizens shows an aging population similar to that of the county as a whole and in line with national trends. The percentage of Tribal citizens over sixty-five years of age is slightly lower than county figures at 22.4 percent (from a 1993 Tribal survey), but the proportional numbers of working-age members are considerably higher and childhood figures are lower. For all of Clallam County, 59.5 percent, and for Sequim, 50 percent of the respective population are of working age (19–65). For the Jamestown S'Klallam Tribe, 71.5 percent of the entire population is of working age and only 6 percent of Tribal citizens are under the age of 18.

Indian families across America also suffer from death and disease rates that far exceed those of the general population. The Indian Health Service (IHS) is the federal agency charged with fulfilling treaty rights to meet the basic needs of all Indian people. With that agency's help, Jamestown has struggled continually to find a way to meet the health needs of Tribal citizens.

The Tribe offers twenty-nine separate social and health programs in the Tribal community center, a modern 3,200-squarefoot facility near Tribal offices. Many of the programs serve Indians in the area who are not Jamestown S'Klallam, and some programs serve both Indians and non- Indians. Since federal recognition, the Tribe has made slow but steady progress toward reviving family and community traditions. These efforts also serve the purpose of combating contemporary social and health issues, such as low self-esteem, unemployment, alcohol and drug abuse, heart disease, as well as meeting basic needs of Tribal Elders and low-income Tribal citizens. The Jamestown S'Klallam Tribe is committed to meeting the basic needs of all Tribal citizens. The Tribe defines basic needs as those necessary to maintain a standard of living that preserves each person's personal dignity. Self-reliance is encouraged within a supportive S'Klallam community framework.

Cultural Resources and Needs

The Tribe conducted a comprehensive cultural resources and needs assessment survey with its members in 1991, and results dramatically illustrated that the Jamestown S'Klallam people know they still have a strong and growing sense of community. They identified a broad array of resources that were direct connections to the regeneration and

What Is Culture?

The Tribe defines "culture" as "All that we are and that we do. All that our people have done for centuries and all that our people do today. All activities: our language, songs, work, play, art, family and life ways that make us a unique group of people."[26]

maintenance of their culture.

Family, sharing, and pride were the overwhelming themes voiced by Tribal citizens when asked, "What is the Jamestown community?" Community ties to traditional Jamestown territory and special places with both sacred and ceremonial meaning were identified as culturally important. Tribal citizens characterized themselves as "independent" and possessing a "progressive nature." They also saw themselves as "more assimilated" than other Indians. Nearly half of the citizens responding had family members from other Tribes; in particular, Creek, Suquamish, Lummi, Port Gamble, Cherokee, Swinomish, Lower Elwha, Makah, Quinault, Umatilla, and Umpqua. Marriage to non-Indians included a broad variety of ethnic backgrounds, including Scottish, Irish, Norwegian, German, English, Spanish, Scandinavian, French, Italian, Mexican, Russian, French- Canadian, Portuguese, and Filipino.

Regardless of multiethnic backgrounds, Tribal citizens recognize and maintain both their Jamestown and Indian identities. Individual responses are illustrative of the broad array of issues Indian people still face today, as well as the inherent strengths of being an Indian and a Jamestown S'Klallam Tribal citizen. When asked what it means to be Indian, respondents collectively defined themselves: "Proud; to know who you are, what you are, and why you are all of these things; we were the first here; to hunt and fish; belonging; persecution; people of who I am and always will be; spiritual being; being called names in my youth because of darker skin; much harassing as a child; in tune with nature and animals; to be alive; frustration that so many generations wasted time fighting racism and white peoples' ignorance; joy over unique and beautiful cultural identity; special rights; ancestors to Native Americans; exclusive organization; honor one's Elders; ancestry; gentle, sharing/giving/helpful; getting back traditions and old ways; strength; getting back land; wisdom; lifeline; to be tough because most expect the worst from natives; smiling while your heart is breaking because they make sport of you."[27]

In addition to language-restoration activities, several other ongoing cultural programs serve not only Tribal citizens, but also other Indians and non-Indians with strong social or economic ties to the Tribe. These include weekly instruction for adults in drum making, basket weaving, and carving. Frequently, specialized classes like storytelling are also offered. The Jamestown Tribe runs or coordinates several programs for individuals with Native American ancestry, and not solely for Tribe citizens. These include

- health screening/health fairs
- home health nursing visits
- vaccinations
- injury prevention
- highway safety programs
- diabetes support
- youth empowerment and afterschool programs
- education and employment assistance
- home-delivered meals for Elders
- mental health counseling and referral
- stop-smoking support groups
- substance abuse counseling
- aerobics classes
- a weekly women's support group

Other programs are restricted to Tribe citizens, and some have income eligibility requirements, such as child-care assistance, dental care, food commodities distribution, food vouchers, general assistance grants, housing improvement and home energy assistance, managed care medical insurance, massage therapy, water aerobics, walking, and woman, infant, and child nutrition (WIC) services. The Tribe also

Indian
ʔəcɬtáyŋxʷ

next-door neighbor
nə́cəwʼtxʷ

Makah
məqáʔə

Lummi
nəxʷyə́mi

hosts an annual gathering, the S'Klallam Qwen Seyu Picnic, which draws Tribal citizens and others from across the United States. This event strengthens both community and cultural bonds. The photos on the next few pages illustrate the crucial preparation, activities, and education that occur at these gatherings.

Legacy of Skills and Knowledge

Tribal citizens identified a vast array of traditional knowledge and skills as available in the community and important to pass on to future generations. The skills and knowledge expressed are an interesting mixture of both traditional and contemporary knowledge, practices, and occupations:

- fishing
- food preparation
- gathering
- hunting
- feasts
- native plants
- preparation of wood and other plant materials
- weaving
- carving
- child rearing

- farming
- logging and lumber mills
- cannery work
- villages/camps
- medicine/healing
- songs
- trade
- language
- music
- dance
- boarding schools

- military service
- storytelling
- drum making
- moccasin making
- basket weaving
- beading
- carving
- baking bread in sand
- spirituality
- loom beading[28]

Steaming clams and oysters in the traditional way at the annual picnic.
(Photograph courtesy of the Jamestown S'Klallam Tribe photo collection)

Drumming and singing at a canoe launch.
(Photograph courtesy of the Jamestown S'Klallam Tribe photo collection)

Traditional salmon grilling at the annual picnic.
(Photograph courtesy of the Jamestown S'Klallam Tribe photo collection)

Children carving a
canoe and singing
traditional songs at
the annual picnic.
(Photographs
courtesy of the
Jamestown
S'Klallam Tribe
photo collection)

Children
learning arts
and crafts and
performing
the wolf
dance story.
(Photographs
courtesy of the
Jamestown
S'Klallam
Tribe photo
collection)

Interviews with Elders

Hazel Monday and Sandy Robinson conducted a number of interviews with Jamestown Elders in 1988.[29]

The following excerpts from these interviews illustrate the strong sense of community and connection to the past that today's Jamestown citizens share.

Mildred "Mickie" Prince Judson

Mickie was born in and lived at Jamestown all her life. Her reflections on early life around Jamestown, during her parents' and grandparents' time, corroborate reports from the scientific literature. Jamestown Tribal citizens made their livelihood from crabbing, sometimes working at a sawmill, and subsistence farming with a few dairy cows. They would also work for other farmers as the need or opportunity presented itself. This pattern—a combination of subsistence farming and crabbing and clamming mixed with wage work—has been a hallmark for Jamestown Tribal citizens since whites entered Jamestown territory in significant numbers. Service to the Shaker Church is a prominent feature of Mickie's recollections. The Indian Shaker Church was an extremely important part of the early Jamestown community. The Sunday dinners and feasts on special occasions were part of the glue that held the community together. Mickie remembers childhood games, a few special gathering places, and food and plants that were gathered and used in particular ways. Although this interview is incomplete, it illuminates the connection to the past and shows that traditional ways are still alive today.

Hazel: Who were your parents?
Mickie: They were Elizabeth Prince, maiden name Hunter.

Hazel: And you've lived at Jamestown all your life?
Mickie: Yes.

Hazel: So what is your birthday?
Mickie: 1917, April 12th.

Hazel: So were you born actually right in Jamestown?
Mickie: Yes, they didn't have hospitals in those days.

Hazel: Harriette Adams was saying that they had to row over someplace and get a midwife when she was born.
Mickie: That's the way; my grandmother used to go around and deliver babies.

Hazel: And what were your grandparents' names?
Mickie: Well, on my mother's side were David Hunter and Elizabeth

Hunter. On my father's side was Betsy and Prince of Wales. That's where my dad was from.

Hazel: So your mother's family was from here?
Mickie: Oh, and my dad come over and married my mother, and for the honeymoon they had their church wedding here. They took off in a canoe and went to Indian Island, and my dad worked in a sawmill over there for a while. Then she got homesick, and by golly she got so homesick that he said, well, I'll take you home, so he brought her back here and got the farm down there, and that's where all his kids were born and raised.

Hazel: What about your grandparents? Did they have an influence on you as a child?
Mickie: My grandfather, he lived over there on Indian Island, and they would come by canoe just for short visits until he was real old and my dad built him a cabin in the back of our house, and he lived in there until he died. But my great-grandfather, I never did know him.

Hazel: What about on your mother's side?
Mickie: My grandmother was just part of the family. Any time anybody was sick in this whole village she helped. She'd go. She was very, very religious, and she would walk all over and do washing and cleaning houses, things like that. You might be in trouble. She would go over there and help out, make soups and kind of help out, you know. My grandfather, her husband, was killed. I think a sheep killed him, kicked him. He was shearing them, and either in his heart or lung and he died. I don't know how old I was, or if I was born yet. I can't remember him at all.

Hazel: What did your dad and mother raise to sell? They had dairy cows.
Mickie: Cream and milk. We canned and ate out of the garden. He was working. Out getting crab and selling them and digging clams for the clam feed so he was just going all the time. And like I say, working for this other farm which was over, he'd walk over there and work.

Hazel: How old were you when you married?
Mickie: Eighteen.

Hazel: And what was your husband's name?
Mickie: Harold James was baby's dad. He was Lummi. They had a big celebration over at Whidbey Island and all the Indians from Vancouver all around the coast would meet over there. We all went over there a bunch of us kids, and I met him over there and he come down several times, and I met his folks over there cause the celebration went

on for, oh, three days or so, but it just didn't work out so I came home and never went back.

Hazel: Did you have a child?
Mickie: The only child I got. Elaine.

Hazel: Sounds like you worked real hard on the farm.
Mickie: I worked hard all my life. I went from one thing to another. First I worked the cannery down here. Then we went into picking peas for the Hogue company and just all kinds of housework and doing domestic work. Working for sick people and things like that. I worked for the government for four years, the Navy department. I work myself up into a mechanic painter. At Keyport, Washington. I got my license and everything for that, and so I was pretty proud of that.

Hazel: Were you raised according to a particular religion, the Shaker Church?
Mickie: Well mostly because we served, see my grandmother lived on this end of town and her brother lived on the other end of town. He was a preacher. One Sunday he would have the Shaker Church come to the house and she would have it the next time, and they would have, like, the Elwhas and the Port Gambles, you know, in for that when they had to shake over somebody, but really it was only more or less, and we had to help serve, my cousin and I, she would work over there and our grandfolks, she stayed with our grandfolks, and of course I stayed with my grandfolks, but my mother then my aunt died. And so we helped her, you know, do the work, setting the tables and things like that, but they would have put stuff up in the summertime and stuff like that and have great big dinners; every Sunday they would have something going on. But like I say it was, if you was around that all the time, and you know you never got to eat at the same time as the rest of them you helped serve, and you ate last, and to this day when we're having big feasts, I can't eat until after it gets all over with. When I stay home and watch other people eat, it seems like I'm full, but after everybody is gone I can sit down and eat.

Hazel: Do you remember any of the games you played as a child, with all the rest of the kids?
Mickie: We played hopscotch and duck. I don't know if you know what that is then, but these nets that you see fishermen, you know they would get those. And they had horseshoes. We played ball but we had no balls to play with. We would use, like I got hit with in the eye with it, it kind of gets soft when it goes on the beach. Bark, we'd get bark. They'd hit it, you know, I was going to catch it, and it hit me in the eye. And I couldn't see for several days. Blackened my eye. It seemed like the balls and everything, they were made of, me and Molly used to

make them out of old underwear and stuff like that.

Hazel: Do you remember any Klallam words or maybe names of places that they used to call places that are different now?

Mickie: Gee, oh, I remember one place over here in Dungeness where there used to be so much fish that my dad would go down there in a wagon and a lot of the people who didn't have cars in those days, but my dad had that wagon and, you know, lived on the farm. We had a team of horses and he would put hay in that, you know, just to, I don't know what you would call it, big rig not smaller than a hay wagon and have sides on it, and just put the fish in there and he would start from that end clear down until everybody would have fish to smoke and they called that Flumatch and I wouldn't know how you spelled that. That was the name of the place just where they had that fish. Brick would know that. And there's some other places. In the summer time, we'd go to Discovery Bay to get these soap berries just like our Indian ice cream. They would dry them up and then in the winter time, why, they'd have, you know, bucket parties, they'd have one woman with the strongest arm beat the ice cream up, you know, and have little wooden paddles from cedar to dip in there. I haven't tasted it in years and years. Marion had some one time at the party we had up there in Blyn. She brought some one time. I was really surprised that she brought that. That's the first time I've tasted that in so long. What did they call that? [supalali] I can't think of it right now. It's awful. You never hear things for a long time and a lot of times I'll just be sitting here and I think you know this little old Indian lady who used to live right here next to us, Mrs. Solman. She could speak very little English, so I used to go over there and help her clean her house and get water for her. So I'd tell now you talk to me in Indian so I can learn how. You know, because mom and them wouldn't, you know, so I'd talk to her. So she'd be sitting there on her

Ruby Prince George

Born December 23, 1913, at a hospital in Port Angeles, Washington, Ruby grew up in Jamestown and lived there for eighteen years. She grew up with her brothers and sisters, Lillian Prince Sullivan, Oliver Prince, Mildred Prince Judson, Mary Elizabeth Prince Holden, and Lyle Prince. She attended the Jamestown Day School and went to the Shaker Church. As a child, Ruby went picking wild blackberries in "back of Sequim." During hunting season, they went in a car east of the mountains to go hunting for deer because "they had bigger deer there. Around Sequim, they only had small areas that you could hunt in. We would go over that way hunting and we would stop on the way going and find out where the mountain berries [blackberries] were and pick a bunch, then go hunting and stop on the way back and pick some more." After she was married, she and her husband went to Clallam Bay and Sekiu for berry trips and deer hunting. Ruby used to work in the Bugge Cannery at Washington Harbor. She remembers (old) Tom Lowe, who "used to work in the cannery until he got too old to stand there and work. Then he would tell us what to do. Most of the workers worked there in the summertime until school would start. The Lowes lived there all the time." Today Ruby lives on the Port Madison reservation in a beautiful spot overlooking a Puget Sound bay. She is eighty-seven years old and has lived in this area for sixty-nine years.[30]

little couch there and she was pretty old. And so she'd tell me in Indian what to do and I'd answer her and she was a funny old lady. She'd get such a big bang out of it. If I'd say something wrong she'd start laughing and I'd have to laugh at her because she looked so funny. Oh, she was a cute little old thing.

Hazel: Do you remember any other kind of vegetation or plants that you used to go out and gather or use?
Mickie: Oh, we used to go out and get these Chinese shoes and urchins. You know those things sticking up all over. We used to go down to Wilson and Ethel (Johnson) and another couple and they'd take all us kids and make a big day out of it and take a lunch you know and we'd go and get these Chinese shoes on big tides and these, like, urchins I was telling you. And they'd be gone all day until they'd have to come home at night and milk the cows and stuff. But we used to go out and get those, and, you know, and there'd be, maybe, and just a big tide in the summertime. And they'd have just one or two meals and that would be it, you know, for the year. Just have that once in a while. But as far as anything else, we didn't eat any seaweeds or anything. Bark, different kinds of barks. They would use for venison, you know, and they'd go out and get that but I never, . . . seemed like I went with my mother once. Cherry bark or something, I don't know what it was. But it wasn't you know, it was just really hard.

Harris "Brick" Johnson
Brick was born and raised in and around Jamestown. He was active in Tribal politics, a musician, and a carver. Brick, like many Tribe members, was exposed to the S'Klallam language early in his life but spoke English to his grandparents when he answered them. He has a broad knowledge of his heritage language but worked on his English, even with his grandparents who understood English but chose to speak S'Klallam with the family. By the 1990s there were no fluent S'Klallam speakers left in the Jamestown community. Brick has detailed memories of education, athletics, stories, games, farming, crabbing, and clamming. He recounts fishing with a gaff hook and provides wonderful details on the crabbing industry as well as making drums, spirit dancing, potlatching, and carving. Brick also tells a story about the bone game and gives a brief tutorial on how Indian names, spelling, and English pronunciations have affected the local area. There is a very direct connection between Brick's memories of the bone game, the spirit society, and crabbing and clamming with the material presented in this book.

Hazel: Brick, let's start by having you tell us about your parents and grandparents, where and when you were born.
Brick: This is Harris Johnson. I was born October 30, 1912, in

Sequim. My grandparents were, on my father's side, Joe Johnson and, . . . I can't remember my grandmother's, anyway, their name was Satimalow. They died when I was twenty-one years old. They died about a week apart. They spoke Klallam Indian to us. They didn't attempt to speak English, only if it was somebody else, other than us, that they were talking to. But we spoke English to them entirely. They understood English as well as we understood the Indian, the Klallam Indian language. We didn't speak it so only I and my older brother knew quite a bit of the language, but we didn't speak it enough to remember it. I wanted to mention that my grandfather on my father's side was one hundred years old when he died. About my grandfolks on my mother's side—my grandmother died before I knew her. And my grandfather also lived to be around hundred years old. And he was a wonderful athlete. He was a baseball pitcher, and he could have gone to the big leagues, but he was a shy man. He even belonged to a team which would have probably, eventually, led him to the big leagues, but he decided he didn't want all the publicity, and he came back home. He was a wonderful athlete, and one of the stories that they tell about him was that he threw a baseball through a two-inch plank, and they talked about that for years and years. But he laughed about it when he was talking to us and explained what happened. He said the ball hit a knot, knocked the knot, and it went through the board.

Hazel: Could you tell about your schooling?
Brick: There was what they called a "day school" here. It was an all-Indian school. It was run by a man named Aaron Taylor, who acted as an Indian agent also. He advised the people and counseled them. The school [was] open until I was in the sixth grade, and then they shut it down and began going to Sequim school. I went to school with the

Lyle Prince

Born September 25, 1927, at the Sequim Hospital, Lyle Prince grew up at Jamestown on part of the forty acres that has been in his family for close to one hundred years. He lived all but twelve years of his life on this land. He grew up with one brother and four sisters: Oliver Prince, Lillian Prince Sullivan, Mildred Prince Judson,Mary Elizabeth Prince Holden, and Ruby Prince George. "My father was born and raised in the Port Townsend area. He lived on Indian Island. He had hardly been in this part of the country, but when he and my mother were old enough to be married, their marriage was set up and they were married down here [Jamestown]. From that time on he stayed here and worked on the farms around the country and had his own farm, too. He worked on the Holland Farm, when it was big cedars (trees). Any schooling he may have had was in Port Townsend. "My mother was the one who liked doing things in the old way. She really enjoyed the fish being barbequed on the sticks. She would have us build two fires so the sand in between them would get hot and we would dig a hole for her to put a big bread dough in to cook. Then she would cover it with sand and after a while we would dig it up. It had a real thick crust and we would take it over and smack it on a log a couple of times and all the sand would drop out. It was good, like a French loaf." Lyle still lives in Jamestown.[31]

sixth grade there, beginning the sixth grade.

Hazel: Was that in the 1920s?
Brick: Don't know what year it was. I didn't graduate from high school. I was a dropout in the eleventh grade, or twelfth grade, I guess it was.

Hazel: I know all Indian groups have a rich tradition of storytelling; in fact, that's how their histories were passed on. Can you remember anyone from your childhood who told stories, or can you tell us any that you remember?
Brick: Before I go on to that, nearly all of our children continued school, all the young people in Jamestown. They participated in athletics; they were all good athletes. Most of us played softball and baseball. We had an all-Indian baseball team and a softball team as well. We were told a lot of stories by our grandfolks, but about, when I was about eleven years old, the Shaker Church suddenly decided that the people who belonged to the church could not tell any more stories because the stories that were told in the Indian language would be obscene, probably, in the English language. Which they weren't when it was done in the Indian tongue. After the church banned them, that was the end of it. Oh, occasionally they might tell them in private, stories. Oh, I forgot all about them, but they had stories for everything that happened. Other stories were about, it would be, like about raven. He was supposed to be the big liar. For instance, he was a pretty tricky guy. . . . When the people were asleep, he would put some of the salmon in their mouth and when they woke up, they would miss their salmon and naturally wonder what happened to all their salmon, but then they would taste the salmon in their mouths and come to the conclusion that they ate the salmon. One thing I'll never forget is that in order to keep kids from running around at night, they made you deathly scared of, like, supposed to be spooks out there, ghosts. And they instilled this in the kids, and to this day, I'd probably be scared to go around the cemetery, for instance [laughter]. At night, they just made you scared of going out in the dark.

Hazel: What kinds of games did you play as kids?
Brick: They had a game they called "pee-wee" where they made a pointed stick, probably two to three inches long. You hit this pee-wee and made it bounce up in the air. And while it was in the air, you hit it with this paddlelike thing. Then you challenge your opponent so many steps, so many jumps to the pee-wee. If he could make it, then he earned those points. Another game was with a ball like a softball game. It was fair game to be hit with the ball, and then you'd change sides if you got hit with the ball. It was a pretty fast game. It was a lot of fun.

Hazel: During the depression in the thirties did your family go back to more hunting and fishing than they had been doing? How were times then for the Jamestown people?

Brick: My father had dairy cows, I think about twenty-two to twenty-five on property of about twenty acres. He also leased the next-door neighbor's, the Wood's, property, which was about another twenty acres. He was able to raise just about enough hay to keep the cows going, but he really was just barely, just barely able to make a living. But we younger people found that we could dig clams on state property, which is now called Graysmarsh. And we would ship the clams to Seattle to different shellfish houses. At that time we sold hundred pounds for one dollar or a dollar and a quarter's worth. Doesn't seem like much, but in those days a dollar was a lot of money. Came out to about fifteen dollars a month. We made it through the depression quite well. There was a time when people were walking around with pitchforks over their shoulders and would work for fifty cents a day, pitching hay and chopping hay for the farmers of the area. I milked cows. Two of us milked fifty cows for forty dollars a month. In 1933 we went to Neah Bay, nearly all the guys in Jamestown. We were in the CCC [Civilian Conservation Corps] camp where we had a house and they fed you. We built the first road from the village to the ocean, to the oceanside. We did everything by hand, everything was done by hand. So they had young men from Laconner, Tulalip, Bellingham. We lived on about forty dollars a month at that time, but it was a lot of fun. It was one of the happiest times of my life. Just about everybody could play some kind of an instrument, so we had house parties where people would take turns playing music. At one time there were two bands, two orchestras in Neah Bay.

Hazel: Tell us how fishing and hunting have changed. And I'd be interested to know what changes you've seen in the Dungeness River itself.

Brick: When I was probably, oh, about twelve years old, I and my oldest brother would accompany our grandfather, Drew [?] Johnson, to catch salmon at the river. We had about a thirty-foot, what we called a "feeling" pole, a gaff hook. And the sports fishermen would get pretty mad. We'd round up the fish, hooking them out of the holes. One of the things we did was go up to what is now called Hurd Creek, which was full of dog salmon. In fact, in those days you could nearly walk across the creek on the backs of these salmon, there was so many of them. We went by horse and buggy in those days. They'd smoke them, some of them they left with salt on them. I'm just about the only one left who knows how to smoke salmon anymore.

Hazel: Brick, I'd like to hear about the crabbing industry in Jamestown. I understand there was a big decline at one time because

of changes in the currents or tides or something in the strait?
Brick: In the old days the Indians would get crabs and ship them to
Seattle by a fleet of small ships, small freighters that plied as far away
as Neah Bay along Puget Sound. A man named Snow was the first
one that began fishing crabs on Dungeness Bay. He was shipping the
crab to the big hotel in Spokane. So there was a big demand for crab,
Dungeness crab. In those days you fished with a long line and dropped
the short lines with a trap off about fifty feet apart. Then all you had
to do was pull up the main line, pull the boat to the next trap and lift
it. So this man, Snow, in order to keep the Indians from finding out
what type of trap he had, he didn't have a buoy. Only he know where
his line was and was able to hook it up himself. You see, then the
Indians made grapple hooks and drags and hooked the line up and
studied the traps and began making the same type of trap and began
fishing. After a while nearly everybody in Jamestown was fishing crab.
And they shipped boxes upon boxes of crab to Seattle on the boat,
probably twenty-five dozen in each box. They were shipped live. Then
the ships stopped coming to Dungeness. The old wharf toppled over
and deteriorated, and they couldn't use it anymore. But then the auto
freights began running, and we sent the crab to Seattle on auto freight,
which was faster anyway. There was a place for the trucks to back into.
We'd put the boxes on there, and we'd slide them on the truck. I began
fishing after I'd get out of school. I had about eighteen traps. I fished
where nobody else was fishing. Everybody else had their favorite spots.
It just happened that I found a spot that was really producing. In those
days you'd catch a dozen or fifteen, or a dozen and a half, in each trap.
In those days you got twenty-five cents for them apiece. Now they're
about five dollars apiece [laughter]. I fished for at least twenty or
twenty-five years. Finally one year the crab disappeared. That doesn't
mean that there was absolutely no crab, they just went down to where
if you set fifty or sixty traps, you could only catch two and a half dozen
a day. They disappeared for no reason at all, which happened in other
parts of the coast—at the bay in Bellingham, another one in Oregon,
California. No one knows what happened to them, why they declined.
But about twenty years ago they came back pretty much again.

Hazel: Tell me about your participation in Tribal affairs and
government.
Brick: When I was about fifteen years old, the Tribe sued the federal
government for money they felt they should have coming for land
that was promised to them but never given to them. So it came to four
hundred thousand dollars, which at that time came out to a little over
seven hundred dollars apiece for each member of the Tribe. At that
time, there were enough of the older people still living. They were
able to compile a history of the Tribe and a genealogy and whatever
so that they could determine who was eligible to receive this, ...

A roll of names was developed. That's a good history of the Tribe. However, we felt that we were not fully compensated, so we went back to Congress again—I don't remember what year it was when we finally pursued it again—Congress thought the same—four hundred thousand dollars. But it wasn't distributed "per capita." The second action was years after the first roll was completed so now all the old timers were gone so it was difficult to establish who should benefit from the money that was received. So at fifteen years old I became interested in the Tribal government. I attended all the meetings during the first case. I was familiar with what they were doing at that time in the suit brought against the government. I've been involved in the Tribal government from the time I was twenty-one years old. I've been secretary and chairman of the Jamestown band at different times.

Hazel: Could you describe how the Klallams made their drums?
Brick: Drums were usually made out of deer hide. They were soaked in charcoal, water with charcoal. After some hours you could scrape the hair off. Then you would have to scrape the fat and whatever else off the skin. I don't know what they used for hoops, whether they curved the cedar or cut logs, hollow logs. Let me tell you about the reason they made drums. They had what they called the "Black Tamanous." It was this secret society. In fact I was told a lot by my grandfather that once he joined the Black Tamanous that you were forbidden to tell about the secrets. I can't think of the word that he used to describe it, but it comes out in English as "the big lie." The dancers often go into a trance when they're doing these dances. They still had what they call powwows. There's three fires, that is all the light or heat that is used in these big potlatch houses. And that's really something to see because everybody in the building usually has a drum and the new dancer is followed around the three fires by the people that are drumming— fifteen or twenty drummers following the dancer around besides all the people sitting watching. Some of the dancers are only seven or eight years old. The dancer gets this power from what they call the "tusstaniin," a staff-like thing with decorations on it. Some of the spectators in the smokehouse are appointed to help the person, could be a man or a woman; when he starts out as a dancer, he's blindfolded. He can't see. And once I was assigned to help this one dancer, and he must have weighed close to three hundred pounds. And I saw he was backing into his seer, and that was when I was supposed to help him. But he kind of scared me because he was swinging his arms back and forth, kind of a . . .[laughter] anyway, finally somebody walked him over and sat him down.

Hazel: Tell me some more about your carving—how you got started and so on.
Brick: We attempted to get people interested in carving. For

111

instance, we tried to get some of the kids, the younger boys, to help me complete totem poles or whatever. They never did actually get interested enough to follow through. In carving, you have to be somewhat of an artist just like . . . it's like music, I think. You're either a musician or you're artistic. You're born with it, I guess. A few years ago I was one of the people who helped to build this longhouse. They had some powwows there after it was built. One day they decided they would have a slahal game and they asked me to participate. They asked me to be the pointer. I told the guy from Quileute that I had never really done that, but I knew how it was done. I beat some of the good players from Lummi. They weren't betting a lot of money like they do in the big games—one thousand dollars or two thousand. Hal George was one of the prominent slahal players. Anyway, they had a pot going, and the opponents had six hundred dollars left there. Hal George said, "I'll cover that!" so he took another six hundred dollars [laughter]. Some of the people were good enough to play, what they call "throwing the bones." You try to guess the left hand or right hand, and they would exchange the bones. You were guessing at the "prime" bone, the one with the black band on it. The one with the bones went into a building, off to the side about twelve feet or so. I was barred from the game. Fun playing and they make a lot of noise with their drums. It's all accompanied by drumbeat and song. There are two sets of bones and your opponent is facing you. If you point one finger down that meant the two inside hands. If you point to one side, it means the two hands on that side, for instance, the left-hand side facing you. The one with the bones works against the one that's left. Then it becomes a real guessing game. If you miss it once then you have to guess, is he gonna move it now or keep it in the same hand? I beat my opponents because I didn't look at the guy with the bones because he was doing all kinds of gyrations. And I did pretty good. Actually I only carved two poles. During the community action days, a group came to me and asked me if I would attempt a totem pole. They said we will buy the trees, we would help to carve the pole. Ended up doing all the work, about four hundred hours' worth, by myself. It was their project, but I thought since I had done all the work myself, the pole belonged to me, so I decided to give it to the Ladies Garden Club which cleaned up an old cemetery and made a park of it. They had an Indian canoe and a few other things like that.

Harriette Hall Adams

Harriette was born on the Dungeness Spit and fills us in with more details on the crabbing industry, education, Shaker Church meetings, and cleaning houses for a living. Harriette's mother was a house cleaner and she followed suit. That led her to a custodial position in the Sequim school district. The family stressed the European American educational system, and Harriette embraced this value.

Her family heritage illustrates the pattern of intermarriage among Northwest Tribes and whites. She, like other S'Klallam Tribal citizens, lost the language. She was involved in the early and formative years of today's Tribe and served as Tribal Chair.

Hazel: This is Hazel Monday, and Sandy Robinson and I are conducting an interview with Harriette Adams this April 14, 9:00 A. M. at her home.

Harriette: My name is Harriette Loraine Hall Adams. I have lived at my current residence sixty-one years. I was born on December 27, 1924, on the Dungeness Spit. My dad rode to Jamestown to pick up Ida Hall who was a midwife at that time. As far as I know we lived on the spit until my mother died. She was rushed to the hospital in Sequim, which was right across from the present middle school, which she had first attended. And so, after she died my dad rafted the house that we lived in from the Dungeness Spit to our present residence. We didn't live in it, but he had it out in the yard for years and finally sold it to Mark Hunter who lived in it until present owners Mickie Judson did away with it. My dad, the Fred Hall family (Fred Hall was my grandfather; Jacob Hall was my father) lived in Discovery Bay. So when the mill shut down or when the state started taking the land, we moved near what is now the Three Crabs Restaurant in Dungeness. That's how he moved to this area and then as far as I remember, Henry Johnson owned the present property that I live on and my grandfather, Fred Hall, bought it from him. I don't know, my dad never did tell me much history. I assume that from the Three Crabs they must have moved back to around the Discovery Bay area because they tell me my grandmother is buried in Discovery Bay cemetery. So my mother was a Puyallup Indian. Her name was Florence Sikey. She had one full brother and then when my grandfather, my real grandmother died, he married her sister,

Robert C. Becker

Robert was born May 2, 1925, in Port Townsend,,Washington. His family lived in Irondale when he was born and moved to Towne Road in Sequim when he was three months old. "Dad worked at what they called the Highway Mill, and that was out at Agnew. Eventually he went to work at Carlsborg Mill. We lived there for a while and then we moved right downtown in Dungeness, and we lived there until we moved up toward Jeff's [his son] place in 1931."He moved to Dungeness when he was three and remembers having appendicitis. At Dungeness they had a big old house on about half an acre. "We always had that whole half acre clear full of a garden."They raised a little calf until it was a cow and "boy,we thought we were in hog heaven when we had our own milk."There wasn't much money."If you had a couple dollars a month, you were lucky. . . . "I fished all my life, and at school, when I would get in trouble because I used to fight when the other kids called me names, and I wouldn't take that, and I would just beat the devil out of 'em because I was a big kid. They knew I was an Indian boy and they would rub it in. Then the teacher would send me home and always send somebody with me, because she knew that as soon as I was out of school, I'd go over to the river fishing. I used to fish all the way home for salmon. I got my share every year that I lived." Robert and his family live in a house in Warden,Washington. He says he will come back to Sequim to live after he retires.[32]

Celia Ellis Sikey, and of course my mother didn't get along with her stepmother, so she got a job on what we call the Reed mansion on the Graysmarsh Farm. That's how my father met her. They, the Sikey family, didn't really accept my dad because he was deformed. He had a terrible hunchback and he was only about four—four feet tall. He was very interested in education so he attended the Jamestown—that was now what we call the Hubble property. He would walk from the Three Crabs area to the school down here. When he went as far as he could here, he transferred to the Cushman Indian School, which was also an Indian hospital. When he arrived there, he wanted to go into, I guess, construction, but because of his deformity, they put him in the tailoring part of the school. He completed the seventh grade there and then I guess moved back to this area. My grandfather, Fred Hall, was paralyzed from the waist down, so I assume that's why my dad came back. After he came back here, the people here in Jamestown were just getting into the Dungeness crabbing business. I'm told my grandfather, because he was paralyzed, he was the bookkeeper for the community. Each family had their own day to ship crabs to Seattle. Each, well not each, but there were shops on the beach side where they took care of their crabs for shipping. They would, I assume, row them to the Dungeness wharf to get on one of the ferries to Seattle, and incidentally it was a Jamestown group of crab fishermen who originally set the size of the Dungeness crab that they would ship. Not too many years ago, the state cut that back a quarter of an inch and now I hear tell that they're going to raise it again to six. But as far as I know my father was a full-blooded Klallam Indian. My mother, I assume, was a fullblooded Puyallup Indian. My dad was what I called a self-educated man. I mean he could talk with the best of them and hold his own and really outdo some of them. Because we both worked for a family who would rose[?] and he would really set them thinking in our discussions. He was a very outgoing person. Interested in everything. You name it and he would talk to you about it.

Hazel: This is Fred Hall?

Harriette: No, this is Jacob Hall. I didn't know much about Fred Hall. I do not know my paternal great-grandparents, just my great-grandmother who took care of my father after my grandmother died. As I said, my father was very interested in education so that's really how I became interested in it myself. I'll tell you education and voting are the two things that he stressed to me. He was gone most of the time because he was a crab fisherman, and he was out delivering these crabs, and he was also a member of the Jamestown Shaker religion. Under that he did a lot of traveling, and as a youngster I traveled quite a bit with him to Port Gamble, Skokomish, Vancouver Island. And looking back, my dad had the first station wagon, you might say, because he always had an old Model T truck and in that truck he would put a wooden frame and cover it with canvas, and at that time you could get canvas quite cheaply from one of the mills in P. A., and he would, there would be Uncle Billy Hall, Aunt Ida Hall, myself, and maybe Margie Collier would travel in that little truck to the Shaker meetings. To me it's amazing that people at that time who had no formal schooling could talk on the Bible for always and always. It's really amazing to me. As I recall, my dad was the most, had the most education of anyone.

Hazel: Well, there are twelve [grandchildren].
Harriette: Now I'm into great-grandkids. Like I said Margie Collier and I were the first two kids to graduate from Sequim High School, and that was in 1942. Prior to that time I assume it was in the thirties. Let's see, forty-two minus eight. We start at the Sequim school about 1934 because they shut down the Jamestown day school. Our teacher was A. Taylor at the time and I really didn't know what grade I was in. I would just go there every day with my sister, but when we went to Sequim, the principal, then Mrs. Smith, talked with the rest of the teachers and said, well, we'll try her in with the rest of the Indian students. So I was put in the fourth grade, and I guess I did okay because I was never moved. It was a two-story wooden building containing eight grades. The government then just used to come once a year and work on the Indian students. Take them upstairs to the storage room or whatever. In fact, when that building was torn down, my husband, Harvey Adams, and Mr. Larsen, Cynthia Larsen's husband, tore it down for the lumber, and a lot of the lumber and windows went into my old house. We had a two-story wooden building. The original part of the building was rafted from Dungeness Old Town and put up here so the lumber from the school I attended ended up as two bedrooms on my house. We just had a class reunion not too long ago and I was really surprised that the two—well, I don't know what you would call it, discrimination that they weren't really retarded but they were slow, in fact one of them said you let me do the asking because I was retarded and wouldn't get into trouble— were the first ones to come up and greet me. I knew everyone in my high school, but none of the students were that friendly. They didn't discriminate; they just accepted us. The one boy who did try to start something, I don't think he forgets to this day the hit I gave him on the side of the face because of the remark he gave on the bus. As I say, I didn't really feel discrimination when I was going to school. They tell me it was there, is there, but I can't see it, so I don't know, maybe it's me. The only education I've had is the twelve years. I've never taken any other classes. My son keeps telling me I should do that. I never knew or even understood our own Klallam language. My cousin Roger Collier could understand it but couldn't speak it. So that's lost to us. I know very few words of the Klallam language.

Hazel: When did you get involved in Tribal activities?
Harriette: Oh, Sandy said I was involved when I was very young, but I wasn't that interested. When was Brick chairman? I can't remember.

Hazel: '69 or '70?
Harriette: Well, after Harris Brick Johnson resigned as chairman, to this day I don't know, really didn't know why he did it. I guess he was unhappy with what his sister and I were doing. So that's when I moved up to acting chairman. Being of an age I think I started to become more Indian. The Indian, as I grew older, even now, Indian ways seem to surface, so I became concerned about the survival of our Tribe. And so as a result, I asked Les Prince, who stems from our chief's family, and Ron Allen, whose father and Joe Allen was involved with our suit with the federal government, I asked them to come on board, which they did. From there it was just gung ho. As a result, Ron Allen became our Chairman and is today. My one regret is that Les resigned from Council and only involved in fishing . . . so that's the way it goes.

Hazel: So you were Tribal Chairman for a while?
Harriette: Yes, the only thing that I can say as acting Chairman of the Tribe is that I kept at least regular Council meetings. They are on records although we didn't have anything to accomplish, we were only involved with STOWW [Small Tribes of Western Washington] but at least I feel, felt our suit against the government. From there we used to live in the U. S. government annex upstairs. We've come a long ways from that. I was married to Harvey Joseph Adams, a member of the Suquamish Tribe, in November 1942. In the late thirties he used to have a hogue pea-raising pea business here in Sequim Valley and my dad, Jacob Hall, had an all-Indian crew. They would come from all over the state, really, and a lot of them stayed here in Jamestown. They stayed with different families. Quite a few stayed with us in our old house because there were empty rooms and that's how I happen to meet my husband. He came down here to work.

Hazel: Why don't I take a look at these [questions] because I know they don't all pertain to you because you didn't attend an Indian Boarding School.
Harriette: No, but my dad did.

Hazel: Do you remember anything he told you about it?
Harriette: No, just that they didn't put him where he wanted to go. From what I hear though, they were, they couldn't talk their language and that was a deterrent because—

Hazel: Were they punished if they did speak their language? I had heard of that before. Did he have to work for the school? Did he ever mention that?

Harriette: I assume that they sold the clothing he made.

Hazel: So he mainly just learned tailoring?
Harriette: Yes, in fact his tailoring iron is buried down there, somewhere down there, on the Battelle property. My cousin Frank Hall lived in what was then the Bugge canning company. He had lived in houses there where the Indians used to go on a yearly basis to work in the canning, but they had this one left over and my cousin Frank and Martin Hunter lived year-round and worked. They took this tailoring iron, it was a heavy metal iron, they took it down there because they dug clams across on middle ground and on the spit across from the Bugge canning company, well, Battelle now. They used this iron to melt the tar on the cracks of their boats. In fact my husband and I used to have a boat down there during clamming season cause we dug clams commercially too. I had just hoped that it would turn up sometime but I guess with all the bulldozing and everything I guess it's lost. Maybe a few centuries down the road they'll find it.

Hazel: Do you remember any . . . I know you said you didn't feel any discrimination when you were attending school, but do you remember any incidents when perhaps a teacher asked you to share some of your heritage with the class?
Harriette: They never did that. I guess the only discrimination was from one of the peers. I mean when they decided to close the school down here, one woman fought tooth and nail about us entering Sequim school because of the tuberculosis. And the ironic part of it is that her oldest daughter died of it. So it wasn't only the Indians that had it.

Hazel: Do you remember any social event between the different Klallam Tribes or maybe between the Klallams and the Makahs?
Harriette: No, I don't. The only social events were local right here. We used to have a Christmas party all the time at the Shaker Church. Where they got the candy and presents I never knew, but it was a joyous occasion in those days. You could have your pick for Christmas trees, you know, and they always put in a huge Christmas tree in there and everybody gathered for that occasion. The other thing I remember, the Shaker Church, if there was a Tribal member who had died, the church bell was rung three times. And then I don't know whether it was called a wake or what you would call it but they would set the body in the casket up in the church for three nights and they always had someone there sitting. The younger people of course did that. Just like I hate to hear a siren go off when I'm on the job, I guess it brings back memories of our church bell tolling when someone died.

Hazel: It must be pretty hard . . . you said as you're getting older you feel more Indian. So it must be hard to look back and think, gee, it's too bad I didn't feel this way when I was a kid.

Harriette: Our next-door neighbor tried to teach me basket weaving, and I couldn't be bothered. Uncle Robert would try to talk while we were traveling from the little acorn ferry to home, but we weren't interested. We might have learned a few stories. Really, I guess the place to go is in Canada. There's so many of those who are related to the Klallam Tribe. People think we stem from there. I remember for years down across the road was the remains of my dad's boat that he used to go across. I guess that's how they did their traveling in those days before he got his little Model T.

Hazel: Was there a lot of intermarriage between the people in this area and the people in Canada?

Harriette: In Elwha or in Neah Bay, but not so much through the Jamestown, no, they went to the white Tribe. I remember when Lizzie Prince, that would be Mickie's mother, every time any one of my children got married she'd say, "Are they Indian?" She was actually against any of our young people marrying Indians. She wanted them to go onto the white Tribes.

Threaded throughout these interviews with Elders are several important themes, including making a livelihood from fishing or the land, adapting and acculturating into the dominant culture, and maintaining and self-governing themselves as a unique and distinct group. Fishing, crabbing, shellfish, and clams are a central mainstay across generations, particularly for men. Farming and work in the sawmill supplemented seasonal fishing. Women labored at menial service jobs like housekeeping, picking peas, or working in the cannery. Intermarriage, particularly to non-Indians, boarding schools, and the Indian Shaker Church acculturated Jamestown people and separated them from their language. At the same time, though, the Indian Shaker Church helped keep the people together as a political and social group. So, the church had both positive and negative impacts on the Jamestown community. Games, the Indian Shaker Church Sunday and holiday socials, interaction with other Tribes in the area, working with Indian associations, like Small Tribes of Western Washington (STOWW) and Northwest Affiliated Tribes, all helped maintain the uniqueness of individuals as Indian as well as the community as Jamestown S'Klallam. Even when boarding schools drew them away from their homeland, the S'Klallam always returned. This has a lot to do with their ability to survive as a Tribe when so many hundreds of Tribes have completely vanished.

Community Services

A traditional Jamestown value is respect and care for the elderly. One of today's most important social and health services activities is the Elders program. The heart of the program includes an annual Elders gathering, monthly Elders luncheons, field trips, nutritional education, and home-delivered meals. The senior luncheons have become so popular that they outgrew the Tribal community center and had to be moved to the casino where there is more available space.

The future of the Jamestown S'Klallam Tribe is its children, and a broad variety of educational activities are held for both younger and older children. A weekly children's after-school program, a two-week summer program, and regular field trips are annual activities. The overall goal of these programs is to raise Jamestown Tribal children with strong self-esteem, as people who are proud and knowledgeable of their unique culture and ready to pass it on to their own children. Much of what the children learn are traditional values and skills they can use today. The children are taught basket weaving, dancing, singing, drumming, carving, and making traditional S'Klallam clothing. They also learn about other Tribes, building self-esteem and pride in their Indian heritage, as well as drug and alcohol–abuse prevention strategies. Certified chemical dependency counselors provide assessment and individual and group counseling. Recovery and family support services are also available.

The Indian Child Welfare (ICW) program provides protection for children who are at risk due to abuse or neglect. The program is run in partnership with families, social workers, foster families, and the court systems, with the goal of family reunification. A community network board brings together all parties to discuss ways to strengthen and support families in contemporary times.

The Tribe also operates a 1,500-volume book and video library, open to Tribal citizens and residents of Jefferson or Clallam Counties. The library's focus is on materials related to the S'Klallam people, Northwest Coast Indian Tribes, and other sources of interest to Tribal citizens. Many of the resources used to create this book can only be found at the Jamestown S'Klallam Tribal Library.

One of the most important priorities for the Tribe is combating negative information or misinformation about being Indian or Jamestown S'Klallam. Racial prejudice and discrimination over time results in erosion of self-esteem. When a person's self-concept is assailed, he or she begins to believe it's his or her fate to be unemployed, uneducated, and unhealthy. The Tribe is committed to providing equal opportunities for success through access to higher education and employment training.

Some of the more important services include the following:
- interview training to prepare for a job search
- career counseling

youth
swéʔwəs

make a basket
čáʔiʔ ʔə cʔ
muhúy̓

beat a drum
x̌əx̌kʷuʔyáʔsən̓

- skills assessment testing
- higher education scholarships
- financial aid

In addition, individual student tutoring is provided in the Sequim School District with coordination by the Jamestown staff.

The overall goal in health services is to promote the physical, mental, and spiritual well-being of Tribal citizens. Health and social services staff works cooperatively to reduce Tribal citizens' dependence on the Indian Health Service (IHS) delivery system. The Jamestown S'Klallam Tribe, unlike other Tribes in Washington, does not have a primary health-care clinic on reservation lands. Establishing a clinic is still a goal of the Tribe. Without a clinic, and given the small size of the Tribe, other solutions to providing health care were investigated. IHS contract health services were rejected as a viable option because of potential management requirements and financial risks. The Tribe now operates a managed health-care program that was the first of its kind in the nation. The program is funded by a self-governance compact with IHS. A feasibility study funded in 1994 indicated that purchasing insurance for Tribal citizens was preferable to the existing IHS system because it provided higher quality care at less expense.[33]

> The Tribe is committed to providing equal opportunities for success through access to higher education and employment training.

Prior to managed health care, Tribal members relied on a broad array of health services provided by the Tribe, including IHS and local community providers in Port Angeles, Sequim, Port Townsend, and Port Hadlock. Some Tribal citizens were able to make the trip to the Lower Elwha S'Klallam Tribal Clinic in Port Angeles, which was built in 1987. However, health care of comprehensive and consistent quality was not available to Jamestown citizens until the managed health-care program began in 1995. This program faces new challenges each year as the cost of health care rises. IHS budgets have never kept up with real costs.

Since 1993, the Tribe has provided staff for health education, medical and insurance billing assistance, transportation, and delivery at individual homes. One of the most popular programs has been home health nursing by the community health nurse. Home visits totaled 477 in 1997, and 630 in 1996. Additional home visits were made for the chemical dependency program. The strong focus of this program is on providing services for the elderly.

In addition to coordinating a basic benefit package of medical services for Tribal citizens, the Jamestown S'Klallam Tribe contracts directly with local dentists on a discounted fee-for-service basis. The Tribe also contracts with a third-party administrator to coordinate a prescription drug program for Elders on Medicare. This contract includes all claims processing and use of the network provider discounts. The monthly pharmacy reports allow the medical director to

Community of the Future

Future plans and plans already underway for the Jamestown S'Klallam Tribe include the following:

- Establishing a child-care center on Tribal land in the Blyn area, then expanding the center into an educational and developmental learning center for both Indian and non-Indian children. A major objective of the center would be to promote cultural awareness, reduce stereotypes, and educate the non-Indian community about the Jamestown S'Klallam Tribe, as well as other Indian Tribes in Washington and elsewhere.
- Adding more educational programs in language, history, arts, crafts, spirituality, and relearning traditions.
- Acquiring more physical Jamestown S'Klallam cultural properties for a future cultural and educational center.
- Exploring the feasibility of an indoor sports center.
- Exploring a continual formal program for youth.
- Developing a Jamestown-specific cultural and spiritual model for use in self-esteem, chemical dependency, mental health, and parenting classes.
- Increasing the community's emphasis on higher education and employment opportunities.
- Building an Eldercare facility in addition to the primary care clinic. The clinic is envisioned as a combined profit/not-for-profit health and wellness center located near Tribal offices.

monitor the appropriateness of medications being used by the Elders. Vision and hearing assistance are also provided through discounted local provider contracts.

Although the Tribe does not have a medical clinic, chemical dependency treatment, as well as community and public health services, are provided directly by Tribal staff. The chemical dependency treatment program is newly housed in its own building a short distance from the Tribal center. Community and public health services are provided either in a Tribal citizen's home or in the health and human services annex adjacent to the Tribal administrative center. In response to unmet needs, the Tribal Council approved a plan to build a dental clinic.

A self-governance compact with the federal government gave the Tribe the ability to identify the major health problems of Tribal citizens. With this specific information, targeted preventive programs have been designed and implemented. To complement the claims data and anecdotal information about the health status of Tribal citizens, the Tribe participated in a "healthy heart" project. The project surveyed Tribal citizens and then analyzed the data to identify behaviors and health problems that put Jamestown people at risk for various illnesses like heart disease. Based on these data, the three priority areas selected for prevention activities were to increase physical activity, increase healthy eating, and decrease tobacco use.

In addition to community-based programs, the Tribe has begun work to establish a local public-health partnership. Working with the local county health department and the other three Tribes in the county, they have been able to draft cooperative agreements intended to clarify public-health jurisdictions and coordinate services. The three main areas include communicable disease prevention and treatment, environmental health, and emergency preparedness.

The other major initiative for Tribal health services in the past several years was to enhance chemical dependency treatment services. An intensive outpatient treatment program for adults began in January 1997. A youth intensive treatment program was begun in March 1997. Continuing services include evaluations, a post-traumatic stress disorder (PTSD) relapse prevention group, spiritual and cultural support, evaluation and treatment of gambling problems, intern training, and community education.

The managed care program continues to develop strategies to provide better services at a lower cost. For example, a prescription drug review for Elders was conducted. With advice from the medical director, savings of five thousand dollars were realized by switching some prescriptions to less expensive over-the-counter medications.

> The universe, which is all the living energy we know of, is a personal place that requires respect through appropriate actions and prolific knowledge of each discrete element and its relationships within the environment.

Important and dynamic changes occurred for S'Klallam families with the influx of large numbers of non-Indians into their territory in the late 1800s. As federal agents began to exert more control, there were significant negative effects on family. However, self-government has allowed the Tribe to proactively address community weaknesses and needs. The cultural heritage that today's S'Klallam people are restoring and attempting to pass on to future generations emanates from the past but also gathers power from the new traditions being created today. There are real challenges in the efforts to restore S'Klallam culture. At the heart of these efforts is the question of what is traditional Indian education. In Indian Education in America, Vine Deloria, Jr.'s fundamental premise that separates traditional Indian education (by Indians, for Indians) from European American education (by whites, for Indians) is that in traditional Indian education, power and place equal personality. The universe, which is all the living energy we know of, is a personal place that requires respect through appropriate actions and prolific knowledge of each discrete element and its relationships within the environment. Deloria argues that education in America today sharply contrasts this view with its stress on reductionist science, socialization to the corporate world, and a repudiation of the sacred or spiritual.[34]

The Jamestown S'Klallam Tribe's overall goals of selfgovernance and self-sufficiency are anchored in the restoration and enhancement of family and community. Today's Tribal members are actively seeking ways to learn and relearn ceremonies, crafts, history, and lifeways practiced by their ancestors.

Slap'u

as told to the author by Elaine Grinnell, Jamestown Elder and storyteller

Slap'u was this great big lady that lived up in the mountains above the village. Now I didn't see her myself, but they told me about her. Anything that my grandmother would tell me I was sure would be very, very, very truthful, and that's all I needed. Oooooh, Slap'u was a big woman. She was big and she was tall; she was just a big woman. Oh, she sounded scary! She had long black hair that went all the way down the back of her legs. And you know that she never combed it; you could tell 'cause it just stuck out bushy all over. They say that she even had one bird's nest behind her right ear, right there. I said, "Ooh Grandma, why didn't she take it out?" She said,"I don't know,maybe she liked to hear the birds singing."Ooh that was awful to me! Did you know she had great big feet? Oh, they were that long and that wide and her toes stuck out like that. And you know that kinda got me too."Why do her toes stick out like that?" "Oh, that was easy," Grandma said."You know when she came down to go digging clams, if her toes stuck out like that, then she wouldn't sink so fast in the sand." But the other thing about her toes spread apart like that, well, you see, the sand and the mud would kinda squirt up between her toes and it made a peculiar sound like squish, squish, squish, squish. Well, one good thing about that is you could hear her coming from a long way off. Yeah!

Well, you know, she had a great big walking stick that she used all the time and the reason that she had that, I think, is because she carried this big cedar bark basket on her back. It was big enough to carry two children. And she had a tumpline around her forehead like this and attached to the basket. And so when she had a load in there, she just kind of leaned forward with her walking stick and then she would move along very slowly. And every step she took she would go,"Uuuh, Uuuh, Uuuh, Uuuh."Ooh, I just hated that sound.

Well, you know, did I tell you that she had this one long hair that came off the tip of her nose? It went all crooked like that. It blew around in the wind all by itself. Kind of like it had a mind of its own. Because when she would start talking to someone, they say that this hair would blow around in the wind like that until it realized who she was talking to and then it would point right at them. Ooh! Can you imagine being pointed at by a hair? That was really scary to me.

Actually, I guess her job was to be up there on that mountain, and then if she would hear some disobedient kids down in the village, well, then she would make a point to come down and pick up at least two. Usually two at a time. And she'd put them in her basket. She'd take them back up in the mountains for a couple of days, you see, and then she'd bring them back. I said, "What did she do to them?" Nobody ever knew. The kids certainly didn't tell. But,

cedar bark
basket
məhúẏ

tumpline
cəŋʔátən

seagull
qʷəní

boy, when they got back, did they ever mind. Oh, they did mind, yes.

There was one day, the tide was way out and the sun was shining just like it is today. The mother says, "All right, children." She says, "It's time to get your basket and your digging stick and we're going down to the point and we're going to dig clams for our family and for those that cannot go digging." Everybody was happy. They just wanted to be out on the beach and doing something. So they all lined up, and as they went through the village everyone started saying, "Can I go with you, can I go with you?" The mother says, "Yes, come on, come on." And away they went and they're all lined up as they walked down to the point. She says, "Everyone bring your basket and your digging stick. You're going to really work hard digging for everyone in your family and for those that can't dig."Well, finally they got down to the point. All the kids just spread out and the clams were so plentiful. In no time they had their baskets just filled with clams.

She says, "Stop. We don't have any more room for clams. We have enough." She says, "It's time to go home." Well, I don't know if you've ever heard children say this to their parents or not, but they said, "Oh, we don't want to go home."They were having such a good time, you see. Well, she says, "Oh, gosh, now what am I gonna do?" She looked about and the sun was still bright and the tide was way out yet. And she decided, well, it's such a nice day, I'll let them stay a little bit longer. She said, "OK, you can stay a little bit longer." But she said, "Don't let the water get behind you." And, you know why that would be? Well, you're way out there and you might become isolated on a little island of sand. The water comes in behind you. And then it would be very difficult to get back to the beach. So it was important to understand that don't ever let that water get behind you when you're way out digging clams.

The kids all promised, "OK, we won't, we won't let the water get behind us." And she said, "One more thing." She said, "You be home before the shadows get long because you know who's gonna come down from the mountains if you don't mind.""Yes, Slap'u!" everybody said. And so with that, she picked up as many of the basket as she could carry and she took them on home.

Finally, the kids went back to play. Oh, they were having such a good time. They were throwing sand at each other. I know kids you know don't do that. But anyway, the kids were throwing sand at each other. They were pushing each other down in the water, and they were throwing kelp at each other and seaweed. That big bulb on the gull kelp. That was always a good one 'cause you could get a hold of the end of the kelp and you could start whipping it around, like this, and if you happen to hit somebody well, if you hit them hard enough, well then the head would break open and it was full of saltwater. And, oh my, that was a good one. Yeah, they were sure having fun, all right. In fact, it was so much fun that they didn't realize the shadows were getting long.

"We better get home," one of them said. And so they all started running for the village. They were running along the beach and they were running as fast as they could. And finally someone says, "Who is that?" And, oh, they came to a sliding stop. In fact, you could just see the sand kind of fly up where they just skidded to a sliding stop. And they started peering and opening their eyes real wide and closing them so they could just kind of peek out of their eyes. Trying to identify who that dark figure was down there between them and the village."Who is it? Who is it? Who is it? I don't know! I don't know!" And so, finally that dark figure turned sideways and they could see a big basket on her back. And finally she turned the other way and she started walking right toward them, and then they could hear that terrible sound. "Uuuh, uuuh, uuuh, uuuh, squish, squish, squish, squish." "Slap'u!" they all yelled together. Everybody took off running in different directions down the beach, and up the beach. One little boy

Slap'u with a basket full of naughty children. (Illustration by Dale Faulstich)

even swam out around Slap'u in the water to get to the village. This one little girl ran through the bushes and she kept running until she was out of breath. She thought, "Well, maybe Slap'u isn't even chasing me. Maybe she's chasing someone else. I hope! I hope!" She stopped running. And, you know when you run really hard your heart's going so fast and you can't breathe—hold your breath. For some reason if you open your eyes really wide and you drop your mouth open you hear better. I don't know. She stood there and she listened. Pretty soon she could hear the birds just zipping out of the trees, leaving their nests and screeching! And as she looked up high she could see a bunch of seagulls were circling, circling, wondering what all the commotion was. They were looking down and those gulls were screaming. Oh no. And then all at once she heard that terrible sound."Uuuh, uuuh, uuuh, uuuh, squish, squish, squish, squish.""Oh no, she's chasing me." And the little girl took off running again. Why, she ran all the way

to the Dungeness River. She thought, "If I make it there, I can run
right down to the edge of the river. I'll come out on Dungeness
Bay. And my uncle, he's gonna be down there and he's gonna be
catching crabs today. He'll save me. He'll bring me back to the
village. Yeah, my uncle, he'll save me."
So she ran and she ran. She got to the Dungeness River and she
thought, well, maybe Slap'u just decided to quit. Maybe she's tired
by now. She listened again. Same thing, all she could hear was
her heart beating. Oh, her face was all flushed, she was so hot
from running. And again she couldn't hear anything but her heart.
And so she took a real deep breath and she held her breath. She
dropped her jaw open and her eyes were so big, trying to look
back through the bushes. And then she could hear that terrible
sound. "Uuuh, uuuh, uuuh, uuuh, squish, squish, squish, squish."
Slap'u!
She took off running down the edge of the Dungeness River. She
ran and ran until she finally came out at the bay. And when she
came through the bushes there was her uncle in his canoe. He was
just kind of paddling along. He was picking up crabs. "Uncle! Uncle!
Uncle!" she said. He said, "What's the matter?" "Slap'u is chasing
me!" "Oh, there's no Slap'u." "Yes there is a Slap'u. She's chasing
me. She's going to take me up in the mountains. Save me. Take me
back to the village." He says, "I can't take you back to the village.
You see, I'm catching all the crab for the people in the village. I
can't leave right now." "She's gonna take me to the mountains."
"No, no," and he smiled. "There's no Slap'u." He pulled on to the
shore. Just as soon as that canoe came up on the beach she said,
"Uncle, come and see. Listen, listen." And so she got him out of the
canoe and he came over to where she was standing. Pretty soon he
could hear the bushes breaking and the birds just tearing out of
their nest. He could see the gulls up there just circling in real tight
circles looking down. They were screaming too. And then he could
hear that terrible sound. "Uuuh, uuuh, uuuh, uuuh, squish, squish,
squish, squish."
"OK," he said. "You get in my canoe and I'll take you out to the
point. I'll take you out on the spit. You hide behind the logs. As
soon as I'm through here, I'll come out and get you and I'll take
you home." "OK, OK." So she jumped in the bow of his canoe and
he paddled her out so quickly. Pretty soon she was out on the
spit. And he said, "You hide right behind that big log. Don't move.
I'll be back." "OK." He put her there and he jumped back into the
canoe. He turned around and paddled back. Just as soon as that
canoe came up on the beach, oh no! The bushes parted and there
she stood in all of her glory! A great big tall woman, long-haired,
the berry bushes hanging from her hair, sticks and leaves were
hanging from her hair. And he looked down at those great big feet
that came out of the bushes, actually first. All these leaves were
sticking up between her toes. She had this great big stick in her
hand. "Hey! you seen a little girl around here?" Gee what a bad voice
she had. He said, "No, I haven't seen a little girl around here." "Are

you sure?""Yeah, I haven't seen any little girl around here."
Now he was lying. So he was looking down but he really didn't
want to look at her anyway because she was so bad looking. And
then there was that hair waving around on the end of her nose. Oh,
that was so bad looking." Did you take that little girl out on that
spit out there?" "Nope, I didn't take anybody anyplace."He looked
down. Oh, he didn't want her to get close to him."You take me out
there on that spit! I want to see if that little girl is there."Oh, gee,
he didn't want her to get in his canoe. Oh, she was bad looking.
Just like that, she jumped right into his canoe. She said, "You
take me out there.""Oh no, not in my canoe."He had a hard time
getting off the beach now. He turned the canoe around. Canoes
usually float real level in the water, but with her weight, which
was considerably more than his, up in the bow, well, he was way
up in the air. He looked at his paddle and he looked down and he
thought,"Can I still reach the water?" He had to bend way over to
reach the water. It was awful.
He finally got going, but you know when you have all the weight
in the front end of your canoe like that, then the back end has a
tendency to swing around. Oh, he was having a hard time trying
to get going. With all that weight, the canoe was definitely heavier
in the front. Well, those crabs started sliding down towards those
great big ol' ugly feet. He was trying to paddle, trying to get going.
He had to bend way over the side. So he said to those crabs, "Bite
her on the toe. Bite her on the toe.""What did you say?" He said,
"I'm just trying to go, just trying to go."
Ooh, she's bad looking even from the back with hair all over, dirty
feet. Those crabs started walking right down towards her feet.
Finally they got there. And he said one more time, "Bite her on
the toe. Bite her on the toe.""What did you say?" He said, "I'm just
trying to go, just trying to go." And he was paddling as hard as he
could. Finally those crabs got down near her feet, and they started
pinching her on those big ol' ankles and those dirty ol' toes. Oh,
how could they do that? They started pinching her all over the
place."Yeeee, yeeee!" she yelled and she jumped straight up in the
canoe.
Well, you know how tippy canoes are. It sailed back and forth,
water just flying, and she was trying to kick one leg and then the
other, getting those crabs off her feet. He says, "Wait, wait, you're
going to tip us over." Too late, she went right over on her back in
the deep water."Oh no," he thought."Even if she's Slap'u, I'm going
to have to save her. Oh, I'm going to have to touch her, oh no. Oh,
oh no, I'm going to have to touch her." Finally, he knew he couldn't
let Slap'u drown. He put his hands on the edge of the canoe and he
looked over the side and you know, a long time ago the water was
so clear you could see all the way down to the bottom, all the way
down there. He finally looked over the side and he could see her
going down, down, down. She hit the bottom and you'd expect her
to come up. She didn't. She kept getting shorter. She kept sinking
in that mud down to her ankles, down to her knees. She kept going

down and all he could see was her face. She was watching his eyes and he was looking down at her face. She kept getting shorter and shorter. He'd never seen anything like this happen before.

Oh no, pretty soon all that long black hair started rising up in the current in the water, and started going baaack and fooorth. Baaack and fooorth. Baaack and fooorth. Baaack and fooorth. And that one hair on her nose was going baaack and fooorth. Baaack and fooorth. Baaack and fooorth. Baaack and fooorth. Oh, he'd never seen anything like that before. He kept watching her and she kept getting shorter and shorter until all he could see was just her face looking right straight up at him. And that long black hair going baaack and fooorth. Baaack and fooorth. Baaack and fooorth. Baaack and fooorth. And that one hair on her nose going baaack and fooorth. Baaack and fooorth. Baaack and fooorth. Baaack and fooorth. Pretty soon all that long black hair was gone and there was only one hair. You know which one it was. Yeah, the one that was right on the tip of her nose. It was like, baaack and fooorth. Baaack and fooorth. Baaack and fooorth. Baaack and fooorth. And then, even it was gone. And he kept watching that spot where she'd gone down and the hair had gone down, and then pretty soon here come these bubbles that started coming up. Bloop, bloop, bloop, bloop. Bloop. Bloop, bloop, bloop. Bloop, bloop, bloop, bloop. Bloop, bloop, bloop, bloop.

And now, when you go down to a body of saltwater, you look very carefully down into the water, you'll probably see some bubbles coming up. Bloop, bloop, bloop, bloop. Bloop, bloop, bloop, bloop. Bloop, bloop, bloop, bloop. Bloop, bloop, bloop, bloop.

That's where Slap'u went down.

4

Self-Government

Traditional Ways

The traditional ways of S'Klallam governance, characterized by diffused, autonomous village leaders with inherited rights and responsibilities, were completely misunderstood and largely ignored by U.S. and territorial government officials. They needed someone to sign away the land and clear the title for settlement and civilization. Where they could not find such individuals, they created chiefs for the sake of convenience. Still, the fundamental values of listening to a good man who gave sound advice and of following many different leaders who had inherited rights or special knowledge and skills persisted in everyday life. It was only the immigrants who could ignore such traditional practices.

Reservations and Treaties

Isaac Ingalls Stevens, the man who led the treaty parties in Washington in the mid-nineteenth century, was well aware that it was a mistake to try and force so many different Indians in western Washington onto a few small reservations. He also knew that Washington Indians could not be excluded from their traditional fishing and hunting grounds because of their way of life. He shared most of the white settlers' negative attitudes toward Indians. He came to his post noted for his outspoken belief in manifest destiny despite Indian rights. His 1854 report on the S'Klallam, which he penned as superintendent of Indian affairs, is worth quoting extensively: "Next to the Makahs are the Clallams, or, as they call themselves, S'Klallam, the most formidable Tribe now remaining. Their country

stretches along the whole southern shore of the straits to between
Port Discovery and Port Townsend; besides which, they have occupied
the latter place properly belonging to the Chim-a-kum. They have
eight villages. . . . Their numbers have been variously estimated, and,
as usual, exaggerated; some persons rating them as high as fifteen
hundred fighting men. An actual count . . . which were supposed to
contain half the population, was made by their Chiefs in January, and
comprehending all who belonged to them, whether present or not,
gave a population of only three hundred and seventy-five, all told.
The total number will not probably exceed much eight hundred. That
they have been more numerous is unquestionable, and one of the
Chiefs informed me that they once had one hundred and forty canoes,
of eighteen to the larger, and fourteen to the smaller size; which,
supposing the number of each kind to be equal, gives a total of two
thousand two hundred and forty men.

"The head Chief of all the Clallams was Lack-ka-nam, or Lord
Nelson, who is still living, but has abdicated in favor of his son
S'Ilaiak, or King George, a very different person, by the way, from the
chief of the same name east of the mountains. Most of the principle
men of the Tribe have received names either from the English or
the 'Bostons,' and the genealogical tree of the royal family presents
as miscellaneous an assemblage of characters as a masked ball in
Carnival. Thus two of King George's brothers are the Duke of York
and General Gaines. His cousin is Tom Benton, and his sons by Queen
Victoria are General Jackson and Thomas Jefferson. The Queen is
daughter to the Duke of Clarence, and sister to Generals Scott and
Taylor, as also to Mary Ella Coffin, the wife of John C. Calhoun. The
Duke of York's wife is Jenny Lind, a brother of the Duke of Clarence
is John Adams, and Calhoun's sons are James K. Polk, General Lane,
and Patrick Henry. King George's sister is the dowager of the late
Flattery Jack. All of them have papers certifying to these and various
other items of information, which they exhibit with great satisfaction.
They make shocking work, however, in the pronunciation of their
names, the r's and f's being shibboleths which they cannot utter.

"It is a melancholy fact that the Clallam representatives of these
distinguished personages are generally as drunken and worthless a
set of rascals as could be collected. The Clallam Tribe has always
had a bad character, which their intercourse with shipping, and the
introduction of whiskey, has by no means improved.

"The houses of the Chiefs at Port Townsend, where they
frequently gather, are of the better class, quite spacious, and tolerably
clean. Two or three are not less than thirty feet long by sixteen or
eighteen wide, built of heavy planks, supported on large posts and
cross-beams, and lined with mats. The planks forming the roof run
the whole length of the building, being guttered to carry off the water,
and sloping slightly at one end. Low platforms are carried round

the interior, on which are laid mats, serving for beds or seats. Piles of very neatly made baskets are stored away in corners, containing their provisions. There are from two to four fires in each house belonging to the head of the family, and such of his sons as live with him. They have abundance of salmon, shell-fish, and potatoes, and seem to be very well off. In fact, any of the Tribes living on the sound must be worthless indeed not to find food in the inexhaustible supplies of fish, clams, and water-fowl, of which they have one or the other at all times. "

"They have a good deal of money among them, arising from the sale of potatoes and fish, letting out their women, and jobbing for the whites."[1]

village
ʔəxʷíy(ə)ŋəxʷ

It is clear from Stevens's report that there were numerous villages with significant populations. For example, in another instance he mentioned an extensive settlement of the S'Klallam on Vancouver Island. Of course, Stevens, for obvious reasons, dwelt on the exaggerations of the population numbers. The fewer Indians around, the easier to extinguish their claims to the land—land that was a prerequisite for statehood. Stevens went out of his way to comment on the S'Klallam's bad character but waxed eloquently on the homes of chiefs at Port Townsend. He was complimentary of S'Klallam canoes, baskets, and dog-hair blankets, as well as the wealth of the Tribe. How all these "drunken and worthless set of rascals" were able to make those canoes and baskets and acquire their wealth, Stevens failed to reconcile. His comments on the abundance of natural resources do hint that in his view, the S'Klallam did not have to work at all to prosper. Anyone familiar with the technology, knowledge, skills, and hard work involved in the harvesting, processing, preserving, storing, and transporting of foods or the building of a canoe would find Stevens's observations hard to believe. By and large, however, in the mid-1850s, Stevens's attitudes reflected those of most of the non-Indians in the territory.

someone
who
speaks for
you
nəxʷscácqən

This report, a year before Stevens entered into a treaty with the S'Klallam, documented his racial and moral biases, regardless of the fine houses, abundance of food, and money he noted. He also mentioned the skins and oil being traded heavily on Vancouver Island and stated that the treaty must stipulate that trade be confined to the American side of the Strait of Juan de Fuca.

When Isaac Stevens received three federal appointments as governor of Washington Territory, superintendent of Indian affairs, and surveyor for the Northern Pacific Railroad in 1853, he was only thirty-five years old and very ambitious. Stevens set a remarkable record for speed when he moved quickly to extinguish the Indians' title to land in the new territory. In the first few months of treaty making at Medicine Creek, Point No Point, Neah Bay, and Point Elliot, Stevens got Indians to cede lands encompassing all of the Olympic Peninsula and most of Puget Sound. Stevens insisted the treaties be read and explained in the Chinook trade jargon (a vocabulary of some three hundred words of French,

English, and Russian origin). His major guidelines in all his treaty dealings included the following principles:

- Put multiple Tribes together in as small an area as possible.
- Help make them farmers by providing each person with a small homestead.
- Save federal money by paying for treaty obligations with commodities.
- Civilize the Indians by providing teachers, farmers, carpenters, and trades educators.
- Stop all raiding among Tribes.
- Stop the slave trade and any trade across territory borders to Vancouver Island.
- Stop the liquor trade.
- Allow the Indians to hunt, fish, and gather in their usual places.
- Eventually end the practice of land held in common by the Tribes.[2]

The treaty-making process and use of Stevens's guidelines in the Puget Sound left large numbers of Indians without reservation lands or federal recognition. Many landless Indians were descendants of Indian and non-Indian marriages who were trying to acculturate to white ways. Most, however, were families who refused to move onto small, crowded reservations with other Tribes who had their own languages and cultures. The only ones who might be able to adjust to the annuity system, which created dependency, were the ones whose reservation was in their traditional territory.

> Many landless Indians were descendants of Indian and non-Indian marriages who were trying to acculturate to white ways. Most, however, were families who refused to move onto small, crowded reservations with other Tribes who had their own languages and cultures.

The S'Klallam received no annuity goods until 1861, two years after Congress finally ratified the Point-No-Point Treaty of 1855 (see the Treaty itself on pages 162-165). Unfortunately, long before treaties were ratified, settlers had already moved on and taken over Indian lands.

Between 1855 and 1915, the situation for Indians in Puget Sound worsened dramatically. Those on the reservation were not productive and successful farmers. Those off reservations, while maintaining their ties to family and traditional village, fishing, and hunting areas, were adopting European American technological innovations when they were useful; but in the light of their weakening position, they remained active and committed to getting their treaty promises and maintaining their treaty rights.

One of the first umbrella organizations to fight for Indian rights in the area was the Northwestern Federation of American Indians (NFAI), formally organized in 1914 by a S'Klallam, Thomas G. Bishop.[3] Bishop pressed the federal government to enroll and

132

provide land for all of the landless Indians in the Northwest on the grounds that treaty promises had never been kept and the condition of Northwest Indians was abysmal. As early as 1911, the Society of American Indians (SAI) was another of several pan-Indian groups voicing similar concerns.[4]

Bishop used individual applications for enrollment on the Quinault Reservation to state his case to the government in 1916. He argued that two or three thousand applicants had rights to be federally recognized because of a phrase used in an executive order issued in 1873, which recognized other fish-eating Indians on the Pacific Coast. Arguments over eligibility, who was already covered under other acts or treaties, and what was the definition of a fish-eating Indian eventually threw the issue to the U.S. Court of Claims, established in 1925. The federal government's position was very clear. Individual claims of treaty violations or enforcement of treaty rights had to be tied directly to Tribal recognition and assertion of rights. In 1916, Charles Roblin, enlisted by the government as a special enrolling agent, began the task of identifying individuals who claimed Indian ancestry and determining to which Tribe they belonged. This was no easy feat. Years of intermarriage, both with Indians from other Tribes and non-Indians, gave rise to a list where applicants, regardless of where they were born or the government's ideas about who was an Indian, responded by providing social connections to one or more groups, village names, or Tribes that a mother or father had joined later in life, for example: "Peter Rogers determined his Tribe by his father's community of origin (Duwamish), not by his mother's ascribed parentage (Suquamish and Skykomish), nor by his residence at Suquamish. But Edward Davis claimed membership in the Snoqualmie Tribe through his mother's father, even though he identified both his parents and his birthplace as Duwamish; and James Thomas identified with the community of his birth and lifelong residence— Snohomish—rather than with the Yakima and Duwamish communities where his parents were born."[5]

When the court of claims opened for business, it heard all claims, including those of unenrolled, landless, and even nontreaty Indians. The real catch in the court of claims legislation was that if a claim was upheld, all treaty annuities, administrative, health, school, and other related expenditures since the treaties were signed could be deducted from any settlement.

Even as the Indian Claims Commission (ICC) recognized that the government had failed to fulfill treaty obligations, they found that the value of Northwest Indian claims was offset by the cost of services already provided. The ICC process was a dead end for Indians on the Northwest Coast.[6] The S'Klallam groups recognized this and chose a different route by retaining their own attorney and suing without using the ICC.

Stevens completed the Medicine Creek, Point Elliott, and Point-

No-Point Treaties in meetings with village representatives between Christmas 1854 and January 26, 1855. Not all villages were represented, but the government's method of naming chiefs (those who could speak for others to sign away their lands) prevailed in these proceedings. When he received no cooperation, Stevens was not immune to outright deceit. Oral history documented that Chief Leschi of the Nisquallies refused to sign and left the treaty meeting at Medicine Creek. Stevens subsequently forged Leschi's mark on the treaty.[7]

Often other seemingly more pressing problems kept land rights in the background. Alcohol, deaths, and poor health did take a toll on the S'Klallam population following contact with European Americans. In 1865, agent John T. Knox dispatched an employee to Fort Townsend "whose duty it is made to keep an eye on those worthless white men who furnish Indians with whiskey, and if possible have them arrested and punished."[8] Annuity goods were also always problematic, whether late, of poor quality, or short of the promise. In an 1863 letter, F. C. Purdy of the S'Klallam Agency writes about the shortcomings: "On taking charge of this agency the first duty devolving on me was to distribute among the Indians their annuity goods. . . . However, after the goods had been unpacked and arranged for giving out, the chiefs in the mean time being present, it was not necessary for me to tell them that the annuity was short. . . . However, after calling them together the evening before commencing to distribute the goods, I stated to them that all the goods in which they were entitled for the second installment had not been received. . . . Hearing this manifested some degree of discontent, especially the S'Klallams, doubting as to whether it was the intention of the government to defraud them or not. The annuities were distributed on the reservation per capita to heads of families. . . . Goods were short of what the invoice called for two hundred and ninety-two dollars and twenty-three cents, making this annuity short twenty-two hundred and eighty-five dollars and sixty cents . . . no small pittance. That it was very reasonable for them to conclude that they were receiving a poor compensation for the rights they had relinquished, which they had no hesitancy in saying, however, not so much on account of this annuity being short, as from a sense of the government heretofore not being prompt in rendering to them their just dues.

"I will close this part of my report by stating that justice demands that the above amount of second annuity that is short should be made good to those Indians."[9]

It took a long time to ratify the treaty in the first place, and then afterwards, annuity goods were always late and never what was promised. The S'Klallams in particular showed their dissatisfaction and accused the government of fraud. This response was exacerbated by the S'Klallam's continuing belief that they were promised that they would be able to live in the old ways, a promise that certainly would require land in their traditional territory. Just five years after signing the treaty, the Puget Sound agent discussed this problem in his report. Agent M. T. Simmons argued that "the Clallams living on the Straits of Fuca . . . should be allowed a reserve at Clallam Bay . . . my reason . . . is that these Indians, reared on the wide waters of the straits and the ocean, accustomed to taking the whale, black-fish, and halibut, cannot content themselves or be made to remain, except by force, on the narrow waters of Hood's Canal, where the reservation is situated."[10]

In 1871 and 1872, agent Edwin Eells tried a strong-arm tactic to get the S'Klallam onto the reservation. He "moved some of their leading chiefs and Indians by force onto the reservation, hoping by this means to draw the whole Tribe, but the effort has not proved successful." As part of this effort, Chief Chetzemoka, known by non-natives as the Duke of York, was brought to the reservation and he "promised to stay."[11] Earlier, in 1854, he had been given a document by the agent for the governor and the superintendent of Indian affairs, recognizing him as "Head Chief of the Clallam Tribe."

Indian agent estimates of the number of S'Klallam that eventually moved to the reservation vary from one-sixth to one-fourth of their population; however, these guesses appear to be very optimistic. If there were eight hundred to one thousand members in 1873 as Eells guessed, the estimated fraction would have meant several hundred people and the reservation could not have housed that number. Agent King in 1868 estimated the S'Klallam population at six hundred and requested the immediate building of a hospital, given his inability to stop various diseases and keep people from dying. He also noted that "a majority of the Indians belonging to this agency reside in the neighborhood of S'Klallam Bay and Port Townsend . . . some 150 miles from the reservation."[12]

Between 1855, when the S'Klallam people signed the Point-No-Point Treaty, and 1874, when the community of Jamestown was founded, their way of life changed rapidly and significantly. The Senate did not ratify the treaty until 1859, so annuity payments did not start until 1861. It is clear from agent reports to the commissioner of Indian affairs that usually less than half the S'Klallam even showed up for the distribution of goods at the Skokomish Reservation. Neither the reservation and assimilation policies, which were intended to civilize Indians by making them farmers, nor the lure of often worthless or useless annuity goods were enough to persuade the majority of S'Klallam people to move onto the Skokomish Reservation. The reservation was not even a good winter retreat, and it was nowhere near their treaty-guaranteed fishing and hunting lands. Edwin Eells's 1879 report to the commissioner of Indian affairs estimated the number of S'Klallam to be about 525 and reported that, despite many attempts, the S'Klallam could not be convinced to move onto the Skokomish Reservation:

different
people
niyaćáʔuŋəxʷ

town
táwn;
šxʷixʷimáy

Cheech-Ma-Ham (Chetzemoka)

In 1808, a child was born at KaTai to Quah-Tum-A-Low and Lach-Ka- Nam, chief of the S'Klallam. He was named Cheech-Ma-Ham (or Chits- Ma-Han). Cheech-Ma-Ham was forty years old when the first white settlers arrived at Port Townsend. The settlers found his name difficult to pronounce, so they changed it to Chetzemoka, and he was given the "royal" nickname Duke of York. His son was called Prince of Wales and his two wives were Queen Victoria and Jenny Lind. His older brother, next in line to become chief, was called King George. King George was the quarrelsome type, unlike the diplomatic Duke. One day, after a disagreement, he packed up all his possessions and paddled off to board a ship for San Francisco, never to return.

The Superintendent of Indian Affairs recognized Cheech-Ma-Ham as chief of the S'Klallam in 1854, holding him responsible for the "good behavior" of his people. At Point No Point, in 1855, Chief Cheech-Ma- Ham signed a treaty giving up all S'Klallam land for a reservation to be shared with another Tribe. Such treaties, pushed by Governor Isaac Stevens and largely misunderstood by the Indians, provoked the Indian Wars in 1855–56.

During these wars, a number of S'Klallam held a secret meeting to decide whether or not to kill the whites in Port Townsend. The S'Klallam deliberated for nine days, during which Cheech-Ma-Ham sent a daily signal of "danger." On the tenth day, the message from Signal Rock was, in essence,"danger is passed." The S'Klallam had given up their purpose.

Cheech-Ma-Ham was considered a hero by the white population and from that point on was immortalized by them. A bronze plaque was eventually placed in the rock he signaled from and a park in Port Townsend bears the name Cheech-Ma-Ham. Prior to his death, Cheech-Ma-Ham named his son, Lach-Ka-Nim (Prince of Wales), chief. It was from Lach-Ka-Nim's nickname that the present-day Prince family name was derived. Cheech-Ma-Ham died in 1888 and was buried in the white cemetery, Laurel Grove, in Port Townsend.

One of the more common photographs of Cheech-Ma-Ham (a.k.a., Chetzemoka or Duke of York). He was fond of dressing in clothes brought by the "Bostons," and this blue outfit is reported to have been one of his favorites. (Photograph courtesy of the Bert Kellogg Collection of the North Olympic Library System)

"The result of all efforts to consolidate these two Tribes on one
reservation has convinced me of the futility of all future efforts to
consolidate the different Tribes of Puget Sound and vicinity on any
one or more reservations."[13] Eells had identified at least ten different
S'Klallam villages, as far as 175 miles from where he was stationed.
His report spoke in glowing terms of the independent and prosperous
S'Klallam people who worked at saw mills, loaded lumber on ships,
worked on steamboats belonging to the mills, or were employed by
settlers to canoe them and their produce to market or to help clear
land and plant and harvest crops. He reported providing three hundred
fruit trees, a variety of agricultural tools, and some building materials
to the S'Klallam who had land they had purchased on their own. He
specifically cited the Jamestown purchase and said, "they have a neat
village; have built a church and school-house, on which, at government
expense, there has been kept up a day school through the entire year."
Agent Eells's 1874 report chronicled a common theme by noting the
S'Klallam still objected to moving onto the reservation. He went on
to report that they supported themselves by catching fish and working
at the mills or for white settlers when needed. Eells organized an
Indian police force that punished drunkenness and "with good effect."
However, he lamented that the total societal effects were resulting in
them dying off rapidly. Eells's 1873 report illustrates several significant
pressures from a rapidly changing world: "The general condition of
the Indians under my charge is much the same as at the time of my last
report. The year has been quiet, peaceful, and prosperous. During the
month of October last I made a distribution of annuity goods to such
Indians under my charge as came for them. In consequence of the
great distance that most of the S'Klallam live from the agency, not half
of that Tribe came for their goods. Less than five hundred in all were
present at the distribution. During the past few weeks I have visited
most of the Indian towns of the S'Klallam. A large proportion of
them live on the southern shore of the Strait of Juan de Fuca, in small
villages from ten to twenty miles distant from each other. They occupy
houses, some of which have floors and windows, and are as good as
many whites inhabit. They subsist by fishing and working by the day
or month for farmers and others. Some have declared their intention
to become citizens, and have taken up claims, and are farming and
accumulating property. They seem to be peaceable and industrious; but
many of them often go across straits, and get liquor in large quantities,
and drink badly. Being so far from the oversight of any one, they drink
without any restraint. Others live at the various sawmills on the sound
and work in them. These are doing well, except they connive secretly
to get whisky and drink badly. I have endeavored to induce them to
come on to the reservation by offering to give them pieces of land
of their own to cultivate. They are very slow to take in such an idea,
because that, first, it removes them so far from their old houses. Then

there is not a cordial good-feeling between them and the Twanas, who are in the majority on the reservation. The reservation is so small that they can have but small pieces of land, and must be thrown in close proximity with those they do not like, and who speak a different language. Then, there is not as good an opportunity to get work near the reservations as there is where they now are; and the opportunities to get and sell fish where they [are] far superior to those near here. These reasons all combine to render it difficult to bring them in any considerable numbers on the reservation. They are diminishing in number, and the most discouraging feature in relation to them is that they have scarcely any children. Consequently, as a nation, when this generation passes away, they will become almost extinct."[14]

Agent Eells's report highlights several important aspects of S'Klallam life immediately after the 1855 treaty. Not even half (about five hundred) came to the Skokomish Reservation to receive their annuities guaranteed by treaty. They still lived in their traditional territory and lived by fishing or working for farmers or the sawmills. Eells focused on the problem of whiskey and lamented he could not do anything about it because of the distance between the reservation where he works and the S'Klallam villages. He was well aware why the Skokomish Reservation would not attract the majority of S'Klallam. It took them away from their "old houses" and kept them from fishing and earning a living by selling the fish. Other problems included the perceived feelings toward the Twana and the small land base available on the reservation. Eells's report mirrored other agents' documents by complimenting some S'Klallam for having houses as good as those of some whites and, in general, being prosperous. At the same time, he spoke of them as being bound to vanish in one generation. Where Eells refers to the accumulation of property, he was undoubtedly referring to the purchase of private lands to found Jamestown. The S'Klallam never agreed or intended to leave their homes and way of life, regardless of white interpretations of the 1855 treaty. There was never room for them on the Skokomish Reservation and they were even then adapting to the new European American economy and in actuality doing very well.

> A number of Indians around Washington had taken homestead claims, but because of federal policy, these claims were legally made null and void, and Indians could not keep settlers from running them off their land and taking over the improvements they had made.

Founding Jamestown

Before 1870, Indians could not acquire unclaimed public lands because they were not citizens. After 1870, the Homestead Act was an avenue for Indians to receive land, but to do so they had to sever all Tribal relations. In 1911, it was noted that only eight S'Klallam had obtained public domain lands. Furthermore, the federal policy required that only the entire Tribe, not individual Indians, could sever

One of the most detailed and comprehensive documents that anyone interested in Jamestown history should read is the federal petition for recognition, with all its supporting documents, available in its entirety at the Jamestown S'Klallam Tribal Library, Blyn, Washington. See Russel Barsh's "Final Determination for Federal Acknowledgement of Jamestown Clallam as an Indian Tribe" (1980). Russel Barsh was the attorney for unrecognized Tribes, and he submitted petitions on their behalf. The history I provide is, necessarily, abbreviated, and much more detail is available in these papers. In addition, see Lane, "Identity, Treaty Status and Fisheries of the Jamestown Clallam Indian Community" and "Brief Report on Federal Government–Jamestown Clallam Relations After the Jamestown Land Purchase in 1874" (both 1977), Jamestown S'Klallam Tribal Library, Blyn, Washington.

Tribal relations. A number of Indians around Washington had taken homestead claims, but because of federal policy, these claims were legally made null and void, and Indians could not keep settlers from running them off their land and taking over the improvements they had made. Many settlers, who read about Indian land purchases in territorial papers, took advantage of the situation.

The founding of the Jamestown community was a tremendously important historical event. Both the federal government and local settlers were lobbying hard to move the S'Klallam over one hundred miles south onto the Skokomish Reservation; however, Edwin Eells, the Indian agent in 1874, had made the judgment that the Skokomish Reservation could not adequately support the Indians who were already there, let alone any new S'Klallam families. The commissioner of Indian affairs' report in 1871 noted that the Skokomish Reservation had been cut up into forty-acre lots but a large amount of the land was "wholly impassable marsh that never can be drained or used for any beneficial purpose."[15]

Facing the prospects of not wanting to leave their traditional territory, increased complaints by settlers, and not being able to secure title to public domain lands, Lord Jim Balch brought together a group of primarily Dungeness S'Klallam. This group of S'Klallam pooled their money and purchased 210 acres just north of Sequim for five hundred dollars, from Richard Delanta, a local settler. The S'Klallam asked the Indian superintendent for building materials and equipment to improve the land. Agent Eells sent lumber and plows and suggested, in keeping with the U. S. assimilationist views, that the land be divided into individual plots, equivalent to each person's contribution. He also suggested the new community be named after Lord Balch. Each family was given water access so, when the land was eventually split up, the plots were long, narrow strips moving away from the beach. The S'Klallam were more progressive than their neighbors and raised the first schoolhouse in April 1878. They were also part of an organized police force, created by the federal government. The schoolhouse doubled as a church. The federal government provided a teacher (clearly recognizing the privately held land as a S'Klallam community with treaty rights) and thirty-one pupils attended classes. There were only about six hundred white residents in Clallam County in 1880, and the only church was at Jamestown. The non-native community did not build a school until after 1910. After 1921, Jamestown students started going to school in Sequim with white children.

Jamestown Tribal citizens were not the only S'Klallam to purchase their own land. Myron Eells, the younger brother of Edwin, the Indian agent, served as a pastor for the Congregational Church for over thirty-three years and worked extensively among the S'Klallam. He reported that around 1880, a group of S'Klallam from Clallam Bay purchased about 150 acres but that around 1891 their land became very desirable to non-Indians and they sold out.

By the early part of the twentieth century, the many villages of the S'Klallam Indians began to firmly establish themselves at three places: Jamestown, Port Gamble, and the Lower Elwha River just outside Port Angeles. When Charles Roblin created a list of unattached western Washington Indians in 1919, Jamestown was the largest settlement. The Jamestown area had attracted S'Klallam from many villages. None of the S'Klallam had federal recognition, but their leaders had clearly been interacting with and receiving services from various federal agencies since the 1855 treaty. The S'Klallam were divided in opinion at the time, some favoring seeking federal status and a reservation but a significant number pointing to the horrendous conditions on reservations and pushing instead for monetary compensation. Congress eventually gave western Washington Tribes the right to sue the U.S. Court of Claims, so the Bureau of Indian Affairs (BIA) began meeting with unrecognized groups.

money
táɬə

something
purchased
sʔíɬəʔ

price
sxʷnánəč

Federal Recognition: The Beginning

In the 1920s, after meeting with BIA representatives, a combined S'Klallam executive committee, acting as a S'Klallam branch of the Northwest Federation of American Indians, composed of Joseph Allen, Wilson Johnson, and William Hall, all from Jamestown, and David Prince and Charles Hopie from Lower Elwha, hired an attorney, William B. Ritchie, to develop and file a brief with the bureau. The BIA and the Department of the Interior supported legislation to settle S'Klallam compensation claims for land taken under the 1855 treaty. While other Tribes used claims money to buy reservation land, the Department of the Interior argued that the S'Klallam had not taken allotted land offered them in a 1911 federal act, which allowed descendants of those under the Point-No-Point Treaty to choose allotments on the Quinault Reservation. Only twenty-two S'Klallam petitioned for land at Quinault, so the S'Klallam had to be paid per capita. The original settlement was reduced from $1 million to $400,000, resulting in $722.32 for each qualified recipient. This much discussed and anticipated "Indian money" was distributed in 1926. The distribution membership committee for all S'Klallam included Joseph Allen, Wilson Johnson, William Hall, David Prince,

Point-No-Point Treaty with the S'Klallam, 1855

Articles of agreement and convention made and concluded at Hahdskus, or Point no Point, Suquamish Head, in the Territory of Washington, this twenty-sixth day of January, eighteen hundred and fifty-five, by Isaac I. Stevens, governor and superintendent of Indian affairs for the said Territory, on the part of the United States, and the undersigned chiefs, headmen, and delegates of the different villages of the S'Klallams, viz: Kahtai, Squah-quaihtl, Tch-queen, Ste-tehthon, Tsohkw, Yennis, Elwha, Pishtst, Hunnint, Klat-la-wash, and Oke-ho, and also of the Sko-ko-mish, To-an-hooch, and Chem-akum Tribes, occupying certain lands on the Straits of Fuca and Hood's Canal, in the Territory of Washington, on behalf of said Tribes, and duly authorized by them.

Article 1.

The said Tribes and bands of Indians hereby cede, relinquish, and, convey to the United States all their right, title, and interest in and to the lands and country occupied by them, bounded and described as follows, viz: Commencing at the mouth of the Okeho River, on the Straits of Fuca; thence southeastwardly along the westerly line of territory claimed by the Makah Tribe of Indians to the summit of the Cascade Range; thence still southeastwardly and southerly along said summit to the head of the west branch of the Satsop River, down that branch to the main fork; thence eastwardly and following the line of lands heretofore ceded to the United States by the Nisqually and other Tribes and bands of Indians, to the summit of the Black Hills, and northeastwardly to the portage known as Wilkes' Portage; thence northeastwardly, and following the line of lands heretofore ceded to the United States by the Duwamish, Suquamish, and other Tribes and bands of Indians, to Suquamish Head; thence northerly through Admiralty Inlet to the Straits of Fuca; thence westwardly through said straits to the place of beginning; including all the right, title, and interest of the said Tribes and bands to any land in the Territory of Washington.

Article 2.

There is, however, reserved for the present use and occupation of the said Tribes and bands the following tract of land, viz: The amount of six sections, or three thousand eight hundred and forty acres, situated at the head of Hood's Canal, to be hereafter set apart, and so far as necessary, surveyed and marked out for their exclusive use; nor shall any white man be permitted to reside upon the same without permission of the said Tribes and bands, and of the superintendent or agent; but, if necessary for the public convenience, roads may be run through the said reservation, the Indians being compensated for any damage thereby done them. It is, however, understood that should the President of the United States hereafter see fit to place upon the said reservation any other friendly Tribe or band, to occupy the same in common with those above mentioned, he shall be at liberty to do so.

Article 3.

The said Tribes and bands agree to remove to and settle upon the said reservation within one year after the ratification of this treaty, or sooner if the means are furnished them. In the meantime it shall be lawful for them to reside upon any lands not in the actual claim or occupation of citizens of the United States, and upon any land claimed or occupied, if with the permission of the owner.

Article 4.
The right of taking fish at usual and accustomed grounds and stations is further secured to said Indians, in common with all citizens of the United States; and of erecting temporary houses for the purpose of curing; together with the privilege of hunting and gathering roots and berries on open and unclaimed lands. Provided, however, that they shall not take shell-fish from any beds staked or cultivated by citizens.

Article 5.
In consideration of the above cession the United States agree to pay to the said Tribes and bands the sum of sixty thousand dollars, in the following manner, that is to say: during the first year after the ratification hereof, six thousand dollars; for the next two years, five thousand dollars each year; for the next three years, four thousand dollars each year; for the next four years, three thousand dollars each year; for the next five years, two thousand four hundred dollars each year; and for the next five years, one thousand six hundred dollars each year. All which said sums of money shall be applied to the use and benefit of the said Indians under the direction of the President of the United States, who may from time to time determine at his discretion upon what beneficial objects to expend the same. And the superintendent of Indian affairs, or other proper office, shall each year inform the President of the wishes of said Indians in respect thereto.

Article 6.
To enable the said Indians to remove to and settle upon their aforesaid reservations, and to clear, fence, and break up a sufficient quantity of land for cultivation, the United States further agree to pay the sum of six thousand dollars, to be laid out and expended under the direction of the President, and in such manner as he shall approve.

Article 7.
The President may hereafter, when in his opinion the interests of the Territory shall require, and the welfare of said Indians be promoted, remove them from said reservation to such other suitable place or places within said Territory as he may deem fit, on remunerating them for their improvements and the expenses of their removal; or may consolidate them with other friendly Tribes or bands. And he may further, at his discretion, cause the whole or any portion of the lands hereby reserved, or of such other lands as may be selected in lieu thereof, to be surveyed into lots, and assign the same to such individuals or families as are willing to avail themselves of the privilege, and will locate thereon as a permanent home, on the same terms and subject to the same regulations as are provided in the sixth article of the treaty with the Omahas, so far as the same may be applicable. Any substantial improvements heretofore made by any Indian, and which he shall be compelled to abandon in consequence of this treaty, shall be valued under the direction of the President, and payment made therefore accordingly.

Article 8.
The annuities of the aforesaid Tribes and bands shall not be taken to pay the debts of individuals.

Article 9.
The said Tribes and bands acknowledge their dependence on the Government of the United States, and promise to be friendly with all citizens thereof; and they pledge themselves to commit no depredations on the property of such citizens. And should any one or more of them violate this
pledge, and the fact be satisfactorily proven before the agent, the property taken shall be returned, or in default thereof, or if injured or destroyed, compensation may be made by the

Government out of their annuities. Nor will they make war on any other Tribe, except in self-defence, but will submit all matters of difference between them and other Indians to the Government of the United States, or its agent, for decision, and abide thereby. And if any of the said Indians commit any depredations on any other Indians within the Territory, the same rule shall prevail as that prescribed in this article in cases of depredations against citizens. And the said Tribes agree not to shelter or conceal offenders against the United States, but to deliver them up for trial by the authorities.

Article 10.
The above Tribes and bands are desirous to exclude from their reservation the use of ardent spirits, and to prevent their people from drinking the same, and therefore it is provided that any Indian belonging thereto who shall be guilty of bringing liquor into said reservation, or who drinks liquor, may have his or her proportion of the annuities withheld from him or her for such time as the President may determine.

Article 11.
The United States further agree to establish at the general agency for the district of Puget's Sound, within one year from the ratification hereof, and to support for the period of twenty years, an agricultural and industrial school, to be free to children of the said Tribes and bands in common with those of the other Tribes of said district, and to provide a smithy and carpenter's shop, and furnish them with the necessary tools, and employ a blacksmith, carpenter, and farmer for the term of twenty years, to instruct the Indians in their respective occupations. And the United States further agree to employ a physician to reside at the said central agency, who shall furnish medicine and advice to the sick, and shall vaccinate them, the expenses of the said school, shops, person employed, and medical attendance to be defrayed by the United States, and not deducted from the annuities.

Article 12.
The said Tribes and bands agree to free all slaves now held by them, and not to purchase or acquire others hereafter.

Article 13.
The said Tribes and bands finally agree not to trade at Vancouver's Island, or elsewhere out of the dominions of the United States, nor shall foreign Indians be permitted to reside in their reservations without consent of the superintendent or agent.

Article 14.
This treaty shall be obligatory on the contracting parties as soon as the same shall be ratified by the President of the United States.

In testimony whereof, the said Isaac I. Stevens, governor and superintendent of Indian affairs, and the undersigned chiefs, headmen, and delegates of the aforesaid Tribes and bands of Indians have hereunto set their hands and seal at the place and on the day and year hereinbefore written.

Isaac I. Stevens, governor and superintendent. [L.S.]

Chits-a-mah-han, the Duke of York, Chief of the S'Klallams, his x mark. [L.S.]
Dah-whil-luk, Chief of the Sko-ko-mish, his x mark. [L.S.]
Kul-kah-han, or General Pierce, Chief of the Chem-a-kum, his x mark. [L.S.]
Hool-hole-tan, or Jim, Sko-ko-mish sub-chief, his x mark. [L.S.]
Sai-a-kade, or Frank, Sko-ko-mish sub-chief, his x mark. [L.S.]
Loo-gweh-oos, or George, Sko-ko-mish sub-chief, his x mark. [L.S.]
E-dagh-tan, or Tom, Sko-ko-mish sub-chief, his x mark. [L.S.]
Kai-a-han, or Daniel Webster, Chem-a-kum sub-chief, his x mark. [L.S.]
Ets-gah-quat, Chem-a-kum sub-chief, his x mark. [L.S.]
Kleh-a-kunst, Chem-a-kum sub-chief, his x mark. [L.S.]
He-atl, Duke of Clarence, S'Klallam sub-chief, his x mark. [L.S.]
Lach-ka-nam, or Lord Nelson, S'Klallam sub-chief, his x mark. [L.S.]
Tchotest, S'Klallam sub-chief, his x mark. [L.S.]
Hoot-ote St, or General Lane, S'Klallam sub-chief, his x mark. [L.S.]
To-totesh, S'Klallam sub-chief, his x mark. [L.S.]
Hah-kwia-mihl, S'Klallam sub-chief, his x mark. [L.S.]
Skai-se-ee, or Mr. Newman, S'Klallam sub-chief, his x mark. [L.S.]
Kahs-sabs-a-matl, S'Klallam sub-chief, his x mark. [L.S.]
S'hote-ch-stan, S'Klallam sub-chief, his x mark. [L.S.]
Lah-st, or Tom, S'Klallam sub-chief, his x mark. [L.S.]
Tuls-met-tum, Lord Jim, S'Klallam sub-chief, his x mark. [L.S.]
Yaht-le-min, or General Taylor, S'Klallam sub-chief, his x mark. [L.S.]
Kla-koisht, or Captain, S'Klallam sub-chief, his x mark. [L.S.]
Sna-talc, or General Scott, S'Klallam sub-chief, his x mark. [L.S.]
Tseh-atake, or Tom Benton, S'Klallam sub-chief, his x mark. [L.S.]
Yah-kwi-e-nook, or General Gaines, S'Klallam sub-chief, his x mark. [L.S.]
Kai-at-lah, or General Lane, Jr., S'Klallam sub-chief, his x mark. [L.S.]
Captain Jack, S'Klallam sub-chief, his x mark. [L.S.]
He-ach-kate, S'Klallam sub-chief, his x mark. [L.S.]
T'soh-as-hau, or General Harrison, S'Klallam sub-chief, his x mark. [L.S.]
Kwah-nalt-sote, S'Klallam sub-chief, his x mark. [L.S.]
S'hoke-tan, S'Klallam sub-chief, his x mark. [L.S.]
Paitl, S'Klallam sub-chief, his x mark. [L.S.]

The first contemporary (1925) S'Klallam council, composed of members from Jamestown, Elwha, and Port Gamble. From left to right, back row: Ernie Sampson, Joe Allen, Dave Prince, Billy Hall, and Peter Jackson. Front row: Tim Pysht, Joe Anderson, Sam Ulmer, Charlie Hopie, and Benny George. (Photograph courtesy of the Jamestown Tribe photo collection)

and Charlie Hopie. The original roll of 1,225 who were identified as S'Klallam was pared down to 533, largely because (in the opinion of agent Walter F. Dickens) the committee tended to recognize only individuals living close to the communities or having regular ties to the communities. Dickens argued for more inclusiveness and added some individuals back on the rolls before the money was distributed. The issue of federal recognition for Tribes in Washington began to receive increased attention by BIA employees and some Washington D.C., legislators.

After the Indian Reorganization Act (IRA) passed in 1934, federally recognized Tribes began to adopt constitutions and establish local governments. The BIA made several efforts to organize the S'Klallam bands in the 1930s in preparation for and in response to the IRA. An umbrella organization bringing all S'Klallam communities together was proposed for Jamestown, Port Gamble, and Lower Elwha in 1934. The BIA staff argued amongst themselves for four years before deciding this combined group could vote on IRA organization and that land could be purchased for them to create a reservation. From 1936 to 1939, the bureau tried to buy land for the S'Klallam in Port Angeles. In 1937, a bureau recommendation was made to create three districts: Elwha River, Jamestown, and public domain (i.e., S'Klallam in Port Angeles). Each district would elect three members

146

to a governing board. The assistant secretary of the interior, however, recommended organizing the S'Klallam as one Tribe or two or more bands. Both Lower Elwha and Jamestown were opposed to district representation and band organization. There clearly was a difference of opinion among S'Klallam during this period about becoming federally recognized, but the suggestion that Jamestown S'Klallam be organized and join Lower Elwha on a reservation was probably what people were most dissatisfied with. The federal government had already approved land purchases at Elwha Valley and Port Gamble. The bureau lost interest in further land acquisition for the Jamestown S'Klallam in the late 1930s.

The Port Gamble S'Klallam were organized under the IRA in 1939. The Lower Elwha S'Klallam received reservation status in 1968, when they finally organized under the IRA. During this period, the Jamestown S'Klallam received no reservation land and were not brought under the IRA. The leadership of the Tribe decided to press for compensation through the Indian Claims Commission. The federal government continued to deal with the Jamestown S'Klallam despite the Tribe's lack of official recognition, and even though their lands were not held in trust by the government but were individually owned. Most of the government-Tribe interaction between 1939 and 1975 revolved around developing and maintaining a water system for the Jamestown community, gaining title to the old school property, developing a constitution, providing Indian Health Service care, applying for federal grants, which were accepted, and adjudicating fishing rights issues. The IRA signaled a significant shift in federal Indian policy. It ended the disastrous allotment act, which was focused on destroying the communal life of Indian people, and it allowed federally recognized Tribes to develop a constitution and begin to stabilize their self-governance activities. This federal initiative has its critics, though, even today. Most IRA governments were founded from a U. S. model that continued to give the BIA far too much control over all aspects of Indian life. The IRA was designed to erode BIA control, but it would take another fifty years before Tribes would begin to strike clauses from their constitutions that provided BIA review of most or all of their decisions.

> Government was not always centralized in the hands of a Tribal Council but, more often than not, was inclusive for all members.

Traditional Tribal governments varied widely in practices and structure. Some Tribes invited participation from all members on a daily basis. Elders and other leaders gained the support of fellow members through a variety of means, such as oral persuasion or inherited rights. Government was not always centralized in the hands of a Tribal Council but, more often than not, was inclusive for all members. There were certainly some highly structured governments with delegated powers, but "democracy" worked in very different ways

Jamestown S'Klallam Leaders: 1930s to 1970s

This record, undoubtedly incomplete because of the lack of documentation by the informal Tribal leadership and the lack of records available from the BIA, is nevertheless important because it was the record submitted by Russel Barsh, attorney for the "Final Determination for Federal Acknowledgement of Jamestown Clallam as an Indian Tribe."

1936: Executive Committee
Wilson Johnson,"president"
Harris Johnson, secretary
David Prince, Jacob Hall, and Lovelle Hall, members

1939:Trust Agreement for Water System
Wilson Johnson, chairman
Lydia Dick, secretary

1944: Council
Wilson Johnson, chairman
David Prince, Jacob Hall, Lovelle Hall, Lydia Dick, and Leonard Wood, members

1946: Council
David Prince, chairman
Jacob Hall, Lovelle Hall, Lydia Dick, and Leonard Wood, members

1948: Council
Jacob Hall, chairman
Lyle Prince, vice-chairman
Harris Johnson, William Hall, and David Prince, appointed council
Same membership as above, but with new members: Harriette Adams,
David Prince, and Cynthia Larsen (from a non-landholding family)
Later that year, Larsen,Adams, and Johnson created an executive
council to work with Chairman Hall and Vice-Chairman Lyle Prince

1966: Council
Charles F. Fitzgerald (son of an earlier leader by the same name), chairman
Harriette Adams,Walt Reyes, Elaine Grinnell, and Art Becker, members

In the early 1970s, the following individuals served in various roles on the council:
Elaine Grinnell, Harris Johnson, Charles F. Fitzgerald, Harriette Adams, Charlotte
Snodgrass, Hannah Johnson,Marlin Holden, and Lyle Prince.

than in the IRA-imposed governments of the nineteenth century.[16]

The IRA ended the 1887 allotment era, which had as its major aim the assimilation of Indian people into mainstream society by taking Tribally held lands and giving them to Indian individuals. The act allowed Tribes to enter into formal legal agreement with corporations and to negotiate issues like hunting and fishing rights with state governments. Tribes gained the extremely important ability to have their own attorneys. The act also attempted to take away the immense control that the BIA had over Indian Tribes and Indian people, but just how that would be realized was not clear within the legislation. It is no wonder that Indian communities were confused and often suspicious of this new deal offer: "During the two-year period within which Tribes could accept or reject the IRA 258 elections were held. ... 181 Tribes (1,229,750 Indians) accepted the act and 77 Tribes (86,365 Indians, including 45,000 Navajos) rejected it."[17]

The Jamestown S'Klallam did not take advantage of the IRA movement and remained federally unrecognized. Although there was undoubtedly some misunderstanding by Indians and non-Indians alike over treaty pledges, the common theme, well known by both groups, was that the Indians never were paid what they should have been paid for their land. In meeting after meeting with Indian agents, federal and state politicians, and whoever else might listen, Indians in Washington State kept the promise and hope alive that one day they would be justly compensated.

When Charles Fitzgerald was elected Council Chair in 1966, the question of federal recognition came back into sharp focus. In 1966, the Jamestown people sought to file a claims suit with the ICC. The BIA initiative to assist Tribes under the IRA had decreased sharply in the late 1930s. The Jamestown S'Klallam had maintained their traditional leadership, after the failed attempts to organize under the IRA, and were poised to work in earnest on a constitution once again. Elaine Grinnell, serving as secretary in 1968, wrote to the BIA for help in working on a constitution. In 1970, Grinnell was elected Chair and a draft constitution was finally submitted to the federal government in 1975. Harris Johnson took over in 1971. In January 1976, the Jamestown people again formally petitioned the federal government for federal recognition. W. Ron Allen, the current Chairman, was elected to office in 1977.

Contemporary Ways

There are several ways a Tribe is able to gain federal recognition, including treaty negotiations and Senate ratification, an act of Congress, or the federal acknowledgement process. In 1978, the BIA published rules for the process (25CFR Part 83/2000). A governing document like a constitution is required that demonstrates how the Tribe governs itself and determines who is a member of the Tribe. There are extensive criteria that have to be met. Geography is also very important. The evidence from the petition has to demonstrate that the group had historically lived in a specific area and was continually viewed as distinct from non-natives. A Tribe has to have some record of identification by and interaction with federal authorities over a continuous period of time. They also may submit evidence of longstanding relationships that identify them as a group who are seen as Indian by a state government. Other evidence can come from

today
ʔáynəkʷ

tomorrow
ʔáʔčikʷáči

yesterday
čiʔáqɬ

149

repeated dealings with a county, parish, or other local government that demonstrate over time that they were seen as a group of Indians. The types of information that can be part of the petition include:

- records in courthouses, churches, or schools
- scholarship from anthropologists, historians, or other scholars
- newspapers

A petitioner can also provide evidence that other Indian Tribes or national Indian organizations dealt with them as a Tribe.

The federal government's process to determine whether a group has always been a "Tribe" is largely focused on proving they have maintained social and political ties from European contact to the present. The Jamestown petition was extremely strong and satisfied all of the applicable criteria. Federal recognition, granted in 1981, was a landmark historical event for the Jamestown people. This event was just as important as the purchase of private property, which formed the Jamestown Village in 1874, or the rights guaranteed by the Point-No-Point Treaty of 1855. The BIA concluded that the Tribe had existed autonomously since contact and was always recognized as a distinct Indian group by non-Indians in the area. In addition, the Jamestown people historically maintained themselves as a cohesive and socially distinct group and always maintained their political integrity and independence. Further, the group was never terminated from any federal relationship. The conclusions of the report speak directly to the strength of the Jamestown application: "The Clallam Tribe was a signatory of the 1855 Treaty of Point No Point. Until that time its ancestral home had been an area along the southern shore of the Straits of San Juan de Fuca, Washington Territory. Its organization was basically that of a group of autonomous bands.

"The Clallam, although required to do so, never took up residence at the Skokomish Reservation, because of adverse conditions there.

"By 1874 a group of the Clallam drifted back to their ancestral area where, under the leadership of Lord Jim Balch, they raised funds and purchased land. All those who came into contact with them at that time identified them as Clallam Indians. At Jamestown they maintained an informal governmental structure.

"During the 1870–1900 period, the Bureau of Indian Affairs provided this group with material aid in the form of agricultural tools and seed, and paid the expenses of an Indian school at Jamestown until 1926.

"This aid continued despite the fact that the Jamestown Clallam had no trust land and no reservation.

"The local Indian agents recognized the presence of a band leader at Jamestown, and dealt continuously with him and his successors. The Bureau of Indian Affairs helped the Clallams organize formally in the 1960s.

"In 1928, 1939, 1954 and 1974 the federal government interceded to protect and improve the Clallams' land solely because an Indian group held it.

"During the Indian Reorganization Act period (1935–1939), the Jamestown Clallam were nearly organized as part of a larger Clallam Tribe with a local autonomy provision in their constitution. Because of the fact that land had already been purchased for two other Clallam groups, there is ample evidence that the Jamestown Clallam were given the choice of moving to another reservation or staying where they were and remaining unorganized. They chose the latter, and so missed out coming under the IRA."[18]

The Jamestown community persevered through very uncertain times while they tried to force the federal government to live up to treaty rights guaranteed since 1855. That struggle continues today. S'Klallam claims were never fully satisfied by the Indian money distributed in 1926. The Jamestown community finally sought and received federal recognition in order to further protect their rights—in particular, their hunting and fishing rights.

> One important principle of international law is that indigenous peoples have always possessed sovereignty.

S'Klallam Government

One important principle of international law is that indigenous peoples have always possessed sovereignty. The much respected Felix S. Cohen's <u>Handbook of Federal Indian Law</u> affirms this, stating that "Perhaps the most basic principle of all Indian law . . . is the principle that those powers which are lawfully vested in an Indian Tribe are not, in general, delegated powers granted by express acts of Congress, but rather inherent powers of a limited sovereignty which has never been extinguished. Each Indian Tribe begins its relationship with the federal government as a sovereign power, recognized as such in treaty and legislation."[19] Thus, the sovereign powers the Tribes retain today were not given to them by the U.S. government. Rather, the powers each Tribal government exercises today are inherent and only limited by what has been expressly taken away by Congress, the courts, or the executive branch.

When North America was invaded, colonial powers only "discovered" lands that other colonial powers had not yet found. Native peoples had a choice to either give up their land or fight. In what was to become the United States, Indian nations were a powerful force to be reckoned with throughout Spanish, British, and early American occupations. Indian wars were expensive and the U.S. government, for the most part, sought peace and treated Indian groups as sovereign nations. It was only after 1871, when the military dominance of Tribes declined, that the United States ended treaty making with Indians.

A standard by which most other Indian law books are measured is Felix S. Cohen's Handbook of Federal Indian Law, edited by Rennard Strickland (Charlottesville, Virginia: The Michel, 1982).
For information on Indian lands, see Carl Waldman's Atlas of the North American Indian (New York: Facts on File Pub., 1985) and Robert N. Clinton, et al., American Indian Law, 3rd edition (Charlottesville, Virginia: The Michel, 1973).
A particularly good general reference for the history of federal Indian law and policy, sovereignty, and the trust responsibility is David Getches, Charles Wilkinson, and Robert Williams, Jr.'s Cases and Materials on Federal Indian Law, 4th edition (St. Paul: West Publishing, 2000).

Since treaty times, American Indian Tribes, nations, bands, and groups have struggled and fought to maintain their sovereignty. The Jamestown S'Klallam are no exception, even though, when compared to most other Tribes, their history is unique since they had to apply for federal recognition. The major challenge facing the council since 1981, when the Tribe received federal recognition, was to develop and implement all the infrastructure of a working government. Of course, federal recognition provided a starting point because of the bureaucracy needed to comply with federal regulations and guidelines on services received from the BIA and other agencies.

A five-member Tribal Council governs the Jamestown S'Klallam Tribe. The mission of the Council is to develop policy. The administration of day-to-day business is the responsibility of staff. From its inception, the Jamestown Council has operated with the belief that success must be created by fostering a balance among past, present, and future. Jamestown Tribal governance has always been solidly anchored in traditional cultural S'Klallam values. When a contemporary Tribe constitution was written in 1975, the Jamestown philosophy was readily evident: "The Jamestown S'Klallam Tribe seeks to be self-sufficient and to provide quality governmental programs and services to address the unique social, cultural, natural resource and economic needs of our people. These programs and services must be managed while preserving, restoring and sustaining our Indian heritage and community continuity."

The Tribe moved quickly to embrace and provide national leadership for one of the most important self-governance initiatives since the 1975 Indian Self-Determination and Educational Assistance Act. The Jamestown S'Klallam Tribe was among the first pilot group of ten Tribes to sign a compact under the Self- Governance Demonstration Project in 1990. The Tribal Self- Government Act of 1994 was passed and signed into law by President Bill Clinton, and in 2000, he created a permanent program with the Tribal Self-Governance Amendments of 2000 (Public Law 106-260). There are more than 270 Tribes and nations currently participating in self-governance. In western Washington, participants include Lower Elwha Klallam, Port Gamble S'Klallam, Lummi Indian Nation, Quinault Indian Nation, Squaxin Island Tribe, Makah Nation, and the Swinomish Tribe. In addition, the Jamestown Tribe has taken on the national role of educating other Indians and non-Indians about self-governance. They participate in a congressionally funded National Self-Governance Education Project, including producing a monthly newsletter, Sovereign Nations. They also have produced a self-governance educational video. The Tribe is committed to assisting other Tribes in their efforts to move toward self-governance and to expanding this initiative with other federal agencies.

One of the major goals of the self-governance project was to strengthen the government- to-government relationship (as provided in the U.S. Constitution) between Tribes and the United States. The Jamestown S'Klallam Tribe has emerged as a national leader in the success of self-governance for Indian Tribes across the nation. Self-governance has proven to be the key to meeting the Jamestown S'Klallam goals of reducing dependency on federal resources and achieving true self-sufficiency. This effort seems to have met with considerable success for the Jamestown S'Klallam Tribe. An additional, if not equally important, benefit has been to reduce the level of federal bureaucracy the Tribe has had to deal with by putting responsibility for planning, fiscal control, provision of services, and accountability in the hands of the Tribe. By far, one of the most dramatic changes in the past two decades is the ability of the Jamestown Tribe to assess, plan, and evaluate its own community's needs, without having to write endless annual grant applications for BIA/IHS or other federal programs based on priorities set in Washington, D.C. The flexibility to reallocate scarce service dollars has resulted in a more relevant, effective, and efficient set of programs for Jamestown S'Klallam community members and in increased exercising of the Tribe's inherent political power.

For example, in 1990 the Tribe reorganized to create better communications and working relationships among the Council, Executive Director, and administrative departments by creating an executive committee. However, the authority and responsibility for governance remains in the hands of the Council, as dictated by the

For a comprehensive history of treaty making and an exhaustive list of other sources on treaties, see Frances Paul Prucha's American Indian Treaties: The History of a Political Anomaly (Berkeley: University of California Press, 1994).
A very comprehensive treatment in two volumes is Vine Deloria, Jr., and Raymond J. DeMallie's Documents of American Indian Diplomacy: Treaties, Agreements, and Conventions 1775–1979 (Norman: University of Oklahoma Press, 1999).
An excellent treatment of precontact European practices and attitudes toward colonialism is found in Robert A. Williams, Jr.'s The American Indian in Western Legal Thought (New York: Oxford University Press, 1990).
A classic nonlegal source is Edward H. Spicer's A Short History of the Indians of the United States (New York: D. Van Nostrand, 1969).

The Jamestown S'Klallam Tribe has taken on the national role of educating other Indians and non-Indians about self-governance.

Tribe's constitution. A modern and future-thinking administration ensures the S'Klallam vision is communicated and implemented across the multifaceted organization. Quality standards are ensured for construction and maintenance of a growing number of Tribal facilities, including the Tribal offices, which are located at the head of Sequim Bay in Blyn, Washington. Administrative functions are

Board Members and Committee Members - 2001

Culture Committee
Margaret Adams, Matt Adams, Janet Duncan, Trina Jeffery, Sandra Johnson, Susan Johnson (Staff Advisor: Kathy Duncan, Liz Mueller)

Education Committee
Beth Anders, Vickie Carroll, Celeste Kardonsky, Theresa Lehman (Staff Advisor: Liz Mueller, Paula Nelson)

Elders Committee
George Adams,Tillie Baker,Ed Blacksmith,Janet Duncan,Walter Hubman,Lyle Prince, Colie Wilson (Staff Advisor:Margaret Adams)

Election Committee
Ann Adams,Danielle Adams,Vickie Carroll (Staff Advisor: Linda Cawyer)

Enrollment Committee
Vickie Carroll, Charlene Dick, Kathy Duncan, Pete Holden, Candy Mair (Staff Advisor: Linda Cawyer)

Fish and Game Committee
Matt Adams, Robin Allen, Don Ellis, Kurt Grinnell, Marlin Holden, Pete Holden, Ken Merritt (Staff Advisor: Scott Chitwood)

Health Committee
Ann Adams, Harriette Adams,Robin Allen, Beth Anders, Lisa Barrell, Sandra Johnson, Theresa Lehman,Candy Mair (Staff Advisors: Dr. Peter Erickson,Danielle Adams,Robin Howell, Cindy Lowe,Vicki Lowe,Carrie Melmed, Bill Riley, Charlotte Stefano)

Housing Improvement Program Committee
Ann Adams, Harriette Adams, Lisa Barrell, Robin Howell, Theresa Lehman (Staff Advisor: Annette Nesse)

Jamestown Community Network Board
Twenty-two Tribal members and local community members (Staff Advisor: Liz Mueller)

Jamestown Seafood, Inc., Board
Harriette Adams, Matt Adams, Pete Holden, Cliff Prince, Lyle Prince (Staff Advisor: Mark Madsen)

JKT Art Board
Matt Adams,W. Ron Allen, Sandra Johnson, Cliff Prince,Marlene Shaw (Staff Advisor: Mark Madsen)

JKT Development, Inc., Board
Ann Adams,Matt Adams,W. Ron Allen,Sandra Johnson (Staff Advisor: Mark Madsen)

JKT Gaming Commission
Jeff Allen,Tom Lowe,Don Salonen (Staff Advisor: Gary Murphy)

JKT Gaming, Inc., Board
W. Ron Allen, Sandra Johnson,Paul Moore, Cliff Prince (Staff Advisor: Mark Madsen) [20]

continually evaluated and upgraded, with the specific goal of enhancing technological strategies. Tribal Council policies, resolutions, and ordinances are implemented and monitored on a continual basis. The Tribe maintains a state-of-the-art financial management system that provides for an annual audit from an external certified accounting firm.

The Tribe is a multimillion-dollar operation. The largest funding source in 2001, for example, was nearly $2 million from self-governance contracts received in a lump sum from the Department of the Interior. Other major funding sources were from the Indian Health Service (also funded under self-governance), the Department of Housing and Urban Development, the Environmental Protection Agency, and the Department of Health and Human Services. A strong indication of the partnership that exists between the Tribe and the State of Washington was nearly $1 million in funding for, primarily, habitat restoration, water conservation, and land

> For more information on self-governance, see Part I: The History and Goals of Tribal Self-Governance (developed by four nations, including the Jamestown S'Klallam Tribe, 14 July 1995). This booklet is available at the Jamestown S'Klallam Tribal offices, Blyn, Washington. There are a large number of brochures and booklets available on self-governance and the Jamestown Tribe. Chairman Ron Allen has taken a leadership role in producing most of these materials. As early as 1989–1990, the Jamestown S'Klallam joined with the Quinault and the Lummi Nations to publish Shaping our Own Future. The Hoopa Valley Tribe joined this national educational initiative in January 1990. A comprehensive evaluation is available: see Rudolph C. Ryser and Leslie E. Korn's Indian Self-Government Process Evaluation Final Report (Olympia, Washington: Center for World Indigenous Studies, 1 March 1996).

The Jamestown S'Klallam Tribal Administration Building, on Highway 101 at the head of Sequim Bay in Blyn, Washington. (Photograph courtesy of the Jamestown Tribe photo collection)

JAMESTOWN S'KLALLAM TRIBE ORGANIZATIONAL CHART–FY 2001

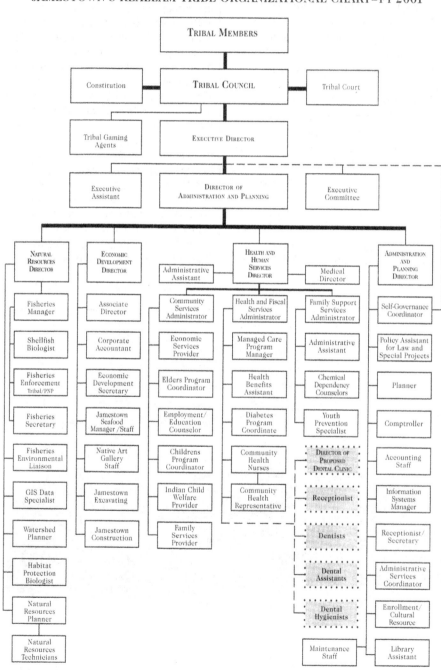

acquisition. Total expenditures from grants and contracts in fiscal year 2001 was $5,923,448.[21]

The Tribe also manages a human resources development program that is dedicated to identifying and hiring highly qualified employees and assisting them with career advancement and meeting personal and professional goals. The Tribe uses Indian preference in hiring, and a primary source of recruitment is enrolled members of the Jamestown S'Klallam Tribe, provided they qualify for the position advertised. However, in the final analysis, the Tribe prides itself on setting the highest professional standards and hiring the best-qualified person for each position.

The Tribe focuses on long-range goals and, in particular, fund-raising strategies. The development of alternative sources of funding for Tribal programs is a major goal because it will eventually reduce dependency on federal programs. Providing the latest communications technology, updating computer equipment and software, and networking all Tribal employees are continual challenges.

Very recently, the Tribe has had to begin more comprehensive research and planning for transportation and housing. Expansion of the Tribe's land base, while working closely with Washington State's Growth Management Act guidelines, has ensured significant changes are in the Tribe's immediate future. The Tribe is working with other agencies to plan a consolidated intersection where U.S. 101 and Old Blyn Highway meet near the Tribal offices. In addition, when new health facilities are built across from the Tribal offices, the current county road will need upgrading to handle increased traffic. The Tribe began to participate in the BIA Indian Reservation Roads program in 1995.

Tribal Housing

The Tribe began participating in the Housing Improvement Program (HIP) in 1983. Three categories of assistance are available to Tribal members with severe financial needs:

A. Repairs to housing that will remain substandard.
B. Repairs to housing that will become standard.
C. New housing.

The Tribe has completed thirty-six projects in category A, thirty-five in category B, and eleven category C projects. If a home is sold after project completion, then repayment is required. Eligibility requirements are stringent and include an income level that is 300 percent below federal poverty guidelines. These programs all involve federal involvement and oversight. Other programs are available, which allow various loans and limited grants to finance construction, down payment and closing cost assistance, renovation, and emergency assistance. The Tribe has funded fifteen projects under this program, which is completely managed by the Tribe. Another housing assistance program available to Tribal residents, as well as everyone else in the county, is provided for low- to very low-income residents in rural areas (funded by the Department of Agriculture—Rural Development).

The future for meeting housing needs is very good for Tribal members. Significant progress is expected as federal and other agencies provide the Tribe with more discretion and oversight of housing funds and projects.

The Allotment Era

There have been innumerable volumes written on Indian treaty rights and the federal government's trust responsibility for American Indians. In its most important form in Indian affairs, both the treaty and the resultant trust relationship focused on Indian land. Millions of acres of Indian land were ceded to the federal government, much of it by treaty, and the remaining lands set aside for Indians were put in the hands of managers or trustees. There were 367 treaties ratified between 1778 and 1868. The basic goal, unmistakably, was that reservation lands were to be beneficially managed so that Tribes could continue to govern themselves and maintain their lifeways. Many treaties spoke specifically about social, medical, and educational services to be provided forever for Tribal people. Allotment of Indian lands was one of the most horrific attacks on Indian Tribes and their significant communal social-cultural-political organization. The combination of acquiring new western lands by the treaties with Great Britain (1846) and Guadelupe Hidalgo with Mexico (1848), along with the gold rush, put tremendous pressure on politicians to open up more land for settlers. Forced assimilation of Indians into white society (a standard practice since first European contact) picked up steam. Every Indian was to be given 160 acres to farm and the rest of Indian lands were to be sold as "surplus." Between 1887 and 1934 (when this policy was reversed by the Indian Reorganization Act), Indian Tribal or communal lands were reduced two-thirds, from 138 million to 48 million acres. The "reward" for accepting an allotment was citizenship (not provided to all Indians until 1924). About 41 million acres were allotted. After allotment, not surprisingly, most of the valuable land was gone (about half of the remaining 48 million acres was desert or semidesert lands). This policy left many reservations checkerboarded with significant numbers of non-Indians who owned land in the heart of reservations. Another important congressional act that was designed to foster assimilation was the extension of federal jurisdiction over seven major crimes committed on reservations in 1885. This act has left a legacy of confusion, contradiction, and inequality for law enforcement on Indian reservations that boggles the mind. The Jamestown S'Klallam escaped allotment because they were in the Far West and not on a reservation. For the reader who wants to know more about allotment, there are hundreds of books and articles on the subject. An excellent starting point for allotment (as well as assimilation or sovereignty) is Albert L. Hurtade and Peter Iverson, editors, Major Problems in American Indian History (Lexington, Massachusetts: D.C. Heath & Co., 1994).

Acquiring Tribal Land

The Jamestown S'Klallam people first purchased land in 1874, but they were not at that time federally recognized. The land was held privately and was never Tribal, reservation, or communal land. The first land the Tribe purchased after being federally recognized in 1981 was 2.1 acres on the waterfront at the head of Sequim Bay in Blyn, Washington. The Tribal headquarters building, social services annex, and community center building They are located on this property, which now has reservation status. The small tract also includes some outbuildings and a caretaker's house. An additional 7.26 acres were purchased just across Highway 101, and these acres are also reservation land. These first two purchases were made because of water proximity and highway access. Sequim Bay, of course, was chosen also because of its location between major population clusters of Tribal citizens and other Indians, located from Port Angeles to Port Townsend. In 1985, the Tribe regained ownership of the 2.9-acre Jamestown Tribal Cemetery. This land was part of the original privately purchased Jamestown settlement, but the county took it in 1902 for nonpayment of taxes. The Tribe worked with the county to return the land, and it is now in reservation status. A burial policy and ongoing maintenance program were established. The growth of Tribal lands, held in common for all citizens, was slow—only about sixteen acres were acquired in the decade immediately following federal recognition. However, by 1994 a total of sixty-two acres near or adjacent to Tribal headquarters was purchased. Today, the Tribe's land base in Blyn has expanded to approximately 174 acres.

Right after federal recognition, the Tribe was considering several options to meet community needs and acquire more land. Staff investigated purchasing the community well at the original Jamestown settlement and applying for a water right with the state. The other pressing issue, over fifteen years ago, was protecting the original Jamestown settlement. The majority of the original property had slipped out of S'Klallam hands and only 30 percent of the original 210 acres remained in S'Klallam ownership. When property was purchased, new surveys seemed to be encroaching on the original plot map, which was completed in 1886 but never officially recorded. The advantages and disadvantages of making the original Jamestown community a reservation were discussed with current residents. In the end, the original Jamestown settlement was never made a reservation.

> Before the Revolutionary War, colonists experimented with offering separate parcels of lands to Indians who might then become "civilized"by breaking away from communal village life.

A Land Consolidation Plan (LCP) was filed with the BIA in 1985.[22] The federal government passed legislation to facilitate all Tribes' efforts to bring lands back into Tribal/reservation status, which had largely been lost during the disastrous allotment era. The Dawes General Allotment Act of 1887 was a new twist to an old idea. Before the Revolutionary War, colonists experimented with offering separate parcels of lands to Indians who might then become "civilized" by breaking away from communal village life.

Decades later, when Congress reversed its assimilationist stance and attempted to rebuild Indian Tribes, one approach they took included assisting Tribes to plan for and acquire a consolidated land base. The LCP does not represent any legal claim upon any land, but it does assist Tribes in securing funding through the Indian Finance Act, which was created to assist Tribes to purchase land for economic development. About 85 percent of the Jamestown S'Klallam LCP is within a twenty-five-mile radius of the original Jamestown settlement. All of the LCP is within original S'Klallam territories and is focused on the original settlement, portions of the usual and accustomed fishing areas (both fresh water and salt water), archaeological sites, and the Tribal headquarters and areas needed for future housing and economic development. The major goal of the LCP is to enhance economic development opportunities. The Jamestown LCP is also intended to position the Tribe to protect and utilize its fishing and shellfish rights guaranteed by treaty. The Tribe's planning division maintains a land database, which is both a current inventory and a basis for planning future land purchases.

Although the Jamestown S'Klallam Tribe could exert its sovereignty and ignore what is happening around them, their basic philosophy of working with other governments and citizen groups is especially apparent in the area of land-use planning. One of the major goals of the Tribe is to ensure that plans complement countywide land-use planning and policies, zoning ordinances, and other regulations.

Jamestown S'Klallam Tribal citizens live in homes they have purchased outside the reservation. The Jamestown Tribal Housing Improvement Program provides assistance to meet the goal of adequate and affordable housing for Tribal citizens. However, severe funding constraints make this area one of the greatest challenges. The Tribe is looking for alternative-funding options to help meet members' needs. Currently, one new home is being constructed annually. Minor renovations and repairs are also being made as limited funds allow. A goal is to develop housing on Tribal lands, as long as the houses can be built to match the lifestyle needs of Tribal citizens as well as federal funding and architectural constraints.

Who Is an Indian?

The determination of who is an "Indian" and what is an Indian "Tribe" depends on who is asking the question and for what purpose. The issue of defining membership in a Tribe is at the heart of the struggle for Indian sovereignty. There is no single, widely accepted definition of who is an Indian. Two common definitions are legal and ethnological. In the legal sense, if a person's ancestors lived in what we call the United States today and that person is also recognized by a federally recognized nation, Tribe, community, band, or village, he or she can probably prove legal Indian status. However, legal entities often (but not always) defer to Tribes to determine their own membership.

Ethnographical considerations include knowledge of the history, geography, language, culture, and lifeways of the Tribe as well as ancestry and recognition by the Tribe. A person can be a legal Tribal citizen but be completely assimilated into mainstream society. Conversely, a person can have only marginal ancestry but be fully conversant in the language and culture, grow up and live on the reservation, and be fully accepted by the community.

> An excellent reference on Indian individual and Tribal identity is Joane Nagel's American Indian Ethnic Renewal (New York: Oxford University Press, 1996).

Scholar Alexandria Harmon argues that Indians and non-Indians around Puget Sound have been continually defining and redefining who is an Indian primarily based on economic, political, and demographic categories shaped by distinctive cultural differences. Historically, a basic issue has always been the multiple individual identities and associations of natives. A single individual was rarely identified with only one village, one house, or even one family. The U.S. government has tried desperately to sort out who is a member of a federally recognized Tribe, assign them to a reservation, and thereby have a way to deal with promises made by treaty, court decisions, and administrative edicts.[23]

Early mixed-ethnic marriages, contradictory federal policies (such as allowing Indians to homestead or take off-reservation allotments), and the failure of providing ample and economically viable reservations all resulted in widespread confusion by the federal government about who could claim to be an Indian. By the late 1890s and early 1900s, increased competition for reservation land assignments highlighted the confusion. Charles Buchanan, a Tulalip agent in 1901, perplexed as to who could be allotted land wrote the Indian commissioner: "Who and what is an 'Indian'? What is a ' Tribe'? . . . In what manner and by what methods can mixed bloods acquire Tribal rights?"[24] Exact answers were hard to come by, both from federal bureaucrats and Indians themselves, who held various ideas about who was a member of which Tribe. Indians from all over the Northwest moved around to work, fish, feast, and attend Shaker gatherings. These folks all considered themselves Indians, regardless of federal definitions and decisions.

Though definitions of who is an Indian vary for legal, ethnographical, or political reasons, in its most basic form, an Indian is a descendant of aboriginal peoples who is also recognized by an Indian community. One of the foremost authorities on Tribal governments, Sharon O'Brien, defines traditional Tribal governments this way: "Although Tribes and their governments varied widely, to be a member of a Tribe meant sharing a common bond of ancestry, kinship, language, culture, and political authority with other members. This feeling of oneness and distinctness from other groups is illustrated by the widespread custom of Indian Tribes naming themselves with a word or words meaning 'the people.'"[25]

Whenever you see the term "Indian" (or "American Indian" or "Native American") used, you need to ask yourself, "Who wants to know and why?" For example, the census bureau uses self-identity and the BIA uses service population (one-fourth degree blood for most purposes). Therefore, the 2000 census identified just over 2.4 million American Indians and Alaska natives, while the BIA estimate was closer to 1 million. The number of people identified as American Indian in the 2000 census was only 0.9 percent of the total U.S. population. However, this reflected a dramatic increase since 1970, when the count was 0.4 percent of the U.S. population. The majority of this increase was attributed to more Americans acknowledging their Indian heritage. The 1900 U.S. census identified just 237,196, or 0.3 percent of the total population.

The Jamestown S'Klallam Tribe is very familiar with these issues because it had to apply for federal recognition even though S'Klallam were the preponderance of signatories to the Point-No-Point Treaty of 1855. The Tribe used the one-quarter blood quantum for enrollment eligibility when it applied for federal recognition in 1981, but changed to one-eighth blood in 1998. When this Tribal referendum was voted on, it narrowly passed, illustrating the controversial nature of who should be recognized as a Jamestown S'Klallam Tribal citizen. The major reason for the change was historical. When the Tribe first began increasingly organized and focused efforts in the 1970s to gain federal recognition, one-eighth-degree blood was the criterion. However, when the application was made, one-fourth was used to conform to BIA practices. The plan was to return to the one-eighth criterion sometime after receiving federal recognition.

Using the one-eighth criterion, the Tribal enrollment before federal recognition was 644. When federal recognition was granted, only 195 individuals met the one-fourth-degree criterion. For the Jamestown Tribe, U.S. census data are virtually meaningless. The 2000 census shows a population of only sixteen. The Tribe has only seventy-one acres in reservation or trust land status. While some of the property has residences, the majority is taken up with Tribal office buildings and the casino. Currently, there are 502 enrolled Tribal citizens and 242 live in Clallam and Jefferson counties, which the Tribe serves with its programs. In April of 2001, the Tribe's service count was 759. This includes citizens as well as Jamestown descendants who do not meet enrollment criteria and Indians or Alaskan natives who are from other Tribes but live in the S'Klallam service area.[26] There are many Jamestown descendants living in Clallam and Jefferson counties who do not meet the eligibility requirements for enrollment. Many have mixed Indian and non-Indian heritage but not a close enough genetic link or cultural tie to be enrolled in the Tribe.

Self-Governance into the Future

Indians in Puget Sound were eventually overwhelmed by immigrants and consequently lost a way of life characterized by wealth, power, rich ceremonial and cultural uniqueness, and the status that distinguished some from commoners and slaves.

Alcohol ravished the entire population, killing where disease had not done that job earlier. The best land was taken and too few small reservations were offered to far too many people. The horrendous, all-consuming cultural change largely occurred in the short time span of roughly half a decade between 1850 and 1900. In the face of these devastating changes, the S'Klallam, who were supposed to be crowded onto the Skokomish Reservation with the Twana after 1855, persevered by adapting to the local economy. They

For a comprehensive treatment of New Deal Indian policies and the self-determination movement, see Vine Deloria, Jr., and Clifford Lytle's <u>The Nations Within: The Past and Future of American Indian Sovereignty</u> (New York: Pantheon Books, 1984).
There are hundreds of volumes on federal recognition. See in particular David Getches, Charles Wilkinson, and Robert Williams, Jr.'s <u>Cases and Materials on Federal Indian Law</u>, 4th edition (St. Paul: West Publishing, 2000); Stephen L. Pevar's <u>The Rights of Indians and Tribes</u>, 2nd edition (Carbondale: Southern Illinois University Press, 1992); and Sharon O'Brien's <u>American Indian Tribal Governments</u> (Norman: University of Oklahoma Press, 1989

became proficient at logging, sawmill work, gardening, crabbing, clam digging, and fishing, and most importantly, they did this by staying home in traditional S'Klallam territory.

The S'Klallam people continue to exhibit traditional family and village values to organize and guide themselves. A variety of leaders, both men and women, have stepped forward to meet religious, judicial, educational, subsistence, or other needs of the community. Indeed, the character traits of paramount importance today—ambition, self-control, modesty, courtesy, generosity, cooperation with other Tribes or groups, and acceptance of each individual's responsibility to protect the environment and to give back to the community—have always been S'Klallam values. They guide the Tribe today just as they did the families and villages of yesterday.

Dramatic changes swept across Indian country when the American Indian Self-Determination and Educational Assistance Act passed in Congress in 1975. This signaled the end of a major effort to terminate the special federal relationship with Tribes that had begun again in the mid-1950s. However, just as the federal government increased efforts to allow Tribes to set their own goals and strengthen their capacity to meet community member needs, the states continued their efforts to control Tribes. Especially at issue were resources with any economic future.

The Jamestown people recognized that they were never going to be able to protect their treaty rights, especially traditional fishing, without federal recognition and Tribal status. In addition, the potential for health, social, and economic development programs could only be accessed by federally recognized Tribes, through the new federal self-determination initiatives. The Jamestown S'Klallam could easily have given up their culture and identity, and assimilated completely into the Pacific Northwest environment. After all, they were renowned throughout the peninsula for their aggressive adaptation to white lifeways and their success at working in the white-dominated economy. In addition, the federal government, while clearly dealing with them as a Tribe and a unique cultural group, did not "officially" recognize them between 1855 and 1981, a period of 126 years. It was the federal government's failure to adequately protect Indian hunting and fishing rights, coupled with the Jamestown people's recognition that they were never going to be able to join other Washington Tribes' struggles to protect treaty rights, that rekindled their interest in becoming a federally recognized Tribe.

The discussions and efforts to seek federal acknowledgment, which had been around S'Klallam territory in one way or another for over 120 years, intensified in the mid-1960s. There were always strong opinions voiced on both sides of the question of whether to seek federal recognition. From the beginning of the federal recognition movement, many Jamestown people saw more negatives than positives in coming under the bureaucracy of the BIA. There was ample evidence of paternalism, dependency, and resource mismanagement with all Tribes across the United States. More important, some Tribal citizens voiced the argument that the Jamestown S'Klallam had made it on their own without the federal government, so why change now? The new faith in the promise of self-determination was in its infancy in the 1970s, but the Jamestown people had to choose. Opposition to seeking federal recognition gradually waned, and in 1975, a revised Tribal constitution was voted on and approved. The Council-Chairman format, which the Tribe had used less formally since the early 1900s, was incorporated in the new constitution.

The Jamestown village was still the heart of political and social activities when the Tribe was struggling with the pros and cons of federal recognition. Tribal citizens at Jamestown opened their homes to smaller meetings and, after the Shaker Church burned down, a hall in Sequim was used for the larger meetings. There were still ten Indian households in Jamestown in 1975. There was a clear indication of a vigorous and continuous Jamestown community from its inception in 1874 through 1975, and this was a major factor in the decision by the federal government to acknowledge the Tribe. Furthermore, regardless of where other Jamestown people lived on the peninsula, they were active in the community, even though most did not hold land at Jamestown. Intermarriage, particularly to non-Indians, and the lack of work on the peninsula meant that there was a large number of Jamestown people who attended social gatherings but were deprived of day-to-day Tribal contacts. When the federal acknowledgement application was made, about 60 percent of the citizens lived on the Olympic Peninsula but a full 85 percent still lived in the state of Washington. One of the major potential benefits of reservation status was to bring community members back home.

How the S'Klallam Became Known as the Strong People

as told to the author by Elaine Grinnell, Jamestown Elder and storyteller

Oh, one day there was a big feast. Many different Indians came. And of course, we just had the traditional foods— salmon, clams, raspberries—all the good things that came from the earth and the water. And then they decided, well, they had to get their work done. They wanted to put up a great big longhouse. Oh, everybody was excited to work together. All the women prepared the food and the men were gathering all the wood for this great big longhouse. First the structure of the longhouse went in, quite easily, with the help of many hands. The sides went up. Everything went up quite rapidly. People all helped when they could. And then all that was left to do was put up the great big pole that would top that longhouse and, oh, it was a big log and it had to go up a long ways. The different Tribes tried to shoulder that log and they just couldn't. They couldn't lift it; it was so huge. Finally it came to the S'Klallam. They had been kinda watching the rest of the Tribes as they failed to pick up that big log. Because they lived right on the straits, they knew what they had to do. Certainly all they had to do was just roll that log down into the water, which they all did. Shoulder to shoulder they rolled that log right down to the water's edge and out and floated the log, and then they all waded out 'til that log was floating to where it was comfortable to get under it. They shouldered the log. They all stood up and they walked out of the water. Oh, what a sight! They walked until they got close to the longhouse and then they got ready and they raised that log up as far as they could and pushed it right up on the roof 'til it was in place. And from then on they were known as the strong people, the S'Klallam.

strong
ʔíyəm

heavy
síq̓i

light
xʷaʔwáwə

5

Interview with Chairman Allen

The honorable W. Ron Allen is Tribal chairman and executive director of the Jamestown S'Klallam Tribe. He is the only elected Tribal Chairman that Jamestown has had since they received federal recognition in 1981. His longevity in this role is unique when compared to Chairmen and Council citizens in Tribal governments across the United States. In addition, Chairman Allen's broad and consistent leadership at the national and regional level stands in contrast to the majority of Tribal leaders.

The honorable W. Ron Allen, Chairman of the Jamestown S'Klallam Tribe. (Photograph courtesy of the Jamestown Tribe photo collection)

Nowhere is the connection between traditional and contemporary ways more aptly illustrated than in the political arena. W. Ron Allen and his twentieth-century predecessors have all distinguished themselves as "good men" or "real men." Their leadership stems directly from the traditional expectations of hard work, seriousness and ambitiousness, self-control, modesty, courtesy, and generosity. These attributes culminate in the shared belief of community first and individual success second. This 2002 interview pulls together all of the threads of the contemporary Jamestown history and puts the successes and challenges in rebuilding the Tribe in perspective.[1] Chairman Allen is in a unique position to help conclude this story and also provide a glimpse of the future.

167

Stauss: What do you see as the strengths of the traditional S'Klallam family?

Allen: The name of the Tribe, "S'Klallam," means strong people, and that meaning has been very reflective of the way that individuals, families, and the community have interacted with each other from the beginning. Early contacts with non-Indian communities and cultures presented many challenges to our Tribe's survival. If I was to characterize what is unique about our qualities or character is the fact that we're strong. We will survive and take care of each other. Our community has always remained a tight-knit community when they were threatened in any way.

Everything that I have read and understand about the way the Jamestown community interacted with the outside society, including other Indian communities, is that they were very protective of their village, their rights, and the people who lived in their village. I think that is true today even though we are more scattered and spread out than we were in the past.

The Jamestown community was always very resilient. Another unique characteristic of the Jamestown community and the S'Klallam people, in general, is our ability to adjust. As the community was exposed to non-Indian cultures, they had to make social and economic adjustments while preserving our distinct identity. While our people were making those adjustments, as a community, they learned how to survive in the growing and developing non-Indian sector.

The Jamestown community had to make adjustments to the various industries that emerged. Our people permeated into those industries in order to pursue new kinds of employment opportunities and earn the income they needed to survive and take care of their families. They were very resourceful, and as new techniques or new tools became available, they utilized them. They didn't resist the use of them as a matter of cultural pride. They looked at them in terms of whether they were practically or pragmatically useful to advance their survival and meet their changing needs.

Stauss: What do you see as the key future challenges that face the Jamestown family?

Allen: I see there are a lot of different challenges. First, other cultural values, non-Indian cultural values, have certainly had a tremendous impact on Indian communities, and the Jamestown people are no different in that matter. Our community has been sharply influenced by those value systems. Those non-Indian value systems and all their influences, particularly the "I" mentality, is something that is problematic for our community because they are more concerned about themselves than the welfare and the future of the community. We certainly are going to have to be very careful about how we preserve our unique Tribal identity. Political decisions must be made in the interest of the community as opposed to the interest of the individual. One of the best examples is while trying to become successful in the business sector, some Tribal citizens may become more concerned about themselves as opposed to future program developments for the community, including health services or programs for the youth or Elders. When you understand the capital investment necessary to provide for the needs for child care, youth services, education, housing, health care, and Elder services, the Tribe has an overwhelming responsibility.

The rapidly rising costs of health care, education, or protecting the environment, which is culturally very important to the community, are very expensive endeavors. Our mission becomes having the ability to direct new resources towards these long-term community needs as opposed to individual needs. This is what I refer to as the balance between the "I" centered individual versus community needs and responsibilities. I do not believe the Tribe has an obligation to generate income for the citizenship, but instead has an obligation to provide a support system to help the citizens become self-sufficient and provide a support system for the special populations of the community, such as Elder and child care. Long-term care for our Elders is a priority for the Tribe. We need to provide them accommodations and assistance to keep them closer and engaged with our community. They have given so much to our children and communities. The Tribe has never had the resources to address all these needs, so it is an area that we need to make a priority.

> "I do not believe the Tribe has an obligation to generate income for the membership, but instead has an obligation to provide a support system to help the members become selfsufficient and provide a support system for the special populations of the community, such as Elder and child care."

However, the goal of providing adequate health care is an area that is incredibly costly. It is one that our society is struggling with in terms of trying to provide an effective system to ensure quality health care, which can improve the longevity of our community. The health-care needs of citizens continues to be very problematic relative to the resources that are available to the Tribe. The health of our community is essential to the interrelationships between families and individuals within the community. We must take care of each other. This value system is both a traditional and contemporary cultural value that has always been a part of our community.

The final challenge I want to emphasize is education. Education goals are becoming more and more difficult to advance. The encouraging footnote is that there are more Tribal youth who have an interest in pursuing their undergraduate and subsequently postgraduate programs. The tough part is finding the resources to accommodate that need. However, education is certainly a priority that the Tribe wants to provide effectively. So far we have done okay, but we need to keep improving.

Now that doesn't necessarily mean that we need, or want, or are trying to steer these youth back to the Tribe once they have graduated and acquired other professional or vocational skills. We know that the spirit will take them wherever the spirit will take them, in terms of where they are going to reside and where they are going to work—whether it's in our own community or whether it's outside our community. Rather, our objective is to assist Tribal citizens to become more self-reliant. This characteristic is consistent with the qualities of our people, i.e., S'Klallam meaning "strong people." If you are self-reliant, and your education base is stronger, then your ability to care for your own needs is enhanced and strengthened, which will guarantee that you will contribute to our community needs, wherever you might reside.

An overall concern that I have in terms of advancing our Tribe's goals and objectives is to avoid, at all costs, causing our people to become dependent on the support services provided by the Tribe. "Indian country" gets criticized sharply for being a "welfare system" which is a system that originated out of centuries of dependency upon the federal government. We don't want that to happen to our Tribal community. So, developing programs that enhance the ability of our citizens to become more self-reliant is a fundamental goal. If you can help the parents to become more self-reliant, then those values and work ethics will get passed on to children. I believe that that makes the Tribe and the community stronger.

Stauss: Let me ask you to talk a little bit about the "I" society. Does the Tribe have any specific plans or ideas or vision about how you combat this negative mindset?

Allen: I think that we are using a variety of approaches and techniques. However, to be able to address positive initiatives requires resources (such as manpower, public relations materials, etc.). For example, we need to coordinate with the public educational system, including developing curriculum and materials that educate the youth about the Tribe and our value systems. We have to raise our understanding of why it's important to adjust to the society that surrounds our Indian community, while preserving our unique, distinct cultural identity, and why these ethics are very important to maintain.

There are also program activities that we can provide within our own Tribal programs, in terms of providing more activities for youth and for Elders. For example, public forums can be utilized to educate and enlighten.

The Tribe is getting better at providing opportunities to meet these goals. One of the impediments is the fact that our community is very dispersed, and it makes it difficult to bring everyone into a forum at the Tribal center. Another challenge is having sufficient staff to coordinate and provide services.

The Bureau of Indian Affairs, the Indian Health Service, and the Department of Education have historically been underfunded to serve the needs of Indian country. Our Tribe struggles to meet the needs of our community. Unfortunately, that scarce funding dilemma puts additional pressures on our Tribe to develop alternative funding resources to assist in meeting objectives.

For example, in our higher education program, even if the Tribe has the resources to advance all our educational objectives, there is still a great need for providing the kind of support that often those students need and may not always get from parents. The Tribe must assist by providing that support as our students weave their way through an educational system that is often insensitive to the special needs of Indian students. The counselors at many schools we use need to help to nurture those students through school. We've probably had more failures than we want to admit, not because our students didn't have the intelligence or they didn't have the interest, but rather they were distracted or discouraged. Unfortunately nobody was there to prod or to reinforce them and to provide the support that they were looking for to move on in their educational goals.

The overall goal for the Tribe's education program is to broaden out the students' horizons and perspectives. There is more to the world than Sequim and our Tribal community. However, it's important that while an opportunity is provided for our students to enrich and grow, we must also provide a safety net to help in that effort. Now I'm not referring to the notion of safety net meaning don't worry about it; you have no risk, so you can go do what you want to do and then you can always fall back on the Tribe. The safety net means that if our students are failing, the Tribe must help provide guidance and support.

Stauss: I was interested in your observation that you are beginning to see more youth interested in higher education. Some Tribal groups around the country are reporting just the opposite because of casino revenues. What do you think is happening in Jamestown?
Allen: If the Tribe's casino were generating literally millions of dollars, we would probably have the same kind of dependency problems. If a person is in a position where they can win the lotto every year, then why would you care about school? Why do you care about an education? Why do you care about having a universal understanding of what's going on in the world and enhancing your own knowledge of the world about you, in all aspects politically, economically, socially, and so forth? You are not motivated because all your desires are being given to you on a silver platter. You are moving through life with an attitude that the Tribe will always provide for your needs. You are not being challenged to learn and make good decisions as they affect you, your family, your children, or your community.

Does it build good citizens? No. In my opinion, it doesn't help, and that is what I find disturbing. Part of our Tribal responsibility is to develop good citizenship as a citizen of the Tribe, as well as a citizen of the community at large.

I firmly believe that our community has to come to grips with the reality that you are a dual citizen, and therefore, you have responsibilities with both the Tribe and U.S./state communities.

This issue provides us with a tremendous amount of political pressure. People are generally more interested in the easy street versus the path that teaches responsible character. At this time, we don't have that problem at Jamestown because we don't have that kind of money. We have had to fight and work hard for every penny that the Jamestown community has ever generated. Everything that the Jamestown Tribe has is because we have earned it. That old-fashioned ethic has caused us to remain strong, resourceful, and responsible. I think it creates and maintains good community character.

I believe that this characteristic has helped us to be successful; yet this success also creates new kinds of problems. It wouldn't surprise me if ten years down the road, when the Tribe has established a stronger Tribal economy, that some will start saying do we really need more programs or buildings? Why don't we just spend this money on ourselves? I think that we will have to establish a fair balance between individual desires and future community stability. We need a long-term plan that looks to the next seven generations.

"I think that we will have to establish a fair balance between individual desires and future community stability."

I say seven generations delicately. People use this philosophy a lot; however, it is not a Coast Salish philosophy. But it is a concept about the future. Are you thinking about the now or tomorrow?

The issue becomes how soon can Jamestown achieve a stable political and economic foundation? What are the operational conditions that indicate that you are stable? Does the Tribe have things in place to take care of its citizenship? My view is that we have to diversify the Tribe's economic base. We have to start generating the kinds of revenue to enhance the governmental community services.

If we are successful and then have to begin making per capita payments, it's going to be a problem with Congress, who will consistently bring up the "means testing" concept to allocate federal resources relative to the Tribal revenue generated by the Tribe's businesses.

Let me give you some examples of what the Tribe should be investing in to prepare for such a dilemma. The Tribe will always have education programs. Right now we have a difficult time providing financial assistance to those who want to go to post-graduate programs. This is an area we should provide more assistance in because there are students we want to get master's and doctorate degrees. We don't have those resources yet. But how do we get in that position? Well, what we do is start generating an endowment fund—a fund that generates regular revenue depending on the market. It generates a revenue source so you are not dependent on the federal government and their potential to cut funds from programs like education.

If the Tribe has an endowment and it generates an educational fund of, say, a hundred thousand dollars a year, then we can provide consistent assistance for as many students that would ever want to go to school no matter what level of education they want to pursue. Hopefully, the Tribe establishes a program that provides enough assistance to avoid the student having to work, so that they can just focus on their studies. As long as you do well in your studies and your grades are good, the Tribe will be there for you.

A second example is health care and it is even more complicated, but we can follow the same approach. What are the health-care services that are needed and where are the resources going to come from? The federal government provides a limited amount of funding, but as medical costs are rising, the Tribe is drawing on reserves to cover these costs. We are going to have to figure out how to address this increasing need.

It doesn't matter whether it is direct medical, dental, or whether its prescription drugs, we need to have a program that can cover that need so that our people know that they are being protected. The Tribe must have an effective health-care program and make it a main priority.

A third example is protecting and sustaining our treaty resources, like salmon and the geoduck resources. We must manage these resources so they are sustainable. The fin fishing is a little more complicated, simply because we have to deal with the habitat and all the other problems out there that impact them. However, it's the Tribe's responsibility to address these issues. That requires staff expertise to deal with the ecosystem, to interface with the development industry, the farming industry, the timber industry, and the townships and cities and so forth. They all have an impact on that environment that affects our fishery. Subsequently, it impacts our culture.

A fourth area is providing for adequate and safe housing. This is another Tribal priority and an area that continues to grow. We are a growing Tribe, and it means we have younger families and the majority of them will need some sort of assistance to get into homes.

"Land is essential to our governmental and cultural identity."

Today, we are managing our businesses to ensure fundamental good business practices, and ensure they are generating the best revenue possible, relevant to market conditions. We use disposable income to address Tribal community priorities and needs. We have so many needs for programs and services and we have a lot to do before

we consider per capita payments. Once you start making them they are
very difficult to stop or reduce.

Another priority is the re-establishment of our land base. The
Tribe and its community are not just about fishing or hunting. We're
also about land. Land is essential to our governmental and cultural
identity. We are never going to recover our land base that was
traditionally ours, which covered over four hundred thousand acres
across the Olympic Peninsula. But, a good land base that preserves
your way of life and the environment, as well as provides for economic
development, is essential to our future.

We are trying to buy back some of the original land in the
Jamestown community, so at least we can preserve some of where
our community originated. The original Jamestown S'Klallam Tribe
provided the opportunity for S'Klallam from across our territory to
become a part of the S'Klallam Tribe. That migration from other
villages changed the character of Jamestown because they are not the
same community as those that were what you would call the original
Jamestown community. So we developed into a little different character
from our original community. But we still embraced S'Klallam values.
They still embraced that unique special identity. But, to preserve our
unique identity we must reacquire some of our original lands.

Our land acquisition goal is expensive. You are buying back at
the current market price. It's not being given to you. I really believe,
though, that we are going to be able to achieve that objective on our
own.

Stauss: You talked about the Elders, keeping them close to the
community. Some Tribes are using gaming funds to develop a place
for Elders to live. Is the Jamestown S'Klallam Tribe moving in that
direction?

Allen: Absolutely. It is clearly an objective of the Tribe. Our Elders are
among our most active group. We have been very blessed with good
staff that has really created a lot of interest and enthusiasm among
our Elders. However, we just need more facilities with more space and
resources to expand the activities we want to provide for them.

Regarding interaction between the Elders and youth, I believe the
youth are interested in what the Elders are doing and learning from
them. The spirit will lead the youth into communicating with them and
learning from them—whether it is cultural activities such as carving,
painting, or basket weaving, or whether it is learning about who you are
and what you are all about as a community. I think the Tribe can assist
by providing the programs and support for this type of interaction and
spiritual steering by the Elders.

Stauss: I know the last fluent Jamestown speakers have passed on.
How important is the language?

Allen: Language is something that is very important to the preservation of the identity of any Tribe. It doesn't necessarily mean that somebody has to be able to speak the language, but that the language itself has been preserved.

It was disappointing to me that many of our Elders chose to not pass the language on and felt that it was time to let it go. My grandmother was one of those that held that view. My grandmother spoke fluent S'Klallam and she made the decision not to teach us. When we were asking to learn how to speak it, she said, "No, because it's a dying language and you need to learn how to speak English." I have a great appreciation for the Lower Elwha S'Klallam teachers and a couple of our Tribal citizens, including Margaret Adams and Kathy Duncan, who have a personal interest in restoring our language.

I think that the youth have an interest in our language and they adapt to it very easily. I believe that it can be restored. Will it be a commonly used dialect that some of our people actually speak with fluency? Probably not. How much is going to be regularly practiced is an open question. I think what's been encouraging is the growing interest. This interest goes back to the Tribal priority of developing cultural programs that can be sustained with dedicated resources.

Stauss: Tell us a little about your own history and, in particular, how you got started in Tribal politics.

Allen: I suppose going back to my earliest childhood roots, my father grew up in the original Jamestown community and my mother grew up in a nearby small community. I grew up in Port Angeles, Washington, because that was where the jobs were, and my father moved us to Port Angeles to find work. However, we spent a great deal of our time in Jamestown. We spent many weekends and summers in Jamestown and so, spiritually, I was always a part of the Jamestown community and the families down there.

In high school and just after high school, I really did not have any particular interest or aspirations about what I wanted to do for my career. Those were the freespirited, peace-loving and anti-war days of the 1960s, you know, when people were wondering what is true about life. I was pretty much caught up in that time myself, and so I never got serious until my late twenties when I went back to school and pursued my college degrees. I graduated from high school in 1966 and it was the mid-70s before I started getting refocused. The next thing you know I became interested in the Tribal arena by accident. I used to play a lot of Indian basketball. I had to go back and get my Indian "blue card." Keep in mind in my family, a couple of my brothers looked very Indian, but I didn't. I took after my mother who was Scottish and Irish. When I used to play a lot of Indian basketball, I'd get carded to see if I was really Indian. The blue card was my evidence that I was a citizen of a Tribe.

We weren't federally recognized. When I asked what do I do to get a card, they said that there was little the Council could do until the Tribe became recognized by the federal government, again. At that time there was an empty seat on the Council. There were a number of citizens who were very active leaders who had spent years and years leading Jamestown, including my grandfather Joseph Allen back in the twenties and thirties. Harriette Adams, who had been on and off the Council for probably forty years, she's the one that persuaded me to get involved. She said we were trying to pursue federal recognition and that Edith Cusack, who at that time was the Vice-Chairwoman, was our point person working on that project. Edith needed help, and they asked me if I would be interested in being appointed to Council and work on this project. I saw this request as the opportunity to get my Tribal ID card and said, sure, I would do that. So I was appointed to the Council in 1975. and at the end of that year the Tribe had an election and I got elected for two years. Then in '77, when I was well engaged in the Tribe, I ran for Tribal Chairman, once again at the encouragement of Harriette Adams, Lyle Prince, and others who were active leaders at the time. Of course, at the same time I was still going through college.

I was on the Tribal Council trying to help complete the recognition process with the lawyers. That effort went on from the 1970s until we received federal recognition in 1981. I had spent quite a bit of time with Edith Cusack, tracking down information and documents. We would go to people's garages and get documents out of boxes to gather evidence that verified the Tribe was an ongoing entity, and that the Tribe sustained its leadership and its distinct cultural continuity.

In 1981, after the federal recognition process was complete, we focused on developing governmental operations. We started up with small grants and a small staff. I was just finishing up my college career and, rather than going on to post-graduate work, I decided to go work for the Tribe in 1983.

From that point forward it was a matter of a simple philosophy that I had—make as much of our scarce dollars stick with the Tribe as possible, so that it didn't flow through and we never saw it again. My agenda was to use money so it stayed with the Tribe and keep building our foundation. That was an important objective and it worked. Little by little we kept moving forward.

If I was to characterize my career with the Tribe, it has been about my passion to make the Jamestown S'Klallam Tribe successful. It's a part of who I am, and I enjoy what I do. I love the Tribe, and I am delighted to be serving it. Quite frankly, at this point in time I can look back and say, " I did good."

Stauss: When did you first get involved nationally?
Allen: I began to get actively involved in the early 1980s. I served

on the Board of the Affiliated Tribes of Northwest Indians and was elected treasurer of the National Congress of American Indians [NCAI] in 1989. In 1995, I was elected as President of NCAI and served two consecutive two-year terms. Because of term limits, I was unable to run for re-election as President and instead was elected to serve a two-year term as first Vice President in 1999.

Stauss: And you intend to continue to be active nationally?
Allen: Absolutely. It's going to be hard for me not to be active nationally. When you develop relationships, expertise, and experience, as well as an understanding of how Washington, D.C., works, it is difficult to back away from the duty to help those who don't understand the national political system and process. It takes a long time to develop an understanding of how the process of both the House and the Senate interrelate, as well as the administration. I have developed a lot of contacts. I know how the White House and its various departments work, including departments of interior, health and human services, justice, and the others.

I don't know exactly how extensively I will continue this involvement. That's a tough question for me. I'm always being asked, am I going to go after some of the high-level political appointee positions in different administrations. I haven't had a real strong desire to pursue those positions. I've always had a greater desire to help my colleagues understand the political system and how to advance your cause.

I love living in Sequim. I love working with the Tribe, and I believe that I can make a difference for twenty more years. I don't see myself slowing down till I'm over seventy years old. I see no reason why not. Why, do I want to go off and travel around the world? I mean, I'm interested, and I've traveled a little bit around the world now. But, I'm more interested in working for our cause than what some would perceive as a prestigious position. They are not as prestigious as you think.

The national forum such as NCAI is always in need of leadership, and I'm not sure how much I should continue playing a lead role. I have no doubt I could run again for President. But, is it the right thing for me? One of my problems right now is where my family is at this time. My son and daughter are both in high school, and I spend quite a bit of time away from them and my wife. So I'm not sure if I should stay active at a national level with all its travel demands. Those are all tough personal choices. It has nothing to do with my energy. I have the energy. I am committed to building national Indian advocacy organizations and making them more effective. It takes time to nurture those organizations. They must sustain the constant challenges undermining their capacity to carry out their mission.

I think in the thirteen years I've been involved in NCAI, I've helped lead it from an organization that had questionable political effectiveness and had a terrible vacillating history of ups and downs from ineptness to strength and then right back to ineptness. Now we have stabilized it and moved it progressively upward. The credibility and integrity of NCAI is unprecedented and improving. I am not patting myself on the back. I just believe that is what we have accomplished over the last decade. Now, what is the next step? I want to see a Hall of Indian Nations in Washington, D.C., similar to an embassy. Indian Country has the resources to make that happen, and all I want to do is put the pieces together. I think to myself, If I get that done, I've made a difference for all Indian Country, including the Jamestown S'Klallam Tribe. Then I think I would move on and let someone else continue to provide the leadership and advance the next steps for the national Indian cause.

Stauss: What do you see in this Hall of Indian Nations? What's the vision?
Allen: The hall would be where NCAI, other national Indian organizations, and Tribal offices would reside. You would bring Indian power together and create a presence in Washington, D.C., in a way that the D.C. powers react by saying, "Whoa! We have to deal with native people." As the saying goes, power not used is power abused. Organizational capacity and physical presence all go together to form a power base. Power bases can backslide, but if you do your job and you do it right, then the foundation should always stay solid.

That project is something that I think we are getting closer to achieving. Right now NCAI doesn't have the money to make it happen, but we will soon. We intend to build the annual revenue from the Tribes, corporate entities, and general public to sustain that kind of operation. I believe that this revenue should be coming in from corporate America, who benefits from Indian country—Pepsi Cola, Nike, Microsoft. Indian country should expect people like Ted Turner, who exploit the Indian name and image, to contribute to the Indian cause. But, we need to develop the organizational capacity to be out there pounding on their doors and challenging them to make contributions.

"We believe in providing a good balance between development and preservation of the natural resources that are a hallmark of the Northwest and our Tribe."

Right now there are not enough Tribal leaders filling those roles and that's because most of us are spending our energies surviving at the Tribal level. Survival is the Tribes' primary responsibility; therefore, many do not have the time and resources to fight the larger cause. My good friend and colleague from the Quinault Nation, Joe DeLaCruz would say, "Not enough Indians to cover the bases." Some of us activist doers have to cover a lot more bases than our fair share. But one of my favorite themes is, "Don't whine about it, just do it."

Stauss: Why has Jamestown had such a tremendous commitment to
the preservation and rebuilding of the natural environment?
Allen: Billy Frank, Jr., our good friend from the Nisqually Tribe,
always said, "We're fish people." Our whole culture and way of life are
about the sea and rivers, its salmon and shellfish. Our Tribe has a high
interest in the protection of the natural resources and environment.
Many of our people make a living off the fishery industry. However,
the number of citizens who actually make a living off natural resources
has dwindled substantially from ten to twenty years ago when there
were lots of fish around.

But that doesn't change our interest in restoring the environment.
We believe in providing a good balance between development and
preservation of the natural resources that are a hallmark of the
Northwest and our Tribe.

There is only so much that we can do to restore the environment.
A lot of damage was done as a result of past development, especially
with timber and farming practices. We believe that you do what
you can in your own backyard. For our Tribe, it has always been the
Dungeness River, the Jimmycomelately Creek, Sequim Bay, Dungeness
Bay—those areas around us that we often refer to as the Dungeness-
Quilcene Watershed. Those were the areas that we decided we must
address and take on managerial responsibilities. We believe that it
is critically important for all interested parties to work closely and
collaboratively together in terms of managing the rules, the laws, and
the regulations that have oversight over these geographical areas.

Our natural resource program is doing things that I think are
innovative in terms of enlightening the public's consciousness to
natural resources and why it's relevant to our specific culture. We have
worked out an understanding with the county and a local foundation
called the Rainshadow Foundation to maintain the Dungeness River
environment. The Tribe and local community have developed a
site, owned by the Tribe, on the river to educate people about the
ecosystem. This project demonstrates how the environment and
ecosystem work with the natural flows of the river systems as the
best way to manage and protect the environment for the integrity of
ecosystems. The project is also about creating the right kind of natural
environments for fisheries to restore themselves.

Another aspect of this restoration initiative is rerouting creeks
and putting them back onto their own natural course. Those kinds of
projects are expensive because you have to reacquire land and divert
the creeks back to their natural course so that they become healthy
again. Our Tribe is doing those kinds of projects in conjunction with
the state, the federal government, including U.S. Fish & Wildlife and
the Army Corps of Engineers. They like our project and know that we
share the same environmental goals.

Last but not least, we are active in what we call water-quality or water-quantity management regimes that have come out of a number of statewide forums on that topic. Our Tribe has taken the lead on a pilot project and developed model forums on how to engage our community and the interest groups who clash over those rights; the irrigators versus the water power people versus the developers versus the agricultural people, and so forth. Now we are working together in terms of how to best manage available water. This is a resource that we thought for years was excessively abundant in the Northwest and it has turned out that it is a finite resource. In fact, it's becoming a scarcity and the challenge is how do you responsibly manage a finite resource that is essential to fisheries and so many other competing interests.

Our quality staff has taken a very strong and effective leadership role on this topic. They have become well informed and kept the Tribal Council and myself informed on the problems and proposed solutions.

Hunting is another area where we have a lot to do to improve our hunting relationship with our sister Tribes and the state. There is a lot of ambiguity about where Tribal territories are today that were traditional, usual and accustomed territories for hunting. We have a lot of collaborative relationship building to take care of around protecting and managing hunting for our community. Hunting is still something that is very actively practiced by many of our citizens and they want the Tribe to preserve that right.

The general public has the perception that Indians are the ones who are killing all the animals, when really it's the non-Indians who have the kills. We're a very small fraction of what is actually taken. But the public thinks that we're the ones doing it because we have different seasons. We try to keep our hunters out of conflicts with non-Indian hunters.

Stauss: You talked about water, salmon, and hunting. Are there other environmental challenges that you see in the future for Jamestown?
Allen: Well, there is no question that the Endangered Species Act is a major concern for the Tribe, as well as it is for non-Indian communities. The Endangered Species Act is something that is not very well defined. What you do as a result of this law and what its impact is on your activities or projects is the question. We have great concerns over it being unnecessarily or inappropriately enforced in a way that precludes reasonable commonsense activities. We have a duty to deal with that law and work with our governmental counterparts, as well as the general community, on how to manage it in a responsible way. We do not want to see any species being extinguished or lost to us because of ineptness or mismanagement.

Stauss: One issue that is in the news today is the Makah whale hunt. Some argue that if Makah are going to hunt whales, all the other Tribes will join in. Does Jamestown have any plans to hunt whales?

Allen: Absolutely not. There is no interest whatsoever. I think the view of most of the Tribes is that the Makah were the ones who were historically and culturally whalers. I don't think that any other Tribe that I know of in the Northwest has any interest in rejuvenating that practice. Historically or culturally, the Salish Tribes never hunted whales. We traded with the Makah people. We would trade them venison and salmon for whale meat, bone, and oil.

Stauss: I know there are some stories about whaling if the animals were seen in a bay.

Allen: True enough. Those were easy kills. We used the blubber, bones, and so forth. Whales do have a tendency to get too far inland and get themselves in a precarious situation and so the S'Klallam, being tough fishermen, would go out and get them. Those are stories I have read as well, but reading between the lines, my guess is that these were anomalies. In my opinion, the S'Klallam people were simply taking advantage of an easy whale hunt that was there and they could use it for subsistence needs.

Stauss: The other controversy, which is in the literature, is to what extent Jamestown people were hunters and went into the dense forest and up into the Olympics. There seems to be evidence on both sides of that controversy.

Allen: I don't know much about that one. I know that they were hunters. How deep did they go into the Olympic Peninsula? We know they traveled extensively into the mountains for gathering, ceremonies, and trade and interaction with other Tribes on the other side of the peninsula. There are stories about the large number of wolves, which may have thinned out the herds, making longer trips into the mountains necessary. We also know there was an abundance of deer, bear, and elk at different times here on the lower slopes. But it's very clear that the mountains were used extensively by the early S'Klallam.

> "Our Tribe has had a consistent, steady leadership and team approach within the council. We have had one rudder on this ship, a strong Tribal council, so that the course we are sailing is a steady course. It adjusts delicately and methodically."

Stauss: What do you see as the past strengths and future challenges for Tribal government at Jamestown?

Allen: First of all, our strength has always been political stability. Our Tribe has had a consistent, steady leadership and team approach within the council. We have had one rudder on this ship, a strong Tribal council, so that the course we are sailing is a steady course. It adjusts delicately and methodically. We address the various needs and problems that surface from time to time as a general course of business. But the fact that we have been so consistent in our leadership, and in our vision with regard to where the Tribe is going and what it is trying to achieve, has been one of the our biggest strengths, unquestionably. Historically, most successful Tribes have this characteristic.

This consistent leadership is moving the Tribe steadily and progressively forward. That's very positive. Every community has its own set of goals and different values. So various citizens of the community have different program or cultural objectives and that becomes their priority for the Tribe. These priorities can be children, homes, or jobs. You have this variety of competing interests and needs and, quite frankly, they are generally legitimate and reasonable needs. We have to delicately balance those needs governmentally. I believe that the Tribe has done a fairly good job with that overall challenge.

In the past, when the Tribe did not have resources, there was limited interest in Tribal leadership roles. But, as we become more successful, a new interest rises for some to want to lead. As the Tribal operations have become more complicated, it is the responsibility of Tribal leadership to prepare and encourage citizens for key roles. We have developed a fairly complete government to interact with the American political system. We have to deal with all levels of the federal, state, and local governments. This political framework is very challenging and it takes years to develop the political knowledge, credibility, and effectiveness to protect and advance the Tribe's agendas. We have been very blessed to have a steady leadership in our community.

A political area that we need to strengthen is our Tribal court system. Fortunately in the past, we have not had an extensive need for a Tribal court system. Law enforcement is an area we are going to have to address. Because of the demographics and political conditions of our community and a growing reservation, my contention is that we probably should work with the local community law enforcement agency. We should work out a unique deal with them in terms of their law enforcement agency understanding the laws that apply on our reservation, as well as the county and state laws. This approach would avoid the problems in cross-deputization scenarios.

I think our Tribal constitution is solid. I was very delighted that the Tribal community approved taking the secretary of interior out of the constitution. We came back to the community for a second time to make that happen. That shows the community understands that you don't need the federal government to "lord over" our governmental activities. If we are going to be a sovereign government, then we must act like one and take away the old paternal symbols and conditions that have been weaved into the many Tribal governing documents that provided excessive and unnecessary encroachment and intrusion on Tribal governmental functions and activities. I believe our Tribal Council two-year terms are too short. They are just not practical for political stability. I would hope our community would be conducive or supportive to either three- or four-year terms for Tribal governmental officials.

Stauss: You talked about in the last ten years the tremendous increase in the capacity of Tribal governments all across the country. How has Jamestown been part of this growth spurt?

Allen: When we were pursuing our federal recognition in the 1970s and the Bureau of Indian Affairs (BIA) federal acknowledgement process became clear, we got quite a bit of assistance from the BIA. Particularly from some key people who were very interested in our Tribe. I think that we were very fortunate that we encountered those individuals. Particularly a woman named Helen Peterson (an Oglala Sioux) who was the head of Tribal governmental services for the Portland area office. She was just a magnificent angel on our shoulder who worked with us to help draft a constitution that addressed some of the governmental issues or challenges that were being raised in the federal recognition petition. We had a couple of good lawyers that assisted us; one of them being Emily Mansfield and the other was Jeff Schuster.

We had a good basic governing document that got us started in terms of how the Tribal government functioned. It clearly outlined the duties and the responsibilities of the Tribal Council versus the general council.

We received formal federal recognition in 1981. We didn't have a lot of turnover in terms of the council, and that made a huge difference in our early developmental period.

The next issue is how the Tribe administers its responsibilities. Often we talk about governmental capacity in two perspectives. One is how the structure of government manages itself and whether or not it's well organized and efficient. The second is how you advance your governmental interests in the political system. The knowledge of how federal and state governments work and how the Tribe should interface with them relative to our legal status. This is where leadership makes a difference, because what you are doing is bringing your credibility, experience, and knowledge with you to effectively represent the Tribal government in these various forms. You are educating political leaders about how this unique government-to-government relationship should work and what the responsibilities and rights are for Tribal governments.

When I refer to Tribal governmental capacities growing exponentially over the last ten, twelve years, it's because of leadership stability and increased resources available to the Tribes. We are able to advance our agenda politically because federal, state, and local government officials have to begin to respect us.

An example of that point is how we manage our natural resources in terms of taking responsibility for the fisheries and hunting or protection of the environment. Our staff and programs are as good as any state or federal system. Our experts are as good and knowledgeable as their experts, and quite often are better.

I think the Jamestown Tribe has been a leader in this area. I think that because of my longevity, energy, and skills, it puts me out front in these forums. I have been very aggressive as a representative of our Tribe in regional and national forums. Not only championing our cause, but also the cause of other small Tribes like ours. Part of this effort is creating a respectful relationship or approach to dealing with all Tribes, small or large. For years there was this unsaid view that the large Tribes, I mean Tribes that have maybe five thousand to ten thousand citizens or more, including the Navajo Nation with over two hundred fifty thousand citizens, are the ones who are truly self-governing Tribes. Tribes of five hundred or two hundred or one hundred really aren't the same and aren't given the same kind of respect. Well, Jamestown and other small Tribes fought hard against that notion. We have the same sovereignty, and it is equal to larger Tribes. I have been one to help champion that mutually respectful issue.

The advancement and implementation of Tribal self-governance in the late 1980s was one of the good examples. As the federal government was looking to empower Tribal governments and transfer these federal functions to Tribal governments, they were looking for pilot Tribes to advance that initiative, and they found all large Tribes. I fought hard to prove that small Tribes can also make this initiative work. That's how the Jamestown Tribe became one of the initial ten Tribes to embark on this initiative.

Stauss: Why did the Jamestown Tribe move into the area of educating all the other Tribes about self-governance?

Allen: I believe the main reason is because of our leadership. Being candid, not a lot of people are willing to spend the time to fully understand how to advance this initiative by studying and researching into how the federal government managed their programs, then using this knowledge to negotiate compacts and then help our sister Tribes understand what to do.

Not a lot of people were willing to make that commitment. They are not willing to handle that responsibility in conjunction with their Tribal responsibilities. It is very difficult to balance and it requires high energy. That is one of my blessings. I have the ability to stay focused on multiple issues, whether they are local issues or whether they are broad national issues, and so we simply have taken the lead. I personally have taken strong leadership roles in those arenas.

The Tribe has also been blessed with some really quality staff. Because they are very good and responsible, it allows me to delegate. They have learned how to make a judgment call on when I need to be involved in the decision-making. I am not required to provide excessive supervision. I let them know that I believe they understand their duties and what needs to be done. They are given the discretion to make decisions unless it's clear that it requires direction from me or the council. That helps me deal with the political issues that I have to deal with versus the day-to-day items that I shouldn't have to address. A lot of Tribal Chairmen get caught up in micro-management. That happens if program directors don't really do their job or make decisions delegated to them. They put the burden on the executive director or Tribal Council. Our operation doesn't function that way.

I also have used electronic technologies to be able to handle multiple tasks at one time and stay in communication with the Tribe. If you have to write, you can do it while traveling. When I travel, I pack heavy. I bring all my computer equipment, supplies, and materials. It is just part of what I do, and fortunately my energy allows me to be able to do that without any problem. It's amazing how much you can get done utilizing the email system. I've always tried to stay at the electronic cutting edge. That allows me to interface with the Tribe or with national organizations or national movements. I've taken great pride in always being accessible to the citizenship and staff even though I travel a lot representing the Tribe.

Stauss: It sounds like a lot of progress is focused upon your leadership and energy. How have other Tribes been successful?

> "My activism and leadership style is about developing relationships."

Allen: It varies from Tribe to Tribe, of course. There are many phenomenal Tribal leaders that I have worked with over the years. When you have additional resources that allow you to bring personnel in to cover other tasks or follow-up actions. What Tribes with good resources are able to do is secure expertise to advise them on different matters.

Stauss: It seems that Jamestown also has been in a unique leadership position in cooperating with local and state governments. Was that a planned strategy?

Allen: It happened primarily because of hard work and leadership skills. Tribes and state/local governments are often engaged in negotiations and are advancing collaborative efforts; however, these co-interests often are competing. It is a matter of having and developing the kind of leadership who can guide those organizations and personalities in a way that they can find common ground.

My activism and leadership style is about developing relationships. If you're going to be an effective leader you have to develop confidence and trust with the top policy people at all levels of government. Knowing what you are talking about and keeping their attention with regard to the issue they are trying to resolve is essential in being effective. They need to believe that you understand the topic and can provide solutions. This is an area where I believe that my leadership has been very effective. I think that I have developed a rapport with a lot of key political people at all levels of government.

Other Tribal leaders who I have high respect for have guided me. I have learned from Joe DeLaCruz of the Quinault Indian Nation, Mel Tonasket from Colville Nation, Sam Cagey from Lummi Indian Nation, and Billy Frank, Jr., at the Northwest Indian Fishery Commission, and numerous others throughout the country. You learn from those other Tribal leaders and you learn from different experiences. Then you can bring that experience and credibility into these forums, i.e., local, state, and national. It helps you find solutions to problems that affect multiple Tribes and other entities. This growth does not happen overnight—you have to consistently work at it.

That is a role I have fulfilled throughout my career. I can come into meetings and quickly assess what's going on. Is the right mix of Tribal leaders there? Are staff and/or lawyers driving the agenda? I assess whether or not the participants are leaders or pseudoleaders. If they don't represent the Tribe politically, then you can't allow them to drag the meeting down. The task is to determine how to advance the agenda relative to who is participating. In particular my goal is to avoid solving the issue in court.

Those are the techniques that I utilize as a leader and that's why I get in the middle of things. When a participant is a Tribal Chairman, their effectiveness is greater, especially when you have experience and a national reputation. You know that's a factor but it's the Jamestown Tribe that gets the credit. You know that's good because it brings collective pride and confidence within the Tribe. We believe that we can get things done.

Stauss: Is there anything else that you see as a key ingredient to the success of the Tribe that we haven't touched upon?
Allen: I think the only other point that I would make is that however we were able to capture the vision and the direction of the Tribe, as a general observation, has been embraced by the citizenship. I believe that if our community ever thought we were going in the wrong direction, they would have stopped us. They would have voted people like me out. They would have voted in new leadership.

I think that our success and our growth has caused our people to believe we were doing the best job possible, and that was a reaffirmation that we were doing the right thing. The mere fact that I have gone through twenty-six years of re-election as a Chairman and Councilman, every two years from 1975 to today, is a reaffirmation that we're doing a good job for our community.

There is no question that some citizens, including some on my Council, have asked me to be closer to home, but even when they say it, in the same breath they say, "But we understand what you are doing to protect our Tribe's rights and interests. So keep doing what needs to be done out in those political forums." Those citizens who get the opportunity to observe what I have to do, in terms of providing regional and national leadership and assistance to Tribes, understand that I have been blessed with some skills and talents to lead. So they have been very supportive of my leadership. That support of my leadership has made a significant contribution.

Stauss: You talked about the Tribe becoming self-reliant. What happens when a Tribe becomes self-reliant but yet there are treaty responsibilities on the part of the federal government? How do you balance out continued federal funding with a Tribe that is totally self-reliant?

Allen: I think a lot of people don't realize that with the 560 federally recognized Tribes in the United States, there is simply not enough money and never will be enough money from the federal system to accommodate the needs of all those Indian communities from Alaska to Florida. It will never happen. It will never happen for Jamestown. It will never happen for anybody else.

As Tribes move forward, some will become independent financially and won't require financial support or assistance from the federal government. This will happen because of their resourcefulness and the success of their business entities. What that will achieve is the ability to spread the limited federal dollars to a more concentrated area of Tribes that don't have the same kinds of opportunities or don't have the same kind of leadership and resourcefulness.

I think Jamestown definitely fits into that mold. I think we are moving aggressively towards the ability to becoming self-reliant. As a Tribe moves towards releasing any right to federal dollars because it no longer needs its share, or maybe it does not want the federal constraints that come along with those dollars, then in doing so, it does not relinquish the federal government's obligation to the Tribe in terms of preserving its treaty rights, its unique government-to-government relationship, and the Tribe's legal rights. There will always be a legal responsibility that the federal government cannot abrogate. No Tribe would ever terminate that obligation of the federal government.

As Tribes are becoming more self-reliant and politically savvy, we have the capability to assure that the federal government maintains its trust duty, and we can be even more forceful because the Tribe knows the political system. We have learned how the political system works, and we're working it on our behalf, like it does for what we often refer to as "mainstream America." That would be one of the political objectives that the Tribe has to advance while utilizing its resources to accomplish its community goals. You have community goals and you have governmental protective goals and they go hand in hand. The strength of your government is relative to how you interface the political system that surrounds you, including local community, state, and the federal government.

Stauss: Jamestown has been very successful in economic development over the last several decades. What would you attribute to that success and what do you see as the challenges for the future?

Allen: First of all, I think that going back to the genesis of the Tribe and the fundamental spirit that has driven our Tribe to be strong and self-reliant has driven us to never want to be dependent on the federal government. I remember the early leaders of the Jamestown community, Edith Cusack, Harriette Adams, Lyle and Les Prince, and Brick Johnson. Those people actually didn't want to become dependent on the federal government. I told the Council, including Harriette Adams, that I would do this if we would pursue self-sufficiency in its truest sense. They agreed with that goal, and so that has always been a mission of mine to push Jamestown in a direction that would allow it to become self-sufficient.

The Jamestown Tribe had a conservative economic strategy, which included investing in capital-intensive businesses that have low risk, low profit margin, and to develop a business track record and then expand. We were pursuing that approach and, of course, we were not generating a lot of money—but we did what we could in terms of bringing some new resources into the Tribe. The fireworks operation was one of our first real businesses. So the stand has a little bit of a symbolic status in the Tribe because it was the first real Tribal business.

The Tribe has had many successes and some failures. We have learned some hard lessons. We have spent literally thousands of dollars on businesses that didn't work. The Tribe has some businesses right now that are just surviving. Our seafood business is holding its own. The art gallery is surviving but is on an upward swing. Our biggest obstacle is location. We have high interest in it because it helps market the products that Indian artists generate and it can become a solid small business. The seafood business is culturally relevant. We struggled with the seafood business for a number of years, but it is so culturally relevant that we must maintain those kinds of businesses as a part of our economic profile.

We really got our start through a couple of federal grants that allowed us to buy some real estate. That was how we acquired two apartment complexes and another real estate investment on Bainbridge Island. They have been very successful and steady. And, of course, that improves our business credibility with outside communities and financial institutions.

Our 7 Cedars Casino and gaming business has the potential to be our biggest impact business and strengthen our entire economic foundation. When Congress passed the Indian Gaming Regulatory Act [IGRA], we realized there was a market opportunity. We ended up joining forces with a company from Las Vegas, and because of our Tribe's business reputation, we were able to negotiate a pretty good agreement from this firm. So, we eventually built one of the classiest casinos in the state.

We were blessed because of our political and business reputation to bring on people who wanted to work with us. Our current manager is outstanding in this industry and he, personally, in conjunction with the quality staff that we have, made this business survive. Now, with our ability to provide Class 3 gaming machines (slots), it has become increasingly profitable.

We are seriously looking at a destination resort that we believe is going to bring a significant amount of new business into the county. We have never wanted to just compete for the entertainment dollar. What we want to do is bring dollars into the county, and of course the resort is what makes that work; something unique, classy, and something that is going to be a well-recognized resort in the entire Northwest, not just on the Olympic Peninsula. We also have a high interest in pursuing a golf course to complement the resort.

Beyond that, we will be exploring some other opportunities. I do think that because we are bold and willing to take risks—-that has had a lot to do with our success. Our reputation is a key reason that the business community asks us to consider different projects.

Stauss: Are your long-term economic development plans going to involve other partnerships or cooperative ventures?
Allen: Yes, but I think that's a projection that is hard to judge. Although, we are very clear that the achievement of a strong, stable, diversified economic base will take a significant amount of time. I would find it hard to believe that we could embark on a destination resort project in the magnitude that we are interested in without a partnership. This is a very sophisticated industry. I think that we could do quite well in terms of adapting to the industry and the marketing nuances that are necessary to assure that it's going to be successful. It needs to be run with the kind of class and customer service standards that we believe are appropriate to the image that we are trying to establish. Therefore, you need to bring people in who are experts.

"We have always worked together through the highs and lows of all of our various experiences. That spirit made a big difference for us as a team."

The Tribe is not afraid of partnerships with the private business community. We learned a lot about how to set up those partnerships in terms of protecting the Tribe's interests and sovereign rights. In the past, we had a propensity to put too many irons in the fire. This approach unfortunately keeps our energies too spread out and not focused on the two or three viable business ventures.

Stauss: The Tribe then is definitely going to stay with the seafood and the art because of the cultural relevance?
Allen: Definitely. There is no question we'll work hard at making them

successful. If they can't make it as profitable businesses, then we still won't let go of them.

Stauss: Do you see expansion in that area or are you trying to stabilize and focus in on a particular niche?

Allen: I think modest expansion. Right now they are breakeven businesses; however, I think that they can become solid businesses, generating modest revenue and jobs.

Stauss: Are there other factors you would point to that explain the Tribe's success?

Allen: Camaraderie and family spirit is a big factor in the Tribe. We developed from the very beginning a unique family relationship. We have always worked together through the highs and lows of all of our various experiences. That spirit made a big difference for us as a team. I have always wanted to make our working environment a place where you enjoyed coming to work. When you look around and you see the art and you see the pictures and you see the fine things that are around here, it makes it an attractive place to come to work. We work hard at not letting our facilities and office get run down and at protecting and preserving what we've been blessed with.

I believe that one of our cultural values is stewardship over what you have been given, and your job is to take care of it. The Jamestown Tribe has done a good job in advancing those values and principles. The people who work for us enjoy that atmosphere, feel good, and it causes people to be willing to work hard and put in tireless hours. Again, I like to refer to my good friend Billy Frank, Jr., whose favorite phrase is, "The cause is worth the cost." I adopted that value and accepted it as a part of the spirit that drives me. Later on in life, after I have retired, I want to look back and say, "We did do good, and we had a good time." I think that's a major contribution to our Tribe's success.

Afterword

Readers of this book who are searching for the traditional S'Klallam Indian defined by static images of language, culture, and spirituality firmly cemented in the distant past risk missing the essence of a truly remarkable story. The Jamestown S'Klallam Tribe in 2003 is a true phoenix, restored from the ashes of genocide, colonial political imperialism, and forced internal family and cultural disintegration.

The rebuilding of the Tribe as a political, economic, and environmental success is an amazing contemporary story. In the short span of a quarter century, they have re-emerged on the Olympic Peninsula as a distinct, visible, and politically important community.

> The rebuilding of the Tribe as a political, economic, and environmental success is an amazing contemporary story.

Vine Deloria, Jr., one of the most influential Indian writers of the day, has provided us with a thoughtful format with which to view challenges confronting contemporary Indian nations. He argues there are four critical areas important to the future: Tribal government reform, economic stability, federal- state relations, and cultural renewal.[1] If we hold this mirror up to the Jamestown S'Klallam story, we find remarkable similarities between the Tribe's successes and Deloria's challenges for the future.

Strong Tribal Governments

Although many of the Tribes in the United States have yet to make fundamental changes in their governments, the Jamestown S'Klallam actually benefited from not being an Indian Reorganization Act (IRA) government. Their original 1975 constitution has been revised, specifically shifting the power away from the Bureau of Indian Affairs

(BIA) and into the hands of the Jamestown people. They are not a large Tribe with too few representatives on the Tribal Council, a major problem for some other Tribes. Jamestown members have immediate and direct access to the elected Council members and the Chairman. The IRA originally was written to give self-government to villages and communities within larger reservations, but that part of the proposed legislation was eliminated.[2] The Jamestown Tribal government does not need reforming as other Tribal governments do. Indeed, their self-governing operations are a national model.

One very visible key to Jamestown restoration has been leadership, particularly on the part of its Tribal Chairman. While the S'Klallam faced significant economic, social, and cultural losses under colonial rule, their underlying character and values endured and are manifested in their Tribal leaders. Generosity, hard work, ambition, modesty, courtesy, and calm—the traditional values that proclaimed the status of a good man, or real man—have served S'Klallam leaders well in contemporary times.

Economic Stability and Sustainability

Deloria argues that "self-government is probably a farce without some steady form of Tribal income to support it."[3] Here again, the Jamestown Tribe has a remarkable record of success. Visionary and stable leadership by Chairman Allen, coupled with professional staff support and Council advice, are hallmarks of this record of accomplishment. However, Deloria put his finger on a critical variable when he argued that "the critical factor in achieving economic stability seems to be in encouraging Tribal officials to develop programs that are perceived by the people as natural extensions of things they are already doing. A natural economy maximizes the use of the land in as constructive a manner as possible, almost becoming a modern version of hunting and gathering in the sense the people have the assurance that this kind of activity will always be available to them."[4] Jamestown community members and their leaders have, for decades, acted out this goal for their future.

Jamestown people are today and have always been fishermen. The Tribe is well down the road toward meeting a major goal—being economically self-sufficient in a manner that enhances, rather than takes advantage of, their environment.

Advantageous Federal and State Relations

Deloria characterizes this future challenge as a goal of having states not infringe on the special relationship Tribes have with the federal government while at the same time accepting Tribes on an equal political footing. This arena, across the United States, is a political lightning rod. For example, Tribal gaming, hunting, and fishing rights off reservations are consistently and vigorously opposed by portions of the non-Indian population.

The Jamestown S'Klallam Tribe has had extraordinary success and has provided model leadership in this arena. They have systematically sought out a mediating and leadership role with state, county, city, and community associations and interest groups. The Tribe has established positive relationships and true partnerships with these groups, as well as exercised strong leadership on Tribal, national, and state issues. The progress the Tribe has made toward self-determination is directly related to their philosophy and strategic plan to cooperate with state, local, federal, and community stakeholders in traditional S'Klallam territory and beyond. The major goals in this area focus on fish, shellfish, water quality, and the other environmental issues that are interwoven into the fabric of economic development.

Cultural Renewal

Deloria's most important challenge for the future is extremely problematic for all Tribes. He argues: "Culture is a most difficult subject to discuss. It is also the single factor that distinguishes Indians from non-Indians in the minds of both groups."[5] In the area of cultural renewal, the Jamestown Tribe has made slow but steady progress. They have not enjoyed the same measure of success with cultural renewal as they have in Tribal governance, economic stability, and environmental protection. This is due in large part to their struggles to develop and build the infrastructure of an independent Tribe. Their relatively small population and their ability to acculturate to the dominant European American influx over the last century and a half, and their ageold practice of intermarriage, have all contributed to a loss of traditional practices and knowledge. The Jamestown S'Klallam Tribe has concentrated first on being a politically viable entity in today's dominant non-native culture. Jamestown clearly still maintains a sense of identity and community, which sets them apart from others. However, it remains for them to recapture more of what was lost.

One of the greatest challenges of the future for the Jamestown Tribe is to provide both traditional and contemporary education for its citizens. Traditional education includes relearning and reinterpreting the language and key aspects of the culture, such as collecting and working with cedar. Contemporary education must focus on the rights and responsibilities of being a Tribal citizen. This includes a knowledge of the special relationship between the Tribe and the federal government, how Tribal sovereignty is and can be exercised, fishing rights, economic development challenges, and myriad other important issues.

Equally important, the Tribe must continue to inform and educate non-Indians on the peninsula about these same rights and responsibilities. The issues that sometimes divide groups of Indians and non-Indians—gaming, fishing, hunting—will continue to flare up and must be damped down with constant educational efforts using every means possible.

The Jamestown S'Klallam have worked hard and enjoyed some success in reviving and maintaining some ceremonies and passing of information on storytelling, cedar gathering, canoe making, basket and blanket weaving, and language restoration. Although it is difficult to judge the level of success, it appears that too few Tribal citizens participate in these opportunities, and Elders have not been asked the right questions when recording their oral histories.

However, citizens have a wealth of cultural and ceremonial information to build upon for the future. The potlatch, guardian spirit, coming of age, naming, and related events are well described in the literature. In addition, Elders and others who have learned stories and ways of life passed down to them are still available to help reconstruct important elements of the culture that are not available today.

Of course, the continuation (tradition) of the most basic elements of culture is everywhere among today's Jamestown people— in the values, beliefs, and practices of Tribal government officials and staff; in the industrious approaches employed to making a living, whether at gaming or renting apartments; and in the deeply ingrained efforts to preserve and protect the environment, to name but a few. The anthropological, and indeed the public's, fascination with traditional culture focuses on song, dance, pageantry, religion, and the like. When S'Klallam people talk about lost knowledge of the old ways, they are anticipating this paradigm. Do you practice the first salmon ceremony? How many of your children know the language? Don't you spirit dance each winter? How many potlatches do you have each year? Where can I get a recipe book for traditional S'Klallam foods?

There is a fundamental struggle at the heart of these questions. The definition of a real Indian has been provided not by Indians themselves but by others—anthropologists, filmmakers, non-Indian popular writers, BIA officials, and other non- Indians. Deloria places the controversy more squarely on the shoulders of anthropologists when he writes, "The conflict between Indians and anthropologists in the last two decades has been, at its core, a dead struggle over the control of definitions. Who is to define what an Indian really is?"[6]

The connection between contemporary Indian ways and traditional ones continues to be problematic for many European American scholars. In the dynamic mix of identity issues surrounding "who is an Indian," one underlying assumption seems to be that if you have lost your language and ceremonies from generations past, how are you any different than any card-carrying member of a political club?

That answer at Jamestown clearly lies in a unique relationship to the land, which is and has always been traditional S'Klallam territory; to fundamental individual, family, and community values; and to character deeply rooted in a traditional S'Klallam way of life, along with a commitment to maintaining the continual self-governance that has characterized S'Klallam villages since long before European American contact.

If Indian people get to define who "really" is an Indian, then it stands to reason they also get to define both their new traditions and which traditions from earlier times they want to continue or recapture and restore. Deloria argues that cultural revival "involves the fundamental problem of determining a contemporary expression of Tribal identity and behaving according to its dictates."[7]

> If Indian people get to define who "really" is an Indian, then it stands to reason they also get to define both their new traditions and which traditions from earlier times they want to continue or recapture and restore.

There is a delicate balance and creative tension between traditional and contemporary knowledge for all Indian Tribes. At Jamestown, the connection to the past and, in particular, the language, stories, ceremonies, spirituality, and inherited treaty rights for descendants, are crucial to maintaining a unique Tribal and community identity. Although individual commitment to the maintenance of the Jamestown culture may vary, Jamestown community members must define, validate, and teach their own history. In doing so, they can define what are acceptable and important new "traditions," which help maintain their sense of uniqueness.

The Future

The Tribe has accomplished absolutely amazing things in the past twenty-five years. They have acquired federal recognition, built a sound economic foundation, taken a leadership role in environmental management, and developed a nationally recognized Tribal government. All of their accomplishments are necessary but not sufficient to meet the goal of rebuilding and strengthening the cultural uniqueness of the Tribe. This is the challenge in the years ahead. The Tribe is in a good position to have continued success. They are a small federally recognized Indian Tribe with political clout and respect equal to larger Tribes across the United States. They are in their traditional territory— their homeland. Other Tribes are not as fortunate. Perhaps most important, the Jamestown S'Klallam are still, as always, fishermen committed to rebuilding the rich fishery and water resources necessary to maintain their way of life.

In future centuries and beyond, the Jamestown S'Klallam will still be practicing their unique ways of life, strengthening and maintaining their families and community, and governing themselves, all in their traditional homeland. They are today and will be in the distant future known as the strong people.

Notes

Preface

1. U.S. Bureau of the Census, "Census 2000 Shows America's Diversity, March 12, 2000," prepared by Economics and Statistics Administration, Bureau of the Census (Washington, D.C., 2000). The press release can be found online at http://www.census.gov/Press- Release/www/2001/cb01cn61. html. Last accessed: May 15, 2002.
2. C. Matthew Snipp, American Indians: The First of This Land (New York: Russell Sage Foundation, 1998), 10.
3. George Brown Tindall and David Emory Shi, America: A Narrative History, 5th ed. (New York: W. W. Norton & Company, 1999), 5.
4. Erna Gunther, "Klallam Ethnography," University of Washington Publications in Anthropology 1, no. 5 (Seattle: University of Washington Press, 1927), 173. 5. See Robert H. Ruby and John A. Brown, Myron Eells and the Puget Sound Indians (Seattle: Superior Pub. Co., 1976).

Introduction: An Overview of the Pacific Northwest Coast Ways of Life

1. Barbara Lane and Wayne Suttles, "Southern Coast Salish," in Handbook of North American Indians: Northwest Coast, volume 7, edited by Wayne Suttles (Washington, D.C.: Smithsonian Institution Press, 1990), 485–502.
2. Gunther, "Klallam Ethnography," 173–78.
3. Wayne Suttles, "Central Coast Salish," in Handbook of North American Indians: Northwest Coast, edited by Wayne Suttles, 453–75.
4. Vine Deloria, Jr., Red Earth White Lies (Golden, Colorado: Fulcrum Publishing, 1997), 36–39.
5. Wayne Suttles, "Introduction," in Handbook of North American

Indians: Northwest Coast, edited by Wayne Suttles, 12–14.

6. Suttles, "Central Coast Salish," 453–56.
7. Suttles and Lane, "Southern Coast Salish," in Handbook of North American Indians: Northwest Coast, edited by Wayne Suttles, 493.
8. The topics of these stories and the thunderbird story are found in Erna Gunther, "Klallam Folk Tales," University of Washington Publications in Anthropology 1, no. 4 (Seattle: University of Washington Press, 1927), 113–70. The thunderbird story is on page 152.
9. Wayne Suttles, "Environment," in Handbook of North American Indians: Northwest Coast, edited by Wayne Suttles (Washington, D.C.: Smithsonian Institution Press, 1990), 16–29.
10. Robert Boyd, Indians, Fire and the Land in the Pacific Northwest (Corvallis: Oregon State University Press, 1999), 6–7.
11. Margaret B. Blackman, "Haida: Traditional Culture," in Handbook of North American Indians: Northwest Coast, edited by Wayne Suttles, 240–43.
12. Ruth Kirk, Tradition and Change on the Northwest Coast (Seattle: University of Washington Press, 1986), 108. 13. Suttles, "Introduction," 4.
13. These terms are found throughout the chapters in Handbook of North American Indians: Northwest Coast in each of the cultural areas under discussion: Central and Southern Coast Salish, Nootkans, Makah, and Quileute.
14. Marjorie M. Halpin and Margaret Seguin, "Tsimshian Peoples: Southern Tsimshian, Coast Tsimshian, Mshga, and Gitksan," in Handbook of North American Indians: Northwest Coast, edited by Wayne Suttles, 276.
15. William W. Elmendorf, The Structure of Twana Culture (Pullman: Washington State University Press, 1992), 322, 333.
16. George Gibbs, Indian Tribes of Washington Territory (Fairfield, Washington: Galleon Press, 1972), 30.
17. Frederica De Laguna, "Tlingit," in Handbook of North American Indians: Northwest Coast, edited by Wayne Suttles, 213.
18. Kirk, Tradition and Change on the Northwest Coast, 205.
19. Suttles, "Central Coast Salish," 466–96.
20. J. E. Michael Kew, "Central and Southern Coast Salish Ceremonies Since 1900," in Handbook of North American Indians: Northwest Coast, edited by Wayne Suttles, 476–78.
21. See Eugene Arima and John Dewhirst, "Nootkans of Vancouver Island," in Handbook of North American Indians: Northwest Coast, edited by Wayne Suttles, 404; Ann M. Renker and Erna Gunther, "Makah," in Handbook of North American Indians: Northwest Coast, edited by Wayne Suttles, 423; Suttles, "Central Coast Salish," 466–68.
22. Suttles, ed., Handbook of North American Indians: Northwest

<u>Coast</u>, particularly Wayne Suttles, "History of Research: Early Sources," 70–72.

23. Richard White, "It's Your Misfortune and None of My Own" <u>A New History of the American West</u> (Norman: University of Oklahoma Press, 1991), 73.

24. Ibid., 69–77. 26. Clifford E. Trafzer, "Washington's Native American Communities," in <u>Peoples of Washington: Perspectives on Cultural Diversity</u>, ed. Sid White (Pullman: Washington State University Press, 1989), 29–37.

Chapter 1: Homeland

1. Ruby and Brown, <u>Myron Eells and the Puget Sound Indians</u>, 44.
2. Ibid.
3. Charles Wilkes, U.S.N., <u>Narrative of the United States Exploring Expedition</u>, vol. 4 (Philadelphia: Lea & Blanchard, 1845), 299.
4. Some of the most useful historical, cultural, and legal information specific to S'Klallam fishing is found in a series of reports prepared by Barbara Lane for use in Indian fishing-rights litigation. Her scholarly work is focused, well researched, and well documented. See "Indian Use of Shellfish in Western Washington and the Indian Treaties of 1854–1855" (prepared for the U.S. Department of the Interior, 1993), Jamestown S'Klallam Tribal Library, Blyn Washington; "Identity, Treaty Status and Fisheries of the Jamestown Clallam Indian Community" (prepared for the U.S. Department of the Interior and the Jamestown Indian Community, 1977), Jamestown S'Klallam Tribal Library, Blyn, Washington; "Identity, Treaty Status and Fisheries of the Lower Elwha Tribal Community" (prepared for the U.S. Department of the Interior and the Lower Elwha Community, 1975), Jamestown S'Klallam Tribal Library, Blyn, Washington; "Identity, Treaty Status and Fisheries of the Port Gamble Indian Community" (prepared for the U.S. Department of the Interior and the Port Gamble Indian Community, 1977), Jamestown S'Klallam Tribal Library, Blyn, Washington. While doing the research on S'Klallam fisheries, Lane found some previously uncited material on S'Klallam fishing sites: see T. T. Waterman's "Puget Sound Geography," microfiche, 1922, University of Washington. Waterman worked with people from several Tribes to obtain the information. A typed copy of appropriate sections of Waterman's geographic sites is included in most of Dr. Lane's reports for the Tribes involved in U.S. vs. Washington, housed at the Jamestown S'Klallam Tribal Library, Blyn, Washington. Lane's reports for Lower Elwha and Port Gamble include Waterman's geographic sites that also pertain to Jamestown S'Klallam. Since most Puget Sound ethnographers were not aware of Waterman's study of geographic sites, the information serves as supplemental material as well as a useful

check on studies by Gunther, Elmendorf, and others. Waterman's
material is in three volumes. Volume 1 includes Makah, Klallam,
Chemakum, Skokomish, Nisqually, Squaxin Island, and the area
bordering Puget Sound; Volume 2 includes Puyallup and the
Seattle area. Volume 3 includes Snohomish and area maps that
pertain to all three volumes. Several decades later, Lane prepared
a report for the Point-No-Point Treaty Council that focused on
the period between 1855 and 1950. (See pages 146–49 to read the
contents of this treaty.) See Barbara Lane, Karen James, and Emily
Mansfield's "Hunting and Gathering Practices of the Skokomish
and S'Klallam and the Treaty of Point No Point, 1855, with
Related Legislation and Regulations, Treaty—1950" (prepared
for the Point-No-Point Treaty Council, 1997), available at the
Jamestown S'Klallam Tribal Library, Blyn, Washington.

5. Elmendorf, The Structure of Twana Culture, 295.
6. Ruby and Brown, Myron Eells and the Puget Sound Indians, 13.
7. Ibid., 16.
8. Gunther, "Klallam Ethnography," 199–200.
9. Ibid., 201.
10. William W. Elmendorf, Twana Narratives: Native Historical Accounts of a Coast Salish Culture (Seattle: University of Washington Press, 1993), 42–43. Some S'Klallam terms are replaced with their English equivalent or rough English pronunciation (both in square brackets).
11. Gunther, "Klallam Ethnography," 198–202.
12. Mickie (Prince) Judson in Tribal historical background paper, 1988, original interview by Hazel Monday and Sandy Robinson, transcript held in Jamestown S'Klallam Tribal Library, Blyn, Washington.
13. Meredith Bridges in Jamestown S'Klallam Tribe Newsletter, June 1995.
14. United States v. Washington 384F US 312 (1974).
15. Jamestown S'Klallam Tribe, "Salmon in the Dungeness River: From Abundance to Emptiness" (Blyn, Washington: Jamestown S'Klallam Tribe, 2000), 2.
16. Ann Seiter, Linda Newberry, and Pam Edens, "Cooperative Management of the Dungeness Watershed to Protect Salmon in Washington State" (photocopied paper, Jamestown S'Klallam Tribe Natural Resources Department, n.d.).
17. "Salmon in the Dungeness River," 4–5.
18. Mark Yuasa, "Return of the King: Salmon Season Looks to Yield Big Numbers," in Seattle Times, 24 June 2001, Fishing section.
19. "Salmon in the Dungeness River," 7.
20. Ibid., 5.
21. "Comprehensive Water Resources Planning: The Chelan Agreement" (Northwest Indian Fisheries Commission, 1990), 5.

The claim agreement is located in Jamestown S'Klallam Tribal offices, Blyn, Washington.

22. Seiter, Newberry, and Edens, "Cooperative Management of the Dungeness Watershed."

23. Jamestown S'Klallam Tribe, "The Dungeness: A River Unraveled" (Blyn, Washington: Jamestown S'Klallam Tribe, 2000), 6.

24. Ibid., 2–3.

25. See Ann Seiter, "What is the Dungeness River Management Team?" (public awareness and education paper, produced by Jamestown S'Klallam Tribe); Ann Seiter, "The Northwest's Water Resources: A Question of Federal, Tribal, State and Local Control" (paper presented at Lewis and Clark College, May 1996). Photocopies of these and other papers by Ann Seiter can be obtained by writing or visiting her at Jamestown S'Klallam Tribe, 1033 Old Blyn Highway, Sequim, WA 98382.

26. Ann Seiter, "Why Form Partnerships with Tribes for Pollution Prevention?" (abstract and outline of presentation at the Partnerships in Preventing Polluted Runoff conference, Wenatchee, Wash., 1998); Ann Seiter, "Putting Process into Practice: Tribal Leadership in Regional Water Planning" (paper presented at the American Water Resource Association Summer Symposium on Changing Roles in Water Resources Management and Policy, Seattle, Washington, June 1993). See also Ann Seiter, Lyn Muench, and Linda Newberry, "Every River Has Its People" (abstract of presentation at the Watershed '96 conference, Baltimore, Maryland, June 1996); Ann Seiter, "Every River Has Its People: The Collaboration of the Jamestown S'Klallam Tribe and the Local Community to Cooperatively Manage the Resources of the Dungeness River, Washington State, USA" (paper presented at Alternative Environmental Conflict Resolution in the United States of America and Chile: Experiences, Perspectives and Methodologies conference in Valdivia, Chile, December 2, 1999).

27. Jamestown S'Klallam Tribe, "Recommended Restoration Projects for the Dungeness River," report, 1997.

Chapter 2: Way of Life

1. Marion Taylor, "Dungeness: The Lure of a River," in Land of the Clallam, by Virginia Keeting (Blyn, Washington: Jamestown S'Klallam Tribe, 1975). This handout pamphlet is available at the Jamestown S'Klallam Tribal Library.

2. Ruby and Brown, Myron Eells and the Puget Sound Indians, 18–19.

3. Gunther, "Klallam Ethnography," 207. The traditional ways reported in this chapter rely heavily on Erna Gunther's work with informants in the 1920s.

4. Ibid., 210.

5. From Lane. See chapter 1, note 4.
6. Gunther, "Klallam Ethnography," 186–87.
7. Suttles, "Central Coast Salish," 453–75. There is no better, more concise source for Coast Salish cultural, subsistence, transportation, and related subjects than Suttles, ed., <u>The Handbook of North American Indians: Northwest Coast</u>.
8. Ruby and Brown, <u>Myron Eells and the Puget Sound Indians</u>, 27.
9. Gunther, "Klallam Ethnography," 241–57.
10. Ibid., 235.
11. Ibid., 233–41.
12. Ibid., 249.
13. This section was written using the Jamestown S'Klallam Tribe 1985 and 1994 Comprehensive Plans; an unpublished paper "Historical Analysis and Strategy for the Future" (Economic Development Division, 1996); and a 1994 Tribal Economic Development Tourist–Oriented Projects Summary document for Tribal council briefing. All documents are on file at the Jamestown S'Klallam Tribal offices, Blyn, Washington.
14. "How One Tribe Started Exporting Its Product," AgExporter 11, no. 10 (October 1999), 8.
15. From Jamestown S'Klallam Tribe quarterly reports and the 2001 "Report to Membership," on file at the Tribal offices, Blyn, Washington.
16. One of the only recent studies I could find on the economic contributions of Tribes in Washington was Veronica E. Tiller and Robert A. Chase, "Economic Contributions of Indian Tribes to the Economy of Washington State" (report prepared by Tiller Research, Inc., n.d.).

Chapter 3: Community

1. I rely heavily here on Gunther's early-twentieth-century observations for insight into traditional S'Klallam practices. See Gunther, "Klallam Ethnography," 184–303.
2. Ibid., 184–85.
3. Elmendorf, <u>Twana Narratives</u>, 141–43. Elmendorf's spelling of S'Klallam terms is sometimes replaced with the English equivalent or the rough English pronunciation.
4. Kerv, "Central and Southern Coast Ceremonies," 476–80.
5. Gunther, "Klallam Ethnography," 282–83. S'Klallam terms are replaced with the English equivalent or rough English pronunciation.
6. Ibid., 285.
7. Ibid., 286.
8. Ibid., 298–99.
9. Ibid., 302.
10. Ibid., 289.

11. Castile, The Indians of Puget Sound, 74–75.
12. Ruby and Brown, John Slocum and the Indian Shaker Church, 74–75.
13. Erna Gunther, "Klallam Ethnography," 306–310
14. Elmendorf, Twana Narratives, 31–32. S'Klallam terms from original have been replaced in some instances with English or with rough translation (both in square brackets).
15. Ibid., 34–35.
16. Ibid., 35.
17. Ibid., 40.
18. Gunther, "Klallam Ethnography," 274.
19. George Pierre Castile, ed., The Indians of Puget Sound: The Notebooks of Myron Eells (Seattle: University of Washington Press, 1985), 208–10.
20. Gunther, "Klallam Ethnography," 274.
21. The description of the disk game is from Paul Kane, Wanderings of an Artist Among the Indians of North America (Toronto: Radisson Society of Canada, 1925), 152. S'Klallam-specific materials on games and gaming can also be found in Gunther, "Klallam Ethnography," 183, 274–80.
22. Gunther, "Klallam Ethnography," 276.
23. Ibid., 277. Chinook jargon replaced with rough English equivalent in square brackets.
24. See Kane, Wanderings of an Artist, chapter 14.
25. The "1991 Tribal Resources and Needs Assessment Survey" is on file at Jamestown S'Klallam Tribal offices, Blyn, Washington.
26. Ibid., 17.
27. Ibid., 9.
28. Ibid., 11.
29. Jamestown Elders were interviewed by Hazel Monday and Sandy Robinson in 1988. The interviews were taped and transcribed verbatim. They are available at the Jamestown S'Klallam Tribal Library, Blyn, Washington. Selected interviews are presented in this volume to provide the reader with a contemporary voice from Tribal Elders. Original spellings and syntax have been retained.
30. Marlene Hanson, Sharing Our Memories: Jamestown S'Klallam Elders (Blyn, Washington: Jamestown S'Klallam Tribe, 2001), 5–6.
31. Ibid., 7–8.
32. Ibid., 29–30.
33. Material on the health-care system the Tribe has developed was obtained from discussions with staff and internal documents, in particular, the 1994 feasibility study findings and the "Managed Care Feasibility Study Report" (1995), on file at Jamestown S'Klallam Tribal offices, Blyn, Washington
34. Vine Deloria Jr., Indian Education in America (Boulder, Colo.: American Indian Science and Engineering Society, 1991), 13–33.

Chapter 4: Self-Government

1. Isaac I. Stevens, "1854 report on the S'Klallam Indians," in Letters Volume 1, Culture and History Collection, Jamestown S'Klallam Tribal Library. My research in this chapter relies heavily on this and other government reports and letters that were collected and photocopied by the Jamestown S'Klallam Tribe from records of the National Archives and the Washington State Historical Society. The Jamestown S'Klallam Tribal Library's collection also includes photocopied excerpts from paper and microfiche copies of the commissioner of Indian affairs annual reports and various reports of Indian agents of Washington Territory and Washington State.

2. Frank W. Porter III, "Without Reservation: Federal Indian Policy and the Landless Tribes of Washington," in State and Reservation: New Perspectives on Federal Indian Policy, eds. George Pierre Castile and Robert L. Bee (Tucson: University of Arizona Press, 1992), 111.

3. Ibid., 110–20.

4. Alexandria Harmon, Indians in the Making: Ethnic Relations and Indian Identities around Puget Sound (Berkeley: University of California Press, 1998), 178–79.

5. Ibid., 181.

6. Porter, "Without Reservation," 117–20.

7. Sid White and S. E. Solberg, eds., Peoples of Washington: Perspectives on Cultural Diversity (Pullman: Washington State University Press, 1989), 10–11.

8. John T. Knox, 1865, Letters Volume 1, Culture and History Collection, Jamestown S'Klallam Tribal Library, Blyn, Washington.

9. F. C. Purdy, 1863 letter, Letters Volume 1, Culture and History Collection, Jamestown S'Klallam Tribal Library, Blyn, Washington.

10. M. T. Simmons, 1860 report, Letters Volume 1, Culture and History Collection, Jamestown S'Klallam Tribal Library, Blyn, Washington.

11. Edwin Eells, 1871–1872, Letters Volume 1, Culture and History Collection, Jamestown S'Klallam Tribal Library, Blyn, Washington.

12. King, 1868, Letters Volume 1, Culture and History Collection, Jamestown S'Klallam Tribal Library, Blyn, Washington.

13. Edwin Eells, 1879 report, Letters Volume 1, Culture and History Collection, Jamestown S'Klallam Tribal Library, Blyn, Washington.

14. Edwin Eells, 23 September 1873 report, Letters Volume 1, Culture and History Collection, Jamestown S'Klallam Tribal Library, Blyn, Washington.

15. Edwin Eells, 1871 report, Letters Volume 1, Culture and History Collection, Jamestown S'Klallam Tribal Library, Blyn, Washington.

16. Sharon O'Brien, American Indian Tribal Governments (Norman: University of Oklahoma Press, 1989), 14–17.

17. David Getches, Charles Wilkinson, and Robert Williams Jr., Federal Indian Law, 4th ed. (St. Paul: West Publishing, 2000), 221.
18. Jeffrey S. Schuster, First Supplement to the Amended Petition for Acknowledgement of the Jamestown Clallam Indian Tribe as a Federally Recognized Indian Tribe Pursuant to 25 CFR Part 54 (Evergreen Legal Services, April 1979) was particularly helpful for political information between 1925 and 1979. A copy can be viewed at the Jamestown S'Klallam Tribal Library, Blyn, Washington.
19. Rennard Strickland, ed., Felix S. Cohen's Handbook of Federal Indian Law (Charlottesville, Virgina: The Michel, 1982), 122.
20. Jamestown S'Klallam Tribe's "Report to Membership 2001" (Blyn, Washington: Jamestown S'Klallam Tribe, 2001).
21. Ibid.
22. Materials used to write about S'Klallam lands included plans, reports, papers, and conversations with Natural Resources Department staff and other Tribal members. The "1994 Comprehensive Plan" (Blyn, Washington:Jamestown S'Klallam Tribe, 1994) and Ann Seiter, "Every River Has Its People: The State of the Dungeness River Report" (Blyn, Washington: Jamestown S'Klallam Tribe, 1997) were particularly helpful.
23. Harmon, Indians in the Making, 1–12.
24. Ibid., 140.
25. O'Brien, American Indian Tribal Governments, 14.
26. Jamestown S'Klallam Tribe Newsletter, issue 3, April 2001, 13.

Chapter Five: Interview with Chairman Allen

1. Interview conducted by the author on April 26, 2000 in San Diego, California, and on June 21, 2001, in Blyn, Washington.

Afterword

1. See Vine Deloria Jr., "The Future of Indian Nations," in Native American Sovereignty, edited by John R. Winder (New York: Garland Publishing, 1999), 356–76.
2. Ibid., 358.
3. Ibid., 370.
4. Ibid., 371.
5. Ibid., 362.
6. Vine Deloria Jr., "Anthros, Indian, and Planetary Reality," in Indians and Anthropologists: Vine Deloria, Jr. and the Critique of Anthropology, edited by Thomas Biolsi and Larry J. Zimmerman (Tucson: University of Arizona Press, 1997), 215.
7. Ibid.

About the Author

Joseph (Jay) H. Stauss received his Ph.D. in sociology in 1972 from Washington State University. He began his career in higher education at the University of Arizona on the American Indian Studies faculty. Dr. Stauss is the author and coauthor of more than twenty-five scholarly works and several texts on issues confronting urban Indians, minority relations, strengthening Indian families, and developing American Indian Studies programs. Dr. Stauss has devoted most of his career to serving in higher education as an administrator. He recently completed a decade as director of the premier graduate Indian Studies program in the nation. With his leadership, the University of Arizona created the first Ph.D. in American Indian Studies in the nation.

About the Illustrator

Dale Faulstich is an artist and woodcarver. He has earned his living producing both commercial and fine art since 1972. Dale's home and studio is located on the North Olympic Peninsula in Washington State, where he lives with his wife, Heather, and their two children.

Intrigued by the sophisticated art created by the indigenous people of the Northwest Coast of North America, Dale's objective as an artist is to create original contemporary objects inspired by long-established aboriginal themes. He also wishes to pay homage to the culture that flourished on the Northwest Coast, and to the ancient, mostly anonymous masters who expressed these cultural ideas.

As a non-native working in a native tradition, Dale enjoys a unique relationship with the Jamestown S'Klallam Tribe of Sequim, Washington. This long-standing collaboration has led to many commissioned artworks. He is currently working on a commission to produce artworks for the Tribe's newly opened casino. This commission includes designing and carving ten totem poles (the largest of which is forty-nine feet tall and six feet in diameter), numerous carved panels, and other carved figures. To date, six of the poles have been completed and installed along with most of the carved panels. The remaining works for this commission are in progress. Dale is involved in various other Tribal projects, as well as teaching an ongoing series of carving classes. He is always available to assist Tribal citizens in the designing and carving of traditional objects.

Dale has created masks, totem poles, steam-bent boxes, animal form bowls, rattles, drums, and ceremonial objects, as well as carved doors, wall panels, furniture, and other pieces with contemporary applications, which can be found in private collections throughout the United States and in many other countries.

Index

H

harvest statistics 55
housing, Tribal 157
hunting 33
  duck 6

I

Indian 160
Interviews 102
  Adams, Harriette Hall 112
  Allen, W. Ron 167
  Becker, Robert C. 113
  George, Ruby Prince 105
  Johnson, Harris "Brick" 106
  Judson, Mildred "Mickie" Prince 102
  Prince, Lyle 107

J

Jamestown
  founding of 139
Johnson, Harris "Brick" 106
Judson, Mildred "Mickie" Prince 11, 102

L

Language, Klallam
  Place names xvi
Leaders
  Chetzemoka 136
  community xxiv
  Jamestown 148
lodging 33

M

Map, historic villages xv
Map. present-day xiv
marriage 36
meals, food preparation 29

N

naming 42
Native American Graves and Repatriation Act (NAGPRA) 44

45854081R00146

Made in the USA
Middletown, DE
22 May 2019